# OpenOffice.org 2 Guidebook

## Solveig Haugland

Published by Solveig Haugland
Learn more at:
http://openoffice.blogs.com
http://www.getopenoffice.org

ISBN 0-9743120-2-9

**Trademarks**

StarOffice is a trademark of Sun Microsystems, Inc. All terms mentioned in this book that are known to be trademarks or service marks have been appropriately capitalized. Use of a term in this book should not be regarded as affecting the validity of any trademark or service mark.

**Warning and Disclaimer**

Every effort has been made to make this book as complete and as accurate as possible, but no warranty or fitness is implied. The information provided is on an "as is" basis. The author and the publisher shall have neither liability nor responsibility to any person or entity with respect to any loss or damages arising from the information contained in this book.

**Sales and Services**

For information about bulk discounts, or for OpenOffice.org or StarOffice learning materials, training, and consulting, please contact:

Solveig Haugland
solveig@comcast.net
http://openoffice.blogs.com

**Credits**

Content, indexing, and publishing: Solveig Haugland

Cover Design: Solveig Haugland

10 9 8 7 6 5 4 3

ISBN 0-97-431202-9

# Quick Contents

# OpenOffice.org 2 Guidebook
# Table of Contents

*To my parents, Palmer and Ethelyn, who have always been loving and encouraging.*

– SH

# Preface

Good software costs a lot of money. Right?

Not really. In fact, no. Whether software is good has little to do whether it costs a lot.

**OpenOffice.org is free**  This means the software is free from any constraints by big corporations. You don't need to worry about paying for it or keeping up to date. OpenOffice.org means you're free. And with this guide, you've got the easy way to work and play with OpenOffice.org since I just give you the simple step by step instructions for the important things.

**OpenOffice.org means you can spend your money on something important**  If you're in the business of making pecan pies, would you rather spend thousands of dollars on office suite software, or on finding great pecan suppliers? If you're in the business of finding a cure for cancer, rescuing people from burning buildings, teaching children, building houses, growing flowers, or anything else, what's more important: spending money on doing those things, or spending money on office suite software?

**Learning to use OpenOffice.org**  You'll find it's pretty easy to get started even if you've never used OpenOffice.org before. Take a look at these toolbars, for instance. Which one is Word, and which one is OpenOffice.org Writer? They're that similar, and that means you'll find OpenOffice.org familiar if you're used to Word.

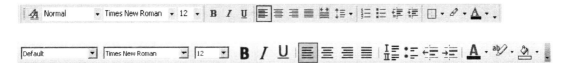

**With OpenOffice.org you can do it all**  OpenOffice.org matches Microsoft Office program for program, and goes a giant step further with a great graphics program, Draw. You get applications for working with documents, spreadsheets, slide presentations, web sites, graphics, and databases—anywhere from Oracle to MySQL to a simple text file.

Putting together a standard document or a letter is simple and quick. Brochures are easy too, with just two clicks to set up columns. And whether you want to just put together a simple budget or do complex statistical or mathematical calculations in a spreadsheet, you'll find the tools you need. You can even create a Web site start-to-finish.

So welcome to OpenOffice.org. It's the best deal you'll find anywhere.

# Acknowledgements

Thanks first and foremost to all the students I have taught over the past few years. Without your questions and emphasis on the jobs you need to do, rather than simply using the software, I wouldn't be able to write a very useful book.

Thanks to all those who contributed suggestions and reviewed the book, through my OpenOffice.org blog. The following is a sincere attempt at completeness; please post on my blog if I accidentally left you out. In no particular order:

* Joao Miguel Neves
* Scott Brawner
* Gordon MacPherson
* Louis Roederer
* Todd Threadgill
* Benjamin Horst
* Pete Holsberg
* Alberto
* Bill Harris
* Miguel Guhlin

Thanks to the OpenOffice.org volunteers, especially those on the users@openoffice.org mailing list, and to the experts on the www.oooforum.org site.

# Part I: Getting Started

# Making OpenOffice.org Work The Way You Want It

# What This Chapter Is About

This chapter is about the things you do when you first start using a program, that becomes automatic later on: starting the program, creating new files, etc. It's also about how to making using a new program as comfortable and convenient as possible. I can't overemphasize how much more useful, efficient, fast, and just plain cool you'll find OpenOffice.org if you set it up to work the way you want it. Take some time to explore this chapter and the subsequent ones in the *Getting Started* part.

# Starting and Running OpenOffice.org

This section covers how to start the program, and open and save files.

## Starting OpenOffice.org

**1**    Start the program as you'd start any other program. Choose the type of document you want to create: Writer, Calc, etc. Here's what it looks like when you start it in Windows and in Ubuntu Linux.

Starting OpenOffice.org on Windows

Starting OpenOffice.org on Ubuntu Linux

**2**    A new empty document will appear.

## Saving a Documents

**1**    Choose File > Save.

**2**    In the Save window, find the directory where you want to save the document.

**3**    Name the document and click Save.

## Creating Another OpenOffice.org File

Once you've got a document open, you can create any kind of other document from within the program instead of starting the program. Here's how.

♦   Choose File > New and select the type of document.

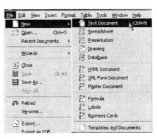

♦   You can also click on the New icon and choose a document type.

# Setting Up Backups and Autosave

The program lets you set up backups and autosave to help save your work.

**1**   Choose Tools > Options > Load/Save > General.

**2**   In the window that appears, you'll see several backup options.

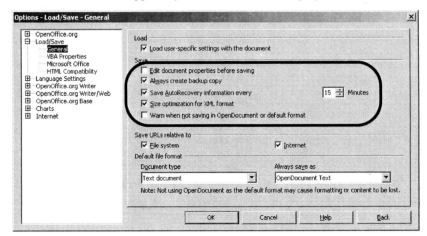

Select the option **Always Create Backup Copy**.

Then select **Save AutoRecovery Information Every**, and specify how often.

**3**   Next, select the Paths item in the left selection panel of the window, under the OpenOffice.org main category.

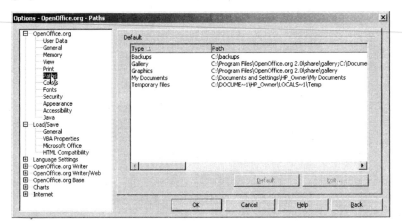

**4**   Select the Backup item, the first item in the list.

**5**   Click Edit.

**6**   In the Select Path window, specify where you want backups created.

**7**   Click OK. You'll see the path in the main options window.

**8**   Click OK to close the window and save changes.

# Making OpenOffice.org Run Faster

The best thing you can do to improve performance on your current computer is to get more memory. The next best thing is to tweak the settings that affect how memory is used in OpenOffice.org. Choose Tools > Options > OpenOffice.org > Memory and set the options as shown. in the following illustration

If these don't help, vary the settings and test further.

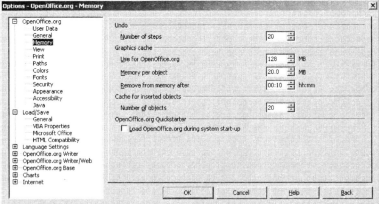

# Changing the Automatic Formatting

You've probably noticed the automatic word completion and other "help" the program gives you. Here's how to control it, and allow only the help that you want.

## Turning Off and Configuring Word Completion

It's extremely annoying when a program does things you didn't tell it to do—and don't *want* it to do. Word completion is one example. Take a look at the example at right. I typed the letters Ope. Maybe I wanted to type OpenOffice.org here, but maybe I wanted to talk about Opera. Regardless, the program pops up the word OpenOffice.org. I find it annoying.

This, however, isn't a problem. You can turn it off or, if you like it, tweak it.

1   Choose Tools > AutoCorrect.

2   If the Word Completion tab isn't in front, click it.

3   If you want to turn it off, unmark the Enable Word Completion option.

Unmark the Enable
Word Completion option
to turn off this feature.

If you want to keep the
feature on, you can
change the key used to
accept the suggested
word, and change the
minimum length of
words the system will
track.

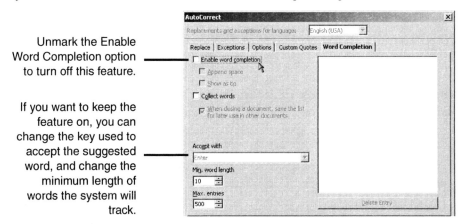

**4**  In the Accept With field, if you want to use a key other than Enter to accept the suggested word, select it from the dropdown list.

**5**  In the Min Word Length field, you can decrease or increase the size of the smallest word that the system will give you a suggestion for.

**6**  Click OK to save the changes.

# Turning Off Other Automatic Formatting

It's not as obvious, but there's a lot of automatic formatting going on, by default, in OpenOffice.org. Some of it can be very frustrating: automatic lists will be applied, for instance, when you type numbers yourself. Turn off everything you don't absolutely love.

**1**  Choose Tools > AutoCorrect.

**2**  Click the Options tab of the AutoCorrect window.

**3**  Unmark everything **except the two checkmarks for the top item**.

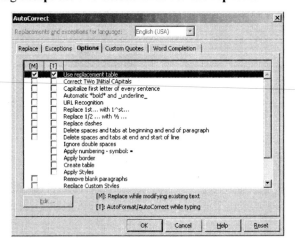

**4**  When you're done, take a look at the options and see if there's anything that you think would be useful. Use the online help to learn more about any particular item. Mark both checkboxes next to anything you want.

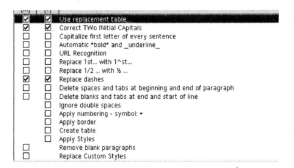

**5**  Click OK.

# How to Find Features You're Looking For

When you first start using a program, it's a bit difficult to find the features you need. Here are a few tips to make that process easier for you.

## When in Doubt, Right-Click

Right-clicking on an item will show you most of the things you can do with an item. When in doubt, select the text or graphic and right-click on it.

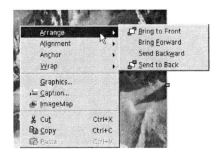

## Put Your Favorite Features on a Menu or Toolbar

The best way to make sure that you always know where a feature is, is to put it in an obvious spot. One way to do that is to take the 10 or 20 features you use the most and just put them on your own toolbar.See *Customizing Toolbars and Icons* on page 17.

## Use the Tooltips

Move your mouse over any toolbar icon and read the tip.

## Use the Online Help

See *Getting Help and Finding More Information* on page 57.

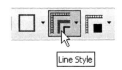

# Using OpenOffice.org Buttons

Most of the icons and buttons you'll see in OpenOffice.org are very easy to figure out and use However, some of them are a little unexpected, or are so important that I want to emphasize them here. Take a look at the following sections so that you'll be sure to know how to use the buttons when the time comes.

## Dropdown Buttons in OpenOffice.org

Usually you simply click on a button or icon, and something immediately happens. In OpenOffice.org, you occasionally need to click on *and hold down* a button the way you would a menu, and then select something.

This procedure will just walk you through using a dropdown button.

1    Choose File > Templates > Organizer.

2    Select the Default category in the left list.

3    Click and hold down the Command button. You'll see that there are several options under the button.

4    Close the window.

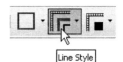

## Icons Look Different in Each Operating System

On Windows, Solaris, Macintosh, and different versions of Linux, some icons look different. This can make following directions a little troublesome when you're just looking for an icon that looks exactly the same as an illustration from a different operating system.

Windows toolbar icons

Ubuntu Linux toolbar icons

However, here's how to make sure you always know what an icon is for. Use the Tool Tips. Move your mouse over the icon and look at the tip that pops up.

## Seeing all Options for Icons With Black Triangles

Usually when you click on an icon, a big formatting window appears, or an action is performed. However, some of the icons across the top in the toolbars, and the icons in the toolbar with a black triangle, give you more options to choose from, before anything happens.

Here's an overview of how the black triangle icons work.

**Here's what happens with icons that have a black triangle, when you click and hold down on the icon.**

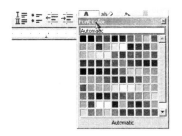 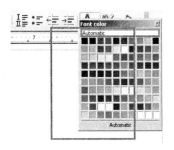 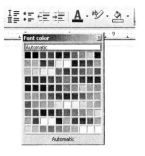

After you click and hold down on the icon, a palette of options will appear. You can just click on one of those options. However, once you make a choice, the whole palette will go away.

Or if you want to display that palette of options for a while, click on the border at the top of the menu. Drag the palette a little to one side, or up or down.

The palette will separate and stay displayed. Then you can click on the palette options to make additional choices and the palette won't disappear.

**Icons on the Drawing toolbar work the same way, but just look a little different.**

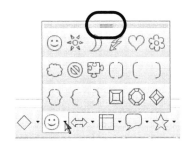

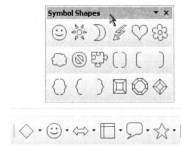

# Using OpenOffice.org Toolbars

You might think that the icons and toolbars are just the way they are, and there's nothing you can do about it. However, it's pretty much the opposite. You can do pretty nearly anything you want to the icons and toolbars.

They look like this to start off with.

But by the time you're done with them you can make them bigger, change the tools that appear on each toolbar, change the pictures for each icon, change the name of a feature as it's displayed in menus, and even make your own toolbar, from scratch.

In this illustration, I've added Page Preview icon to my main toolbar and I used a picture I took as the icon. You also can choose exactly which toolbars are displayed, of the many available.

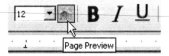

## Making Icons Easier to See

1   Choose Tools > Options.

2   Under the OpenOffice.org category of the Options window, find View.

3   Select the **Large** item from the Icon Size list.

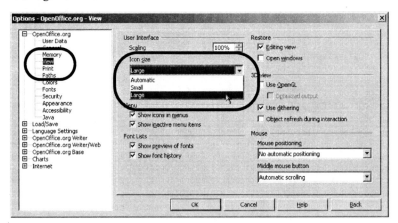

4   Click OK to save your changes and close the window.

# Seeing All the Icons on a Toolbar

If you increase icon size or shrink your window, you won't see all the icons at once. Your icon for changing text color, for instance, might disappear. Here's how to see the indicators that some icons are hidden, and how to get to them.

**1**   Shrink the window to about half its usual size.

**2**   Find the set of arrows at the right side of the toolbar.

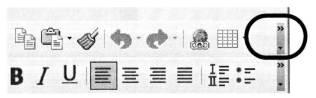

**3**   Click the downward-facing arrow. You'll see the names of all the icons that there isn't currently room to display on that toolbar.

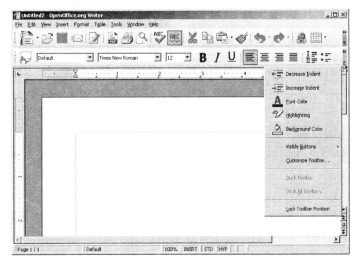

**4**   Select the function you want.

**Note –** You'd normally want to select the text you want to apply the function to first; for instance, if you want to indent text, you'd select that text, then click on the double arrow, then select the function you want.

## Accidentally Hidden Toolbars

You can move the toolbars around wherever you like by dragging the dotted vertical line. However, this means that sometimes they're not in the best position. If you're looking for a toolbar and can't find it, look for something like this.

The circled part is the first icon of the Bullets and Numbering toolbar, which has gotten squished in the upper right part of the work area.

To drag the toolbar to a place where it has more room, click and hold down on the light dotted vertical line at the left side of the squished toolbar.

Then drag it down to below the other toolbars, making sure that a thick dotted border around the toolbar area is visible.

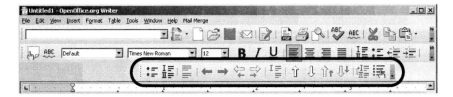

When you release it, the toolbar will have room to show all the icons.

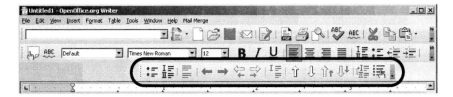

## Viewing Toolbars

OpenOffice.org shows you the basic toolbars when you open a new document. Here's how to show or hide any of the many others.

1   Choose View > Toolbars and look at the options that are displayed. There are a lot of choices, including pretty specialized ones.

**2**    From that list of options, select Bullets and Numbering. That will display the specialized list toolbar. Use this anytime you want to do complicated indented lists.

**3**    Click the X in the upper right corner to close it.

**4**    Check the bottom of the work area. If this toolbar isn't displayed, Choose View > Toolbars > Drawing.

**5**    Choose View > Toolbars > Drawing again to hide the toolbar.

# Docking and Other Ways of Displaying and Positioning Toolbars

The 2.0 OpenOffice.org interface lets you drag around the toolbars. Here are some general guidelines to review before beginning the exercises.

◆    **Showing or not showing** – If you want a toolbar to show, just choose View > Toolbars > *name* and it'll show. (There needs to be a checkmark by the toolbar for it to be displayed.)

If it's floating and showing, just click the X to make it go away.

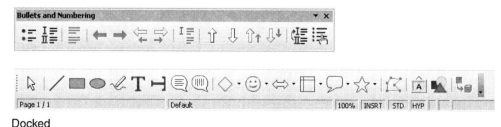

◆    **Floating or docked** – The toolbar appears *floating* or *docked* on the toolbar. Docked just means it looks like a normal toolbar and it's next to the other toolbars. Docked is generally a better approach.

Floating

Docked

## Docking a Floating Toolbar

If you've got a floating toolbar that you want docked, follow these steps.

**1**    Drag it to where you want it near the other docked toolbars.

**2**    A dashed outline of the toolbar will show where it'll end up.

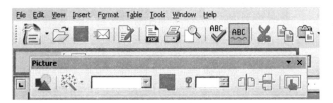

**3**    Release your mouse. The toolbar will appear with the other toolbars where you released it.

**4**    If necessary, click and hold down on the vertical dashed line and drag it right or left to reposition the toolbar.

## Making a Docked Toolbar Float

**1**    Locate the vertical dashed line at the left side of the toolbar.

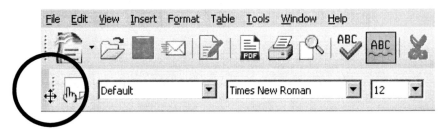

**2**    Drag it to the work area.

**3**    A dashed outline of the toolbar will show where it'll end up.

**4**    Release your mouse. The toolbar will appear, floating.

# Customizing Toolbars and Icons

OpenOffice.org lets you do a lot of customization to show the toolbars you want. You can also choose exactly what icons you want—and don't want—on your toolbars.

## Specifying Icons Displayed on the Toolbars

The OpenOffice.org developers put what they think are the most commonly used icons on the toolbars, but those aren't the only ones available. You can add others that you like better, and remove the ones there already that you don't use.

**1**    Click on the downward-facing arrow on the formatting toolbar. In the list that appears, choose Visible Buttons.

**2**     A list of all the icons available to put on that toolbar will appear. To show an item, find one without a check mark next to it and select it.

**3**    To hide an item, find an item with a check mark next to it and select it.

## Changing a Toolbar Icon

If you or the users in your organizations are used to different icons, you can change them here.

**1**    Choose Tools > Customize.

**2**    Click the Toolbars tab.

**3**    Select the toolbar that the icon is on.

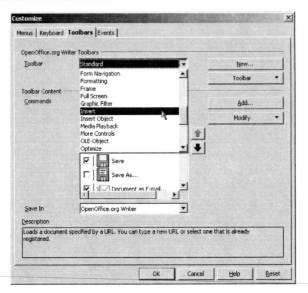

**4**    Select the icon.

**5**    Click and hold down on the Modify button, and choose Change Icon.

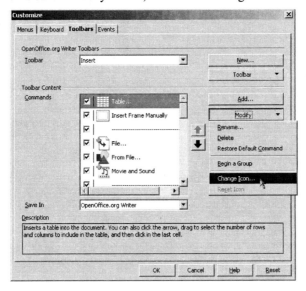

**6**    The icons window will appear.

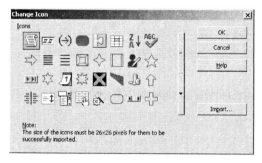

**7**    Select the icon you want by doing one of the following:

*    Select one from the list.

*    Import a new icon from a .png file. The file must be 26 pixels by 26 pixels.

---

**Note –** The icons that you select will be smaller than the standard icons, if you've changed your icons to be large, as in *Making Icons Easier to See* on page 12.

---

**8**    Click OK.

**9**    Click OK again; the icon will appear next to the item you selected.

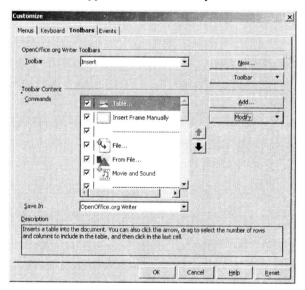

**10**    You'll see the new icon on the toolbar.

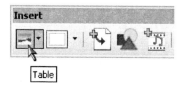

# Changing the Text for a Menu Item

Let's say you're in charge of setting up OpenOffice.org for the users in your organization, and you're trying to make the software as similar to your old office suite as possible. Perhaps users are used to seeing "Print Preview" instead of "Page Preview". You can change OpenOffice.org to use the phrase you want.

**1** Be sure you've got the program open for the menus you want to affect.

**2** Choose Tools > Customize.

**3** In the Customize window, click the Menus tab.

**4** Select the menu and icon that you want to change.

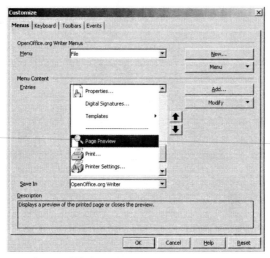

**5** Click and hold down on the Modify button, and choose Rename.

**6** Type the new name for the item and click OK.

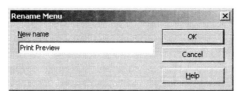

**7** If you want, move the item up or down in the menu.

**8** Click OK.

**9** The item will be displayed with its new name in the modified menu.

# Adding an Icon to an Existing Toolbar, or Creating a New Toolbar or Menu

Many features are not shown on the default toolbars, or are hard to get to as icons. It's helpful to modify an existing toolbar, or create your own toolbar, with icons you use frequently. You can use icons from other toolbars, or icons that aren't shown.

In this example, I'll show how to create a toolbar for Calc with several printing-related icons. **However, you can also use the principles in this procedure to simply add an icon to an existing toolbar, or to add a menu.**

**1**   Be sure you've got the document open for the menus you want to affect. If you want to affect a Calc toolbar, for instance, be sure you've got a spreadsheet open.

**2**   Choose Tools > Customize.

**3**   Click the Toolbars tab to modify or create a Toolbar, or the Menus tab to modify or create a menu.

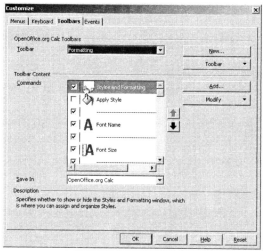

**4**   Create or modify a toolbar or menu.

◆   To create a new toolbar or menu, click New, and in the window that appears, type a name and click OK.

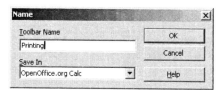

The new toolbar will appear, with no icons in the list. Click Add.

◆   To add an icon to a toolbar or menu, click Add.

**5**   In the window that appears, you can select any icons you want to add to the toolbar or menu.
It's a bit annoying to scroll through all the categories, so when you're looking for something in
the future, expect to take some time.

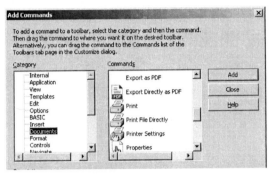

**6**   If you want to add your own icons, select them and click Add after each. Click OK when
you're done adding the icons, then continue to step 7.

If you want to add the print icons for the Calc printing toolbar, follow these steps.

♦   Select the Documents category.

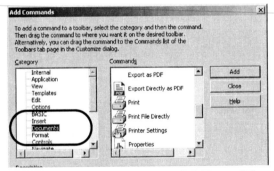

♦   In this category, you want to add the Export as PDF, Export Directly as PDF, Print, Print
File Directly, and the Printer Settings icons. Select the first icon and click Add, select the
next icon and click Add, and so on.

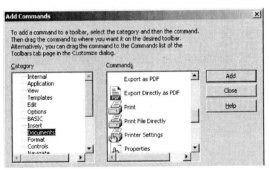

◆ Select the View category and find the Page Preview icon. Click Add.

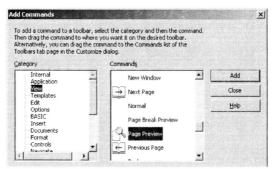

◆ Select the Format category. You're looking for several icons which aren't together; I've shown them together here.

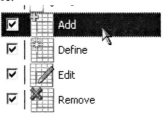

Scroll through the list and as you find each, click Add.

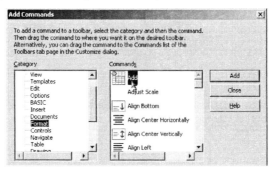

◆ You're done adding icons, so click OK.

**7**    The toolbar or menu is shown in the main definition window. Click OK.

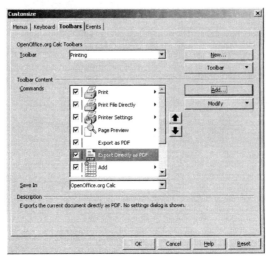

**8**    The toolbar or menu should be displayed in the work area.

If the toolbar isn't displayed, choose View > Toolbars > *toolbar name*.

# Setting the Ruler Unit of Measure

**1**    Choose Tools > Options > OpenOffice.org Writer > General.

**2**    Select the unit of measure for the horizontal and the vertical ruler.

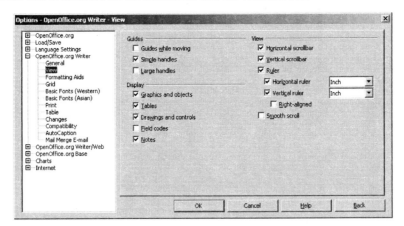

**3**    Click OK.

# Working With OpenOffice.org and Microsoft Office

**IN THIS CHAPTER**

# Introduction to Working With Other Office Suites

There will always be people out there using different office suites than you are. They aren't just Microsoft Office users; there are people using WordPerfect, LaTeX, various options for Macintosh, and more. Learning to work with people using other office suites will be useful regardless of the office suite you're using.

I'm going to address working with Microsoft Office in this chapter since that's mostly what you'll encounter. Additionally, many of the tips will work fine for improving compatibility with any other office suite.

So let's focus on a few key points:

You've converted from Microsoft Office to OpenOffice.org. You need to open those old Microsoft Office files, for one thing. You also need those files to look good. And you also need to still work with Microsoft Office users; how do you give them the files they can open and (if necessary) edit?

* *Opening and Saving Microsoft Office Files in OpenOffice.org*
* *Formatting Issues Between Office Suites*
* *Working With Microsoft Office Users*

# Opening and Saving Microsoft Office Files in OpenOffice.org

To open a Microsoft Office file, just start OpenOffice.org and choose File > Open. Select the file you want. If you want to convert multiple Microsoft Office files to OpenOffice.org format at once, use the converter; see *Converting Documents to OpenOffice.org Using the Conversion Wizard* on page 31.

## Using Microsoft Office Documents in OpenOffice.org

It's a simple process—just choose File > Open or File > Save. You can follow these step-by-step instructions, as well.

### Opening a Microsoft Document

1    In OpenOffice.org, choose File > Open.

2    Locate the Microsoft document on your computer.

3    Click Open. The document will appear in OpenOffice.org.

### Saving a Microsoft Document in OpenOffice.org Format

If someone sends you a Word document, and you're just going to keep it, you'll probably want to just save it in OpenOffice.org format. Here's how to save to OpenOffice.org format.

1    Open the document in OpenOffice.org and choose File > Save As.

**2** Click on the file type dropdown list. Select the one that makes sense for your document: OpenDocument Text, OpenDocument Spreadsheet, etc.

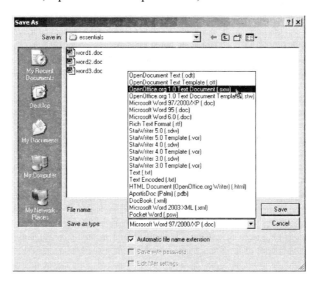

**3** Click Save to save the document.

# Formatting Issues Between Office Suites

When you open a Microsoft Office, WordPerfect, or other document in OpenOffiec.org, the document might not look exactly the way it did in the original program. Sometimes it will, but not all the time. Here's an example: a document in OpenOffice.org Writer, and the same document saved as a .doc and opened in Word. The cute red graphical bullets, specific to Writer, were lost. Otherwise, it looks pretty good, including the drawing object.

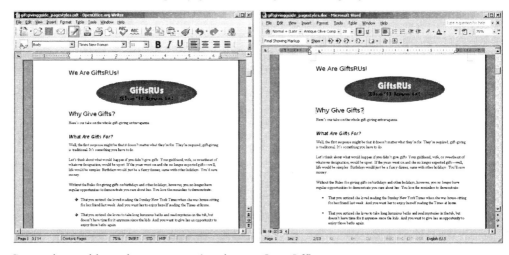

Conversion problems, however, aren't unique to OpenOffice.org.

- Take a complex document from Word 95 to Word 2003, or vice versa (if possible) and you might some interesting differences.

- If you're working with Word 2003 on a computer has a big set of fonts, and you take a document created on that computer to a computer with Word 2003 but fewer fonts, you might have differences.

- Take a Word document from one platform to another, and you might encounter problems.

Anytime you change the program, program version, or environment (fonts and operating system) for a document, there's a chance things will change. It's an issue with software in general, not only OpenOffice.org.

That said, how do you deal with specific issues between OpenOffice.org and Microsoft? That's what this section is all about.

# Overall Formatting Solutions

This is the section with all the formatting solutions. I've grouped them into general guidelines, specific fixes, and setup.

## Margins, Fonts, and Font Size

Fiddle with the margins. Different margins can drastically change how text flows on a page. Also tweak the font, and font size to make them match the Microsoft documents. See *Changing Margins* on page 102 and *Making Text Look How You Want It: Basic Formatting* on page 71.

## Default Fonts

Change the default fonts used for new documents to match the fonts used in the Microsoft documents you're opening. See *Setting up Default Fonts for New Writer Documents* on page 44.

## Default Template

Change your default template to match the main characteristics of the Microsoft documents. See *Specifying a Template as the Default Template for New Documents* on page 43.

## Default Tabs

Change the default tabs slightly; increase them a little or decrease them a little nd see what happens. See *Setting up Default Tabs* on page 90.

## Hyphenation and Other Text Flow Options

Change hyphenation, text flow, and other items in the Text Flow tab of the Paragraph Formatting window (choose Format > Paragraph). See *Reference to Advanced Paragraph Formatting* on page 82. Use this approach only if you're familiar with these advanced features.

## Use Formatting Windows, Not Tabs or Carriage Returns

Sometimes the document you bring from Microsoft Office into OpenOffice.org just wasn't formatted well in the first place. Carriage returns and tabs instead of wrapping the text can be one issue. Show the tabs and carriage returns, and other typographical marks so that you can more easily see what might be causing the formatting programs. See *Viewing Carriage Returns and Other Formatting Markups* on page 93 to understand these marks. You'll probably just want to delete any tabs or carriage returns in the middle of a paragraph. This will help a lot.

Follow the guidelines in *Guide to Good Layout and Formatting* on page 141. By formatting in a more automatic way (that is, using the formatting windows) and less manual way (using carriage returns and tabs), you create a document that's less likely to break when going between programs, computers, documents, or operating systems.

# Solving Problems With Specific Pieces of Text or Graphics

Occasionally you'll just have formatting problems with a few pieces of text rather than the flow of a whole document. Here's how to fix those.

### Return the Formatting to Default Mode

If text formatting is decidedly odd, select the text and choose Format > Default.

### Anchor Graphics to Paragraph or Use Frames to Group Items

If graphics are behaving oddly, right-click on each and choose Anchor > To Paragraph. Then reposition the graphic. See *Positioning Graphics* on page 206.

If this doesn't do what you want, and you don't want to have graphics layered on top of each other, create a frame. Text boxes and graphics that aren't solidly tied together in Microsoft Office might come flying apart in OpenOffice.org, and frames tie them together. Choose Insert > Frame, set size options and click OK, then cut and paste items into the frame. See *Frames* on page 214.

### Use Graphical Bullets

If bullets are being weird, try graphical bullets instead of font bullets (normal bullets). See *Applying Different Types of Bullets* on page 125.

# Setting Up OpenOffice.org Compatibility

OpenOffice.org 2.0 has many new settings to help you improve compatibility between Microsoft Office and OpenOffice.org. Which ones you use depends on how you formatted the original documents, your fonts, and other variables, so you'll need to experiment a bit. Here are the items to play with.

### Font Replacement

If you're on Linux and coming from Windows, or just have limited fonts, you can substitute all the fonts you don't have with the best fonts you do have.

Choose Tools > Options > OpenOffice.org > Fonts. Select a font in the Font list and in the Replace list, and click the green checkmark to put it in the list. Click OK.

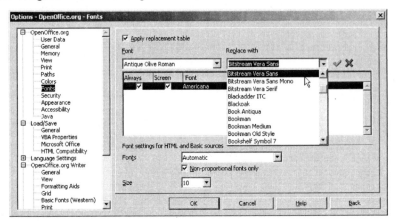

## Compatibility Settings

One of the recent additions is this window. How they each affect your documents depends on your setup. However, you should check each and see if it helps with conversion. See the online help for more information on each. I particular recommend, however, trying the **Use Printer Metrics for Document Formatting**. This option ties the fonts to the default printer you're set up to use. It doesn't work for everyone but I've seen it really clean up documents.

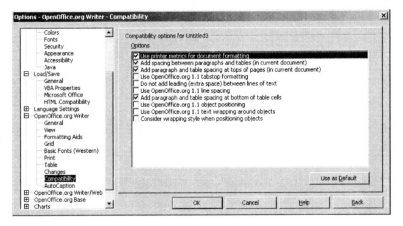

## Spreadsheets

Choose Tools > Options > OpenOffice.org Calc > General. Select one item to test and click OK. Open a Microsoft Office spreadsheet and see the effect.

Some of the options are good ways to tweak how spreadsheets behave so that you're more comfortable with the program, but some will help you with compatibility.

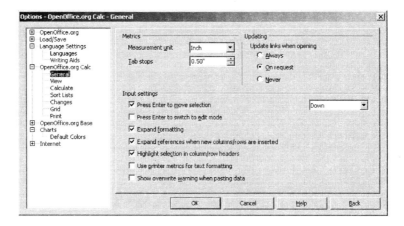

### Saving in Microsoft Format All the Time

This might be what you need, if you're constantly exchanging documents with Microsoft Office users or if your organization doesn't want to deal with the possibility of having two different document formats. All Writer document will be saved in .doc Word format all the time, and the same for Impress with Powerpoint format and Calc with Excel format. See *Always Saving in Microsoft Format* on page 34.

# Converting Documents to OpenOffice.org Using the Conversion Wizard

You can open any Microsoft Office document and save it in OpenOffice.org format, but sometimes it's convenient to have a faster approach: the document converter.

- ◆ Your Microsoft Office templates will work with OpenOffice.org, once they're converted to OpenOffice.org template format. If you have more than five or ten, converting them one at a time can take too long. Just slam the templates through the wizard using the steps in this section. Then you're ready to follow the directions in *Using Existing Writer, Calc, and Impress Templates in OpenOffice.org* on page 39.

- ◆ If you or your organization have been using Microsoft Office for more than, say, a week, you're going to have a bunch of documents to convert.

- ◆ OpenOffice.org 1.x documents are in a different format than 2.x documents, and need to be converted.

For these reasons, and no doubt more, the Conversion Wizard is very useful. Follow these steps.

**1**   Create a directory for the copies that you will create with the converter: for all the documents
or for each separate directory. You might do this, for instance.

Your current files, in
Microsoft Office or
OpenOffice.org 1.x format.

A new set of empty directories
where you'll have the conversion
wizard create new
OpenOffice.org 2.0 copies.

**2**   Choose File > Wizards > Document Converter.

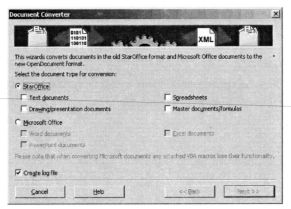

**3**   What you select depends on what you need to do.

♦   If you're converting from Microsoft Office, select Microsoft Office and all types of
documents you want to convert.

♦   If you're converting from OpenOffice.org 1.x, select StarOffice and all the types of
documents you want to convert.

**4**   Click Next. In this window, specify where you want to convert from, and where you want the
copies to go, for each type of document. Once you set it up in one set of fields you can copy
and paste the paths to the other fields.

You want to specify the smallest directory you have set up; note that the example shows the **\reports\annualreports** directories, not just the **\reports** directories.

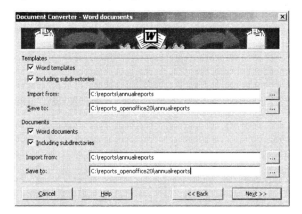

**5**  Click Next and fill in the information it asks you for.

**6**  In the Summary window, review the information, then click Convert.

**7**  A progress message will show what's happening. When the conversion is done, you'll have converted copies in the target directories.

# Working With Microsoft Office Users

How you work with Microsoft Office users all depends on what they need to do with the documents you're sending them. For instance, does Betsy in the city courts office need to *change* your report, or does she just need to read it, print it, or file it somewhere for reference?

If they don't need to change the document, your situation, and theirs, is much simpler.

| What the Person Receiving the Document Needs to Do | What You Should Do |
| --- | --- |
| Change the document by adding their own changes or content. | Send a Microsoft Office version of your document. See *Making Microsoft Office Versions of Your Documents* on page 34. To avoid formatting problems, see *Opening and Saving Microsoft Office Files in OpenOffice.org* on page 26. |
| Read it, file it, send it to someone else, but not change it. | Send a PDF version of your document. There are never inter-office-suite formatting problems when you use PDF; this is absolutely the best option to use if the person you're sending the document to doesn't need to change the file itself. See *Making Documents Everyone Can Read With PDF* on page 35. |

# Making Microsoft Office Versions of Your Documents

When you need to send documents to Microsoft Office users, and those users really do need to edit the documents, here are some options.

## Emailing Your OpenOffice.org Document to Microsoft Office Users

**Note** – You can use this feature to email an OpenOffice.org document in standard OpenOffice.org format, as well. Just choose Email as OpenDocument instead.

This is the slickest and quickest approach.

**1**   Just choose File > Send > and choose to send as Word (in spreadsheets, this will show as Excel; in presentations, this will show as Powerpoint).

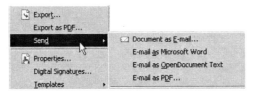

**2**   Your email program will start, a new email document will be created, and your Microsoft-format document will be attached to it. If the correct email program doesn't start, see *Setting the Default Email Program* on page 55.

The same procedure is currently available for sending a PDF version of the document. See *Emailing a PDF Attachment* on page 54.

## Saving Your OpenOffice.org Document as a Microsoft Document

Save the file in the correct format, then attach that document to your email.

**1**   Choose File > Save As. You'll see that you can choose a variety of formats.

**2**   Select the format that makes sense for your document that ends with 97/2000/XP: Microsoft Word, Microsoft Excel, etc.

**3**   Click Save.

## Always Saving in Microsoft Format

If you're always going to need a .doc , .ppt, or .xls version of your documents, you can just set up OpenOffice.org to use that format all the time.

Choose Tools > Options > Load/Save > General. In the Default File Format area, choose to save Text documents as Word 97/2000/XP documents, and so on. Click OK.

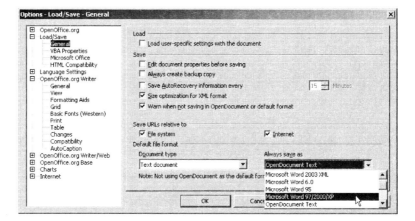

When you save documents, you'll get this message. Click Yes. You can also mark the checkbox to not show the message anymore.

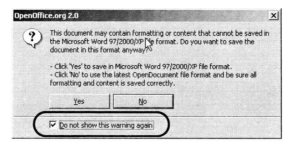

Now you don't have to take additional steps to put your document in a Microsoft Format—it already is. Just email your document to Microsoft Office users as is.

# Making Documents Everyone Can Read With PDF

You're going to work with people who use Microsoft Office, WordPerfect, LaTeX, plain old text editors, Lotus, and other programs. There's no way you want to waste time sending them all a document in the format of the program they use.

Even if you just work with Microsoft Office users, there are disadvantages to sending them .doc,.xls, or .ppt files if you don't have to. They can change the documents, and if you don't want them to be able to, that's a problem. There are potential formatting issues between OpenOffice.org and Microsoft Office, just as there are between different versions of Microsoft Office.

You can solve all these problems by sending out your documents in *Adobe PDF format.*

# Saving Time With Templates and More

## Templates: The Key to Efficiency

Templates are one of the greatest time-savers around. Templates are just a special kind of document that holds frequently used formatting and content such as canned text, signatures, placeholder text, etc. With a template, you can just make one document and use it as the basis for other documents, instead of redoing the formatting and retyping the content every time.

## Creating a New Category for Templates

There are a few default categories for templates: My Templates, Presentation Backgrounds, etc. However, you'll want to have some more specific categories to keep yours well organized.

**Note** – You will use these categories when you create one template at a time, or bring in one at a time. If you just point to a directory that already exists, then that directory will be the category. See *Preparing and Organizing Your Templates* on page 39.

1    Choose File > Templates > Organizer. Right-click in the left column, **on one of the categories**, and choose New.

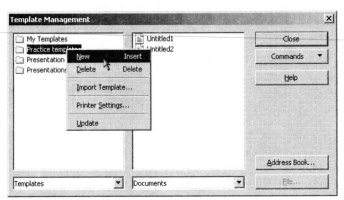

2    An untitled category will appear.

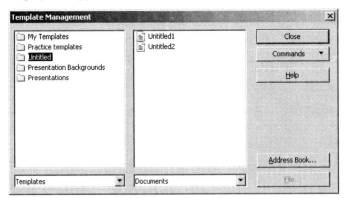

**3    Immediately** type the category name.

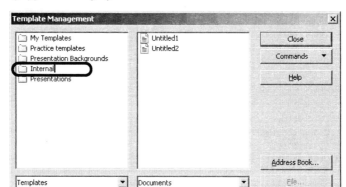

**4    Click Close.**

Now, when you choose File > Templates > Save, File > Templates > Organize, or access your templates, the new categories will be displayed.

# Using Existing Writer, Calc, and Impress Templates in OpenOffice.org

You're convinced—you agree to use templates. Or you've been using templates all along and you've got these great templates from your old office suite, or you've found some cool new OpenOffice.org templates and you want to use them. What do you do to incorporate the templates into OpenOffice.org?

There are several different approaches, so you can pick the one that works best for the templates you have.

## Preparing and Organizing Your Templates

There are just a few things to do first so that the templates are easy to find.

**1**    If you downloaded a .zip file of templates off the Internet, be sure to unzip them first. (Right-click on the .zip file and choose to expand or unzip.)

**2**    If you're using Microsoft templates, convert them to OpenOffice.org format first. See *Converting Documents to OpenOffice.org Using the Conversion Wizard* on page 31.

**3**    Set up the directories in a logical manner so you can find them during this procedure, and so that later when you make documents based on them, you will know what you're getting.

The templates can be on the server, or on each user's computer, depending on what works for what you're doing.

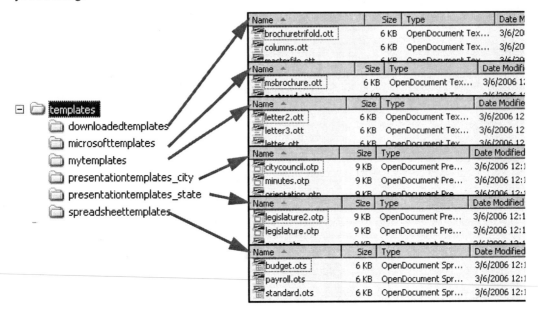

## The OpenOffice.org Templates Directory

Once you've converted and organized your templates correctly, copy your templates or template directories to this directory: openoffice.org directory\share\template\*language*\

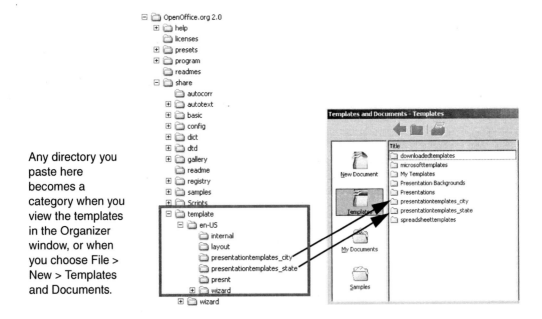

Any directory you paste here becomes a category when you view the templates in the Organizer window, or when you choose File > New > Templates and Documents.

## Importing a Single Template From Any Location

If you've got a template already on your computer or at another location, you can import it into the templates list. Once you do this, it will show up when you choose File > New > Templates and Document.

**1** If you don't have a good category to put the template in, make one using the information in *Creating a New Category for Templates* on page 38.

**2** Choose File > Templates > Organize.

**3** Select a category in the left column, to import into.

**4** Click and hold down on the Command button; select Import Template.

**5** Locate the directory where the template to import is, and select the template.

**6** Click Open.

**7** In the organizer, click Close.

**8** Close the window. When you or other users choose File > New > Templates and Documents, you'll see the new template in the My Templates category, along with any other templates already there.

# Creating a New Template

It's all very well to use other people's templates but the real power is in making them yourself. It's pretty simple.

**1** Create a new document—spreadsheet, text, presentation—and format it the way you want. Add any content you want to be in the template.

**2** If you don't have a category where the template should go, see *Creating a New Category for Templates* on page 38 and make a category.

**3** Choose File > Templates > Save.

**4** In the Templates window, select the category it should go in.

**5**    Name the template by typing the name in the New Template field.

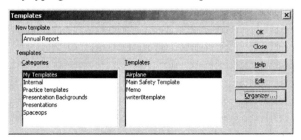

**6**    Click OK.

# Converting Microsoft Templates to OpenOffice.org Format

If you've got Microsoft format templates you like, you can use them in OpenOffice.org. You need to get them into OpenOffice.org template format first.

◆    You can open them one by one, choose File > Save As, and choose to save them in the OpenDocument Template format.

   However, as you've already gathered, this would take a long time to convert 2,980 templates. If that's how many you have.

◆    It's better to use the batch converter utility instead. See *Converting Documents to OpenOffice.org Using the Conversion Wizard* on page 31. Then continue to your favorite method in this section for setting up existing templates so you can access them through OpenOffice.org. You'll probably use *Preparing and Organizing Your Templates*.

# Creating a Document Based on a Template

You can follow these steps to make any type of document based on a template, including presentations. However, if you'd like to use the Impress wizard to create presentations, see *Creating and Running Presentations* on page 343.

**1**    Choose File > New > Templates and Documents.

**2**    Click on the Templates icon.

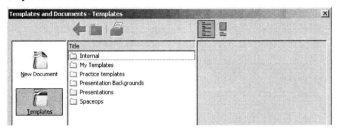

**3**    Select the category where your template is and double-click it.

**4**    Select the template and click Open. The template will open as an untitled document.

**5** Start creating your document. Save it as a normal document; this will happen naturally so you don't overwrite the template.

# Setting up How New Documents Look

You can specify exactly what formatting, styles, and content appear when you create a new document, by specifying the template that's used. This is one of the best things you can do to save time and make OpenOffice.org do exactly what you want.

## Specifying a Template as the Default Template for New Documents

When you choose File > New, it's not just a blank new document you're getting. It's based on the internal OpenOffice.org default template for Writer. You can specify a different template to use.

**1** Make the template that you want to show up when you create a new document. See *Creating a New Template* on page 41.

**2** Choose File > Templates > Organize.

**3** Select the appropriate category.

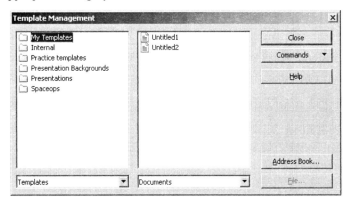

**4** Double-click the category. All the templates in that category will appear.

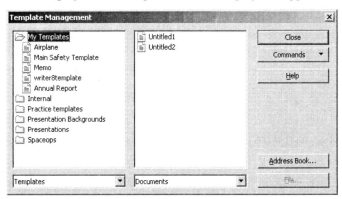

**5**    Right-click on the template you want, and choose Set as Default Template.

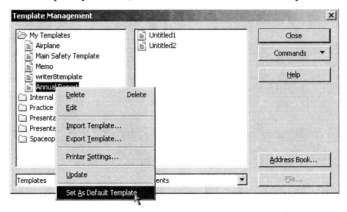

**6**    Click Close.

## Reverting to the Default Template

To revert to the default template, choose File > Templates > Organize. Right-click on any template category and choose Reset Default Template > *typeoftemplate*.

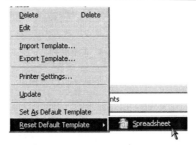

# Setting up Default Fonts for New Writer Documents

Templates are one way to mold OpenOffice.org new documents to your will. However, a quicker way if you aren't picky is to just set up the default fonts. By the way, this is overridden by the process in *Specifying a Template as the Default Template for New Documents* on page 43.

**1**    Choose Tools > Options > OpenOffice.org Writer > Basic Fonts (Western).

**2**    Select the fonts and font sizes you want to use.

**3**    Click OK.

When you create a new text document, those settings will be used.

## Font Replacement

If you don't like the fonts in the documents people send you, or if you just have very limited fonts, use the Font Replacement window.

**1** Choose Tools > Options > OpenOffice.org Writer > Fonts.

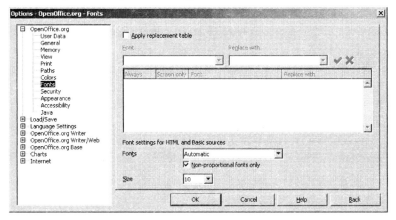

**2** Select Apply Replacement Table.

**3** In the first dropdown list, select the font you don't have or don't like, and in the second list, select the font you want to use instead.

**4** Click the green checkmark.

**5** The fonts will appear in the replacement table list. Choose whether to use the replacement all the time, or only onscreen.

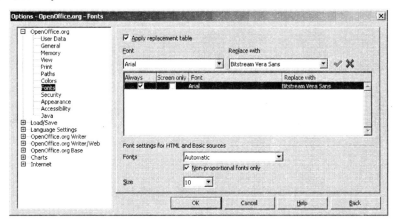

**6** From the Size list, specify a font size.

**7** Click OK.

# Shortcuts for Frequently Used Text

Templates are about document-scale efficiency. If you use a particular document or set of formatting over and over again when you create a particular type of document, templates are for you.

However, let's say you also use a particular phrase frequently in many different types of documents. You don't want to mess around with a template just to hold that text, since you don't use it all the time, but you use it in many different situations.

There are two options for this: a lightweight quick approach, and a heavy-duty approach.

## Creating a Shortcut in the AutoCorrect Window

1   Be sure OpenOffice.org is running with a document open.

2   Choose Tools > AutoCorrect.

3   Click the Replace tab.

4   In the **Replace** field, type the shortcut for your word, and in the right-hand **With** field, type the actual word you want to appear in the document.

   For your name, for instance, you'd type your initials in the Replace field and your name in the With field.

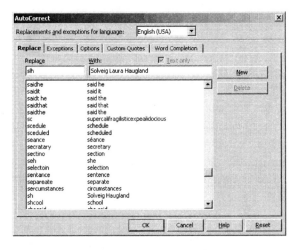

5   Click New. The shortcut and phrase will appear.

6   Before leaving the window, click the Options tab. Be sure that the top two checkboxes next to Use Replacement Table are marked. These mean "Use everything in the Replace tab."

7   Click OK.

8   In a blank Writer document, type the shortcut you specified, **followed by a space.**

slh ·〗

**9**   The replacement phrase you specified will appear.

Solveig·Laura·Haugland ¶

# AutoText

Let's say you've got this text, with some formatting, that you use frequently. The text might occasionally include a logo, as well.

> Yours truly,
>
> Magenta Golightly
> Program Director, *Elbow Grease Division*
> **magenta@elbowgrease.hardwork.com**

The shortcut in *Creating a Shortcut in the AutoCorrect Window* on page 46 won't work since this text has multiple lines, formatting, and sometimes a logo.

The right way to insert this text automatically is with an AutoText entry.

---

**Note –** The AutoText is available in any document, and is stored in the AutoText directory at Tools > Options > OpenOffice.org > Paths. You can change this directory, if you want, by clicking the Edit button and specifying a new directory.

---

## Creating an AutoText Entry

**1**   Create and format the text you want to insert and include any graphics you want.

**2**   Select everything you want in the autotext entry. Be sure to select all of every line, so that you won't get some lines of the autotext entry on the same lines as other text.

|                    |                    |
|:------------------:|:------------------:|
| **Select this way** | **Not this way**  |

**3**   Choose Edit > AutoText.

**4**   If you want to create a new category, click Categories, type a category name, and click OK.

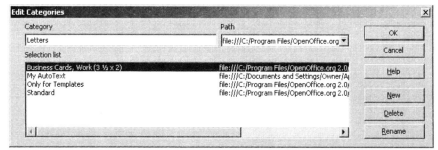

**5**    Select the category that you want the autotext to be in.

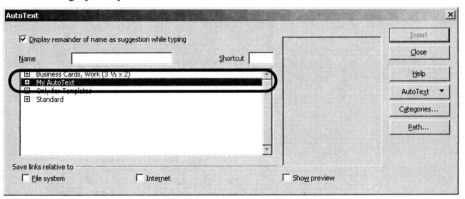

**6**    Type the name of the entry and, if you want, change the shortcut that automatically appears. You can use the shortcut when you insert the item.

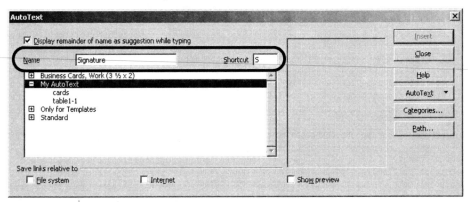

**7**    Click and hold down on the AutoText button and choose New.

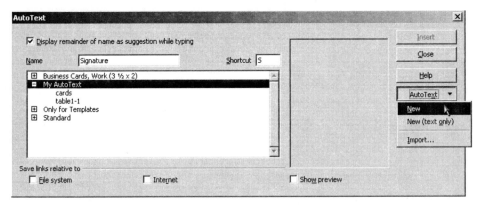

**8**    The entry will appear in the main list area, in the category you selected.

## Inserting an AutoText Entry

**1**  Go to the place in your document where you want the entry to appear.

**2**  Insert the entry using either of these ways.

   ◆  Choose Edit > AutoText, select the category and item, and choose Insert.

   ◆  Or type the shortcut, then immediately press F3.

## Specifying the Path to the AutoText Files

When you choose Edit > AutoText, the AutoText window has a Path button. Click that Path button and you'll see the location(s) where the AutoText entries are stored. If you want to copy your AutoTexts to another location, on another user's computer or the network, use this window to determine where the file is. If you want to point a user to another AutoText location, add the path using this window.

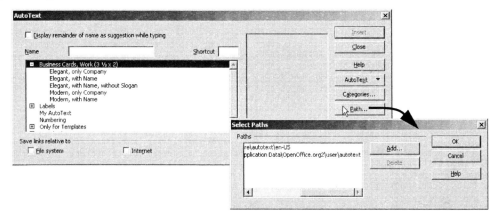

**4**

# PDF, Publishing, and the Web

# Why PDF Is an Incredibly Useful Feature

What are the problems you encounter when you give someone a document you created?

* They might not have the same program you created your document in, so they might not even be able to open the document
* They might not have the same fonts you used on their computer, so the document will look different
* Depending on how you inserted any graphics in the program, they might not have those graphics so the document will display placeholders instead of graphics
* They might encounter other problems related to a different operating system or other factors which affect how the program looks
* They might, accidentally or purposefully, change the content of the document, thus introducing inaccuracies
* Different fonts, settings, and other document attributes might cause problems with printing
* And so on

These are serious problems. One approach, which is not feasible, is to have everyone in the whole world who ever might exchange documents, use exactly the same fonts, operating system, printers, and software. Any IT director who's even tried to make that happen in the same company knows it's impossible, so trying to do it on a world-wide scale isn't in any way feasible.

So what else could solve the problem?

You need to be able to make your document into a format that contains all its own formatting and fonts, and which anyone can open. You'd need the document to be uneditable, so that no one could take that document and change it around, introducing errors. And if the ability to create and read this document format were available to anyone with a computer, for free, that would be even better.

That's what PDF is: portable document format. Everyone can read PDF format documents for free, and you, since you're using OpenOffice.org, can make your documents into PDF for free.

## What PDF Is

PDF is a way to "freeze" any document, whether it's originally in Word, Writer, Excel, Text, Photoshop, etc. The "frozen" PDF document looks exactly like the original, and can be opened using many free programs including the free Adobe Reader program. Adobe Reader or another PDF reader program is on pretty much every computer in the world.

When you need to send a document to someone else, you just:

* Convert it to PDF (this creates a PDF copy of your original). In OpenOffice.org this is free; there are programs that cost hundreds of dollars that do it, as well.
* Send that PDF document to whoever needs it.

## Using PDF With Microsoft Office Users

Needless to say, PDF is a great way to exchange documents with anyone using a different office suite or operating system. There are no formatting problems between users since the PDF document is "frozen" with all its formatting attributes. Anytime you need to send out a document, whether to another OpenOffice.org user or someone with different software, try PDF.

**Note** – If the people you're sending documents to need to change your document, rather than just printing it or saving it, then you'll need to use Microsoft Office format. See *Making Microsoft Office Versions of Your Documents* on page 34.

# Printing to PDF

If you need to have a PDF copy of an OpenOffice.org document, here are two ways to make it.

## Making a PDF the Quickest Way

**1**  Open a document.

**2**  Click the PDF icon on the top toolbar.

**3**  In the Export window, name the PDF copy of the document and put it in the location you want.

**4**  Click Export.

**5**  Find the PDF file on your hard disk and double-click it; it will open in Adobe PDF reader.

## Making a PDF With More Control

**1**  Open a document.

**2**  Choose File > Export as PDF.

**3**  A window will appear where you can specify what the PDF file name should be and where you want it to be created.

**4**  Click Export.

**5**     The PDF options window will appear.

Specify the range of pages to put in
the PDF. Separate nonconsecutive
pages with a semicolon such as
1-10;15;20-25

Reduce the size of the resulting
PDF file by reducing the quality and/
or resolution of graphics.

Leave Tagged PDF marked to
export hyperlinks.
This will convert OpenOffice.org
notes to PDF notes.

This refers to blank pages that are
inserted when you use some of the
existing page styles.

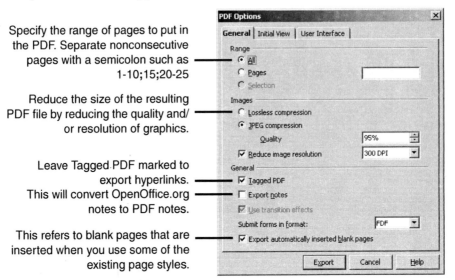

**6**     Select the options you need; you don't have to make any changes.

**7**     You can set the values for Initial View and User Interface tabs if you need to control exactly
how the PDF opens for users; see the online help (press F1) for more information.

**8**     Click Export.

**9**     Find the PDF file on your hard disk and double-click it; it will open in Adobe PDF reader.

# Emailing a Document as a PDF Attachment in One Step

If you just want to get a PDF version of your OpenOffice.org document to someone else and you
don't care about having a PDF of it around your hard disk, use this. It's a very slick, easy approach
and I recommend it for anyone getting started with PDF.

## Emailing a PDF Attachment

**1**     Open the OpenOffice.org document.

**2**     Choose File > Send > Document as PDF Attachment.

**3**     The PDF options window will appear. Generally, you can leave these options as is. (You can
also specify just a range of pages, if you don't want to send the whole file.)

**4**     Click Export.

**5**     Your email program will start, if it hasn't started already, and you'll see a new email document
from you, with the document in PDF format attached.

# Setting the Default Email Program

Use your operating system tools to set the default email program. This will vary by your operating system but here are two examples.

In Windows XP, go to the Control Panel, choose Internet Properties, and set the default email program.

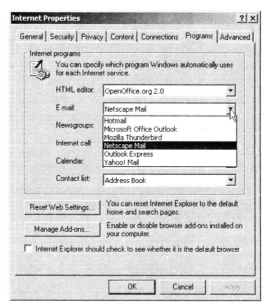

In Ubuntu Linux, choose System > Preferences > Preferred Applications.

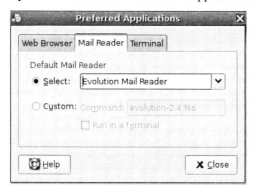

# Getting Help and Finding More Information

# How to Get More Information

If by some chance this book doesn't answer all your questions (it won't, since it's under 20 pounds), you're going to need to get some of your answers from somewhere else. How do you do that?

Everyone has their favorite ways to get information; here are the ones I suggest.

# Using the Help

1   In any OpenOffice.org document, press F1 or choose Help > OpenOffice.org Help. The main help window will appear.

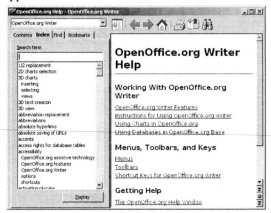

2   Click the Find tab.

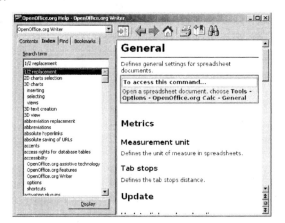

**3** Type the word you want to find in the Search field.

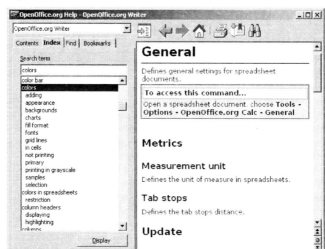

**4** In the results that appear, double-click on any item that looks like what you want.

**5** You'll see help on the topic.

# General Tips

Here's a list of things that work pretty well.

◆ When in doubt, right-click on the item in question and look at the options.

◆ When you want to figure out where a default setting is stored, try Tools > Options. When you want to figure out where automatic behavior is coming from, try choosing Tools > AutoCorrect. Check the Options tab first, then the others.

◆ Some of the icons like **B** **I** and **U** are self explanatory; some are harder to figure out. The tooltips are an excellent way to find your way around OpenOffice.org. Move your mouse over any of the icons in the work area and hold it there. You'll see a small tip describing what the icon does.

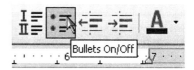

# Using Other Resources

If you'd like to go online, here are some places to start.

## Using Online Forums and the Mailing Lists

* The users@openoffice.org mailing list is an excellent resource. Search the archives first, then email the list. Subscribe to the list first; set it to Digest so you don't get overwhelmed.

* The dev@openoffice.org mailing list is good for more advanced questions about development, macros, etc.

* The oooforum.org site is chock full of marvelously smart people who give great help for simple or advanced questions.

## Blogs and Sites

My blog is at http://openoffice.blogs.com. Use the categories to find topics.

Some great blogs and sites are:

* openofficetips.com
* openofficetutorials.com
* learnopenoffice.com
* taming-openoffice-writer.com

This isn't all, by any means. Try google.com, or technorati.com, to find other resources.

# OpenOffice.org Training

If you need to help a group of OpenOffice.org users learn the program, consider bringing in an instructor to get everyone up to speed at once. You can email information and instructions to people until you're blue in the fingers but there's very little to match having people sit down in class for a day or a week and focus on learning the program. Training resources are outlined at http://openoffice.blogs.com.

# Part II: Writer Text Documents

6

# Text Formatting in Writer

# Creating and Opening Text Files

Here are the basics for creating, saving, and opening files.

## Creating a New File

1   Open a new spreadsheet document by starting the program and choosing OpenOffice.org > Text Document, or just choose File > New > Text Document if the program is already running.

2   The new document will appear.

---

**Note** – Within OpenOffice.org. you can choose File > New to create any kind of new document: Calc; Draw or Writer or the other options. Choose File > New > Text Document; a new text document will appear.

---

## Opening a Text Document

1   Choose File > Open or click the Open icon on the main toolbar.

2   In the Open window, navigate to where the file is stored and click Open.

## Saving a Text Document

1   Choose File > Save or click the Save icon on the main toolbar.

2   Navigate to the location where you want to save it, type the name, and click Save.

# Selecting, Copying and Other Tips

Everybody knows how to select text, right? And copying and pasting—well, it's intuitive, right? No serious book needs to cover those topics.

Well, in theory. But do we know for sure? Nobody really remembers when they learned those skills, of course. If you come from a command-line background, "obvious" mouse stuff isn't obvious. Plus, I'm also covering a few power tips in this section that are a little less well known, including selecting non-consecutive text.

## Selecting Text and Objects for Formatting

Here's how you select items: not just the mechanics, but what order, and shortcuts.

---

**Note** – See *Copying, Pasting, and Arranging* on page 421 for additional tips on copying and pasting objects.

---

### Select First, Then Format

Let's say you have a document with the phrase Save the Badger.

| |
|---|
| Save the Badger |

You want the word Badger to be bold, like this, at right.

| |
|---|
| Save the **Badger** |

There are two things: the word that you want to format, and the formatting. **Which do you do first?**

In some early computer programs you would say "I want something bold" and then specify what you wanted bold. However, in OpenOffice.org and most other programs these days, you want to say "I want to do something to this word" and then say "I want it to be bold." The short version of this is that you should always:

- Select the word
- ***Then*** apply the formatting

So here's how it works with the badger example.

Select the word Badger

Then click the Bold icon on the formatting toolbar.

The word **Badger** is now bold.

Save the **Badger**

## What You Need to Select for Paragraph-Wide Formatting Like Margins and List Numbering

As we just saw, some formatting is applied to particular characters. If you want something orange or bold, you select just the characters you want, and apply the formatting.

However, let's say you want a paragraph indented, or you want to make a few separate lines (separate paragraphs) into a list. It doesn't make sense to indent just a few words within a paragraph. The whole paragraph is affected, period. And likewise you couldn't have one word in a line part of a list, and the rest not.

This means that you don't have to baby OpenOffice.org as much when you're applying these paragraph-wide things. You just have to click *somewhere in the paragraph*, then apply the formatting.

If you wanted to indent this paragraph, you just click somewhere in it. That's all. (The cursor is circled.)

Rain, rain, go away; come again another day. I am going to go out of my mind if we have any more rain and that's just not going to be pretty.

If you want to indent two or more paragraphs, you can select it like this. You don't have to select all of every paragraph.

> Rain, rain, go away; come again another day. I am going to go out of my mind if we have any more rain and that's just not going to be pretty.
>
> I'm not really sure I remember what the sun looks like.

If you want to make these three paragraphs into a list, it's the same as the previous example—just select at least part of each line that you want to put in the list.

> Things I could do if it weren't raining.
> Go hiking.
> Take pictures.
> Lie in the hammock.

Then apply the formatting you want.

## Selecting One or More Characters by Dragging

The standard way to one or more characters is to click to the left or right of the text you want to select, keep holding down the mouse, drag it so that all of the text you want is highlighted, then release.

1    Click and hold down the mouse button at the edge of the text you want.

> Rain, rain, go away; come again another day

2    Drag in the direction you want to select

> Rain, rain, go away; come again another day

3    Keep dragging til you've got all the text you want

> Rain, rain, go away; come again another day

4    Release your mouse.

## Selecting One or More Words by Double-Clicking

Most of the time, you'll want to select a word or more. I.e. you want away, not just aw.

In this case, the easiest thing to do is double-click the word. There's no dragging; just double-click the word and you've got it. It's more precise, too.

Let's say you want to select three words. Double-click the first word, then move the mouse toward the next one. The whole next word gets selected—you don't have to precisely select all the letters in that word. Keep on going and it works the same way.

Before, it didn't matter where you started but with this approach, start with the farthest-left word.

**1**    Double-click the farthest-left word.

> Rain, rain, go away; come again another day.

**2**    Move your mouse slightly to the right. The whole next word is selected even though you didn't move your mouse as far as the right end of the word.

> Rain, rain, go away; come again another day.

**3**    Keep moving til all the words you need are selected.

> Rain, rain, go away; come again another day.

## Selecting a Sentence by Triple-Clicking

You could select a whole sentence using either of the previous approaches. But there's an easier way. Just triple-click one of the words in a sentence, and you get the whole sentence selected.

> Rain, rain, go away; come again another day. I am
> going to go out of my mind if we have any more rain
> and that's just not going to be pretty.

## Selecting a Paragraph by Quad-Clicking

Click rapidly four times in a row on a word and the whole paragraph is selected.

> Rain, rain, go away; come again another day. I am
> going to go out of my mind if we have any more rain
> and that's just not going to be pretty.

## Selecting Non-Consecutive Characters or Paragraphs

Let's say you've got this text. You want three of the phrases and one of the paragraphs bold.

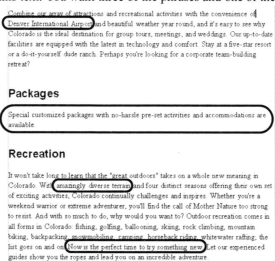

They're not consecutive so you can't just select them using the ways I've described so far.

It'd be annoying to have to select every one of them separately and format them. Select, format; select, format; etc. Imagine if there are 187 separate pieces, and if you have to make each bold, blue, 14-point, and a different font. That's a lot of work.

However, it's much easier when you select all the items, then format just once. Here's how you do it: select one word (or character), hold down your Ctrl key on your keyboard and select the next word or character (keeping Ctrl held down), and so on. When you're down, release the mouse and the Ctrl key, and apply your formatting.

The same goes for paragraphs. Select the first paragraph using the approach of your choice, hold down Ctrl, select the next paragraph (keeping Ctrl held down), and so on.

Here's how the document looks with the previously shown chunks selected.

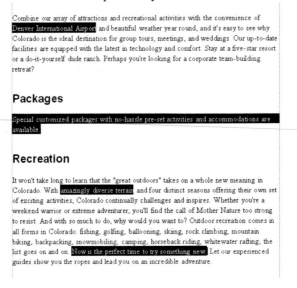

Now you can just click Bold, apply color to the text, delete the text, or do any other formatting just once. Everything you've selected will be affected.

# Copying, Cutting, and Pasting

Let's say you've typed a paragraph, and realize that you need to use it seven pages later in the same document. Or you just need to move that paragraph to another place in the document. Never retype it: just copy and paste, or cut and paste.

## Copying and Pasting Text

You want some text to be where it is, but in another place too.

1    Select your text or a graphic.

**2**    Copy. You can do this by clicking the Copy icon but it's quicker to hold down the Ctrl key on your keyboard and press **C**. Release the keys.

**3**    Go to the place where you want the text to be, and click in the spot where the text should appear.

## Packages

**4**    Paste. You can do this by clicking the Paste icon. It's quicker to hold down the Ctrl key on your keyboard and press **V**, then release the keys.

**5**    The copied text will appear.

## Packages

Special customized packages with no-hassle pre-set activities and accommodations are available|

### Cutting and Pasting Text

You've got some text or a graphic that should be somewhere else. You want to get it out of where it is and put it in another place.

It works the same way, but you should Cut instead of Copying. To cut, select the text or a graphic and either use the Cut icon. You can also hold down the Ctrl key on your keyboard and press **X**, then release the keys.

Then paste as usual. Be sure to paste quickly since the text will be lost if you copy or cut something else before pasting.

### Copying, Cutting, and Pasting Objects

This works just like it does for text. However, **before you paste, you have to click somewhere else in the document.** Otherwise, the pasting will just replace what you copied instead of duplicating it.

Click on the object, copy, then click on a blank space in the document, *then* paste. The pasted item will appear next to the copied item.

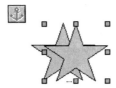

# Undo and Redo

If only life were as easy as undoing in a software program. Let's say you are typing away happily, try to do a standard formatting command, and all of a sudden something weird happens. You have no idea what you did but the document looks very weird. That's where the Undo feature comes in very handy.

## Undoing

Click the Undo icon, or hold down the Ctrl key on your keyboard and press **Z**, then release the keys. If that doesn't do it, repeat. The Undo can go back several steps.

## Redoing

If you find you want to just repeat a step over and over again, or if Undo took you to a bad place, use Redo. Click the Redo icon. You can also hold down the Ctrl key on your keyboard and press **Y**, then release the keys.

## Power Undo and Redo

Normal undo and redo undoes and redoes the most recent act. Keep clicking or pressing Ctrl Z or Ctrl Y to do more. You can redo or undo a bunch of steps at once if you click and hold down on the Redo or Undo icon. Just click on the black triangle, then select the items to undo.

## Setting up the Number of Undos

By default, you can undo up to 20 actions. You can change this by choosing Tools > Options > OpenOffice.org > Memory and finding the undo setting.

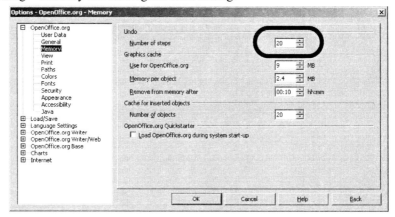

20 is a lot, but if you want more, just increase it. However, it's possible this might make the program run slower so don't increase it too much.

# Making Text Look How You Want It: Basic Formatting

Let's say you've got a document with some key information that you're going to distribute, or post on the bulletin board. Right now, it looks like this.

Some of it's more important than the rest, though, isn't it? You want to highlight the title and make sure people notice it. You want to emphasize the other important information like times and subheadings, and you might just want to change the font of the headings, the body text, or both.

All this just means you need to use the formatting tools to make the document's appearance bend to your will.

## Specifying Font and Font Size

**1**    Select the text that you want to format.

**2**    Use the dropdown list at the top to select a different font. Choose any font.

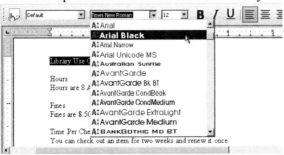

**3**    Use the dropdown font size list at the top to change the font size.

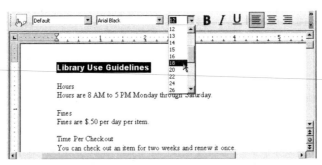

## Applying Bold, Italic, and Underline

You'd like to make each of the main categories, like Online Resources, stand out so it's easy to tell what kind of information is available.

**1**    Select the text that you want to format.

**2**    Use the Bold, Italic, and Underline icons to format the text as needed.

## Specifying Text Color

**1**    Select the text that you want to color.

ANNOUNCEMENT REGARDING
INTERLIBRARY LOAN

**2**    Locate the Text Color icon at the right side of the work area, shown here.

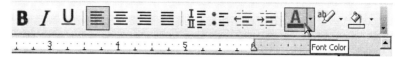

**3**    Click and hold down **on the black arrow** by the text color icon; the color palette appears.

**4**    Click on the border at the top and drag the color palette slightly either left or right.

**5**    Find a color you like in the palette and click on it to apply the color to the selected text. If you don't like the color, apply another.

**6**    Close the color palette when you're done.

**7**    The text is selected so won't show the true color while it's selected. Click on some other text in the document to see the true color of the text.

You can also apply a background color to a character, or to the whole line, with these icons.

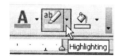

# Using the Format Paintbrush Icon to Repeat Formatting

I think that the best way to apply formatting to lots of pieces of text is to use the approach in *Selecting Non-Consecutive Characters or Paragraphs* on page 67. Select all the text to format, then apply the formatting once. This works for all types of formatting. However, you can do it another way with the Format Paintbrush icon.

## Repeating Formatting Just Once

**1**    Select some text that's formatted the way you want it.

**2**    Click the Format Paintbrush icon.

**3**    Your cursor will look like this.

**4**    Select some other text you want to apply the same formatting to.

**5**    Release the mouse. The formatting will be applied.

*Packages*

Special customized packages with no-hassle pre-set activities and accommodations are available.

*Recreation*

It won't take long to learn that the "great outdoors" takes on a whole new meaning in Colorado. With **amazingly diverse terrain** and four distinct seasons offering their own

## Repeating Formatting Several Times

You can double-click the Format Paintbrush icon if you have several pieces of text to apply formatting to.

**1**    Select some text that's formatted the way you want it.

**2**    *Double-click* the Format Paintbrush icon.

**3**    Your cursor will look like this.

**4**    Select some other text you want to apply the same formatting to. Release the mouse. The formatting will be applied.

**5**    Repeat the previous step for every additional piece of text you want to apply the same formatting to.

**6**    When you're done applying formatting, click the Format Paintbrush icon (just once).

# Aligning Paragraphs at the Left, Center, Right, or Fully

Standard text is often just left-aligned, but for headings, you sometimes want the text centered; for quote citations you might want the text left aligned; and so on. Here's how to apply center, left, right, and fully justified alignment.

**1**    Click anywhere in the text to align. This is formatting that will apply to the whole paragraph so you don't need to select every piece of text.

> ## Locations to Stay and Things to Do
>
> Combine our array of attractions and recreational activities with the convenience of **Denver International Airport** and beautiful weather year round, and it's easy to see why Colorado is the ideal destination for group tours, **meetings, and weddings.** Our up-to-date facilities are equipped with the latest in technology and comfort. Stay at a five-star resort or a do-it-yourself dude ranch. Perhaps you're looking for a corporate team-building retreat?

**2**    Locate the centering icon in the toolbar, or the alignment you want.

**3**    Click the centering icon. The paragraph will change its alignment.

> ## Locations to Stay and Things to Do
>
> Combine our array of attractions and recreational activities with the convenience of **Denver International Airport** and beautiful weather year round, and it's easy to see why Colorado is the ideal destination for group tours, **meetings, and weddings.** Our up-to-date facilities are equipped with the latest in technology and comfort. Stay at a five-star resort or a do-it-yourself dude ranch. Perhaps you're looking for a corporate team-building retreat?

# Indenting Paragraphs by Dragging, and Using the Indent Icon

You can easily make specified text start in farther from the left or right than the rest of the text. This is useful if you want text centered within a narrower area to make it look better, or if you just want text to start farther in from the left to allow for a big margin before a book is bound.

**Note** – This procedure is for indenting a selected paragraph, not changing the margins for the whole document.

## Indenting

1    Select the text to indent.

2    Click the Increase Indent icon once to indent the text to the next tab. (The next tab is based on the default tabs and is usually a half inch; see *Setting up Default Tabs* on page 90.)

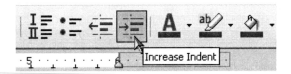

3    Keep clicking the Increase Indent icon as necessary.

## Dragging the Text Margin Markers

If you want more precise control over how far in the text goes, use these steps.

1    Select the text to indent.

2    Position your mouse over the icon at the left side that looks like an **hourglass**.

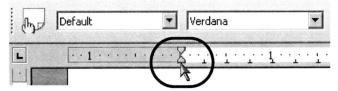

**Note** – The icon to drag is immediately on top of the page margin line, so doing this is a bit tricky. If your mouse turns into a left-right arrow, you've got the document margin, not the text margin. Moving the hourglass changes the margins *only* for the text you've got selected.

3    Drag the hourglass to the place where you want the left side of the text.

**4**   Repeat this step on the right if you need to indent the text there too. Position your mouse
over the icon that looks like the lower half of an hourglass.

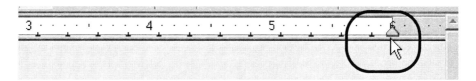

**5**   Drag the right text margin icon to where you want the right side of the selected text to end.

# Specifying Single, 1.5, or Double Line Spacing

Here's how to automatically apply more spacing between each line of text.

**1**   Select the text to change line spacing for. You only need to click somewhere in the
paragraph, though you can select all the text.

**2**   Right-click on the selected text and choose Line Spacing and your spacing choice.

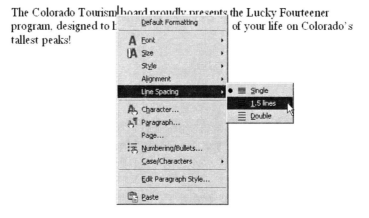

You can also use the appropriate icon on the formatting toolbar.

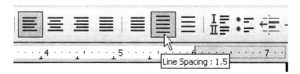

**3**   The spacing will change.

The Colorado Tourism board proudly presents the Lucky Fourteener

program, designed to help safely have the time of your life on Colorado's

tallest peaks!

# Formatting Using the Paragraph and Character Windows

The choices on the formatting toolbars are effective but somewhat limited. That's where the advanced formatting windows come in. If you haven't played with these, you're going to be surprised at how many options you have.

## Reference to Advanced Character Formatting

Select the text you want to format, choose Format > Character, pick the tab for the type of formatting you want to do, mark the options you want, and **click OK**.

### Character Formatting Window: Font Tab

Select the font, font style (bold, etc.), and font size you want. A preview of your selections is shown below.

If you're having problems with spellchecking, be sure that this is set to the language you're using.

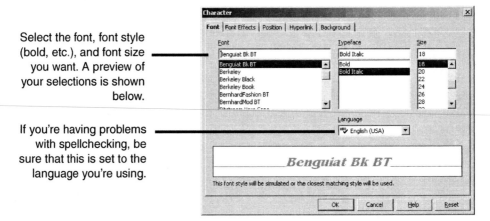

### Character Formatting Window: Effects Tab

Select additional formatting options like underlining, color (for the underlining or for the text), strikethrough, etc.

Select effects like all caps or title case, relief, outline, shadow, etc.

The preview area shows the effect of the current selections.

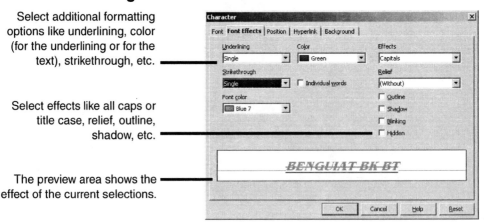

## Character Formatting Window: Position Tab

Select character position options like super or subscript, then specify the amount to raise or lower and the size.

Rotate text.

Change character width.

Specify how far apart the characters are (as opposed to the width of each).

The preview area shows the effect of the current selections.

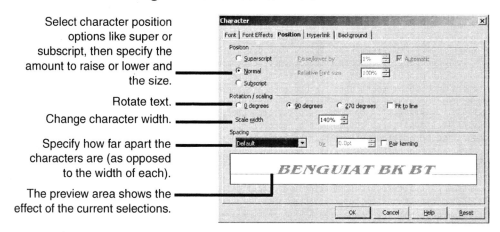

## Character Formatting Window: Hyperlink Tab

Specify the URL to link to.

Specify whether the target URL will open in a new blank browser, or another option.

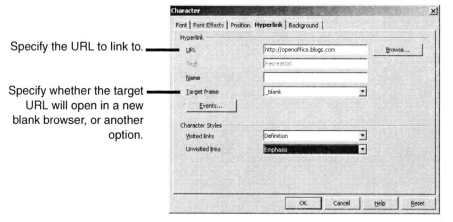

## Character Formatting Window: Background Tab

Select No Fill or the color you want in the background.

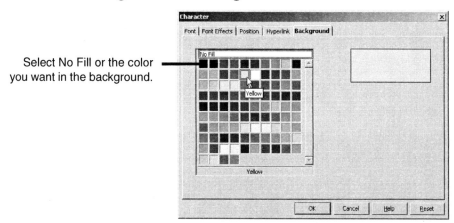

# Hyperlinking Text

**1**    Select the text.

> forest. From family-friendly vacation rentals and luxurious ski resorts to elegant historic
> properties and the reliable national hotel and motel chains, you're sure to find the perfect
> place to base your Colorado adventure

**2**    Choose Format > Character and click the Hyperlink tab.

**3**    Type the URL, and set other options such as selecting **_blank** as the target frame if you want
        the link to open in a new browser window.

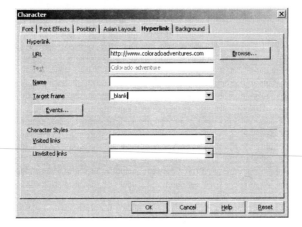

**4**    Click OK.

**5**    The text will be linked.

> forest. From family-friendly vacation rentals and luxurious ski resorts to elegant historic
> properties and the reliable national hotel and motel chains, you're sure to find the perfect
> place to base your Colorado adventure.

## Removing a Hyperlink

To remove the link, right-click on the linked text and choose Default.

## Applying Advanced Formatting Using the Character Formatting Window

You've seen all the pictures of the windows. Here's a walkthrough with all the steps. Let's say you've got some more complex formatting you want to do that the dropdown lists, etc. on the icon bar can't take care of.

**1**    Open the document and select some text you want to jazz up.

**2**    Right-click on the text and choose Character, or choose Format > Character.

**3**    Click the Position tab.

**4**    Specify a scale width, perhaps 140 %.

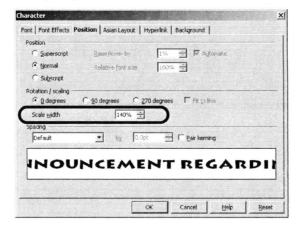

**5**    View the preview of your selection at the bottom of the window.

**6**    Click the Effects tab.

**7**    Select a different text color.

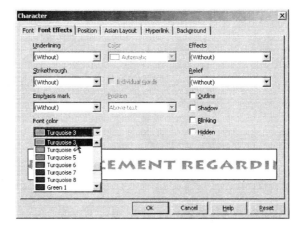

**8**    Select the Outline and Shadow checkboxes.

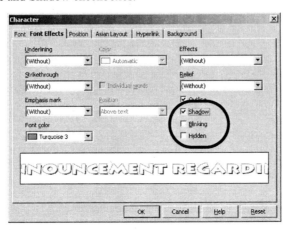

**9**    View the preview of your selections at the bottom of the window.

**10**    Click OK to apply the formatting selections to the text.

# Reference to Advanced Paragraph Formatting

There's actually not much on the toolbar that gives you good paragraph-level formatting. The Paragraph formatting window includes a lot of very powerful features for complex indenting, spacing below paragraphs, and other text flow items.

## Paragraph Formatting Window: Indents & Spacing Tab

This is the workhorse power center of paragraph formatting. When you want to do exact spacing for a paragraph above, below, left, right, and for each line, use this tab.

**Before Text** is the left indent; **After Text** is the right indent. **First Line** is a separate indent for the first line of text.

Specify the spacing above and below each paragraph. Typical settings are 0 or .02 above and .08 to .12 below.

Single is usually fine, though you can set a specific height by selecting **Fixed** line spacing and roughly .20 inches.

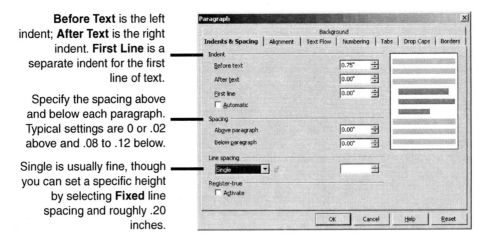

## Paragraph Formatting Window: Alignment Tab

You don't get much more here than the same alignment icons from the toolbar.

Specify the alignment of the paragraph.

For justification, select additional options for the last line of the paragraph.

Select an alignment option for oversized or undersized characters in the paragraph relative to the rest of the text in the paragraph.

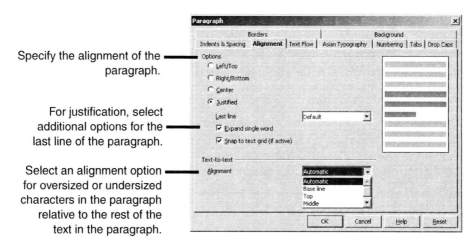

## Paragraph Formatting Window: Text Flow Tab

This is a very powerful, somewhat complex tab. If you care about hyphenation, widows and orphans, and other complex text flow issues, you will love this tab. If you want to automatically switch from one page style to another (styles are covered in *Saving Enormous Time and Effort With Styles* on page 147), this is your tab. Otherwise, don't worry about it.

Turn this on for automatic hyphenation and the number of characters to allow.

Select Insert and a page style if you want to switch to a new page style, and new page number, each time the current paragraph formatting is encountered.

Specify options for keeping the text with the next paragraph, and short lines (orphans and widows).

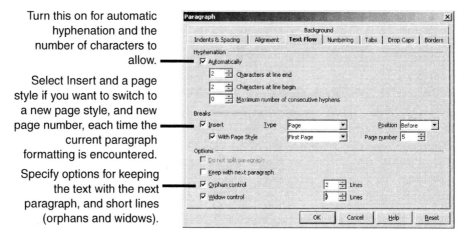

## Paragraph Formatting Window: Numbering Tab

This is another powerful, complex one that you probably don't need to know about. I don't do paragraph or line numbering and I'm not sure how many people do.

This is where you come to if you need it, of course. The Numbering Style field is an option that we'll cover when we get to styles.

Select a numbering style that you create, or from the existing list, if you want this paragraph formatting to always be linked with a particular list style.

Select this option if you want to restart the list numbering with this paragraph.

If you are doing line numbering, specify these options.

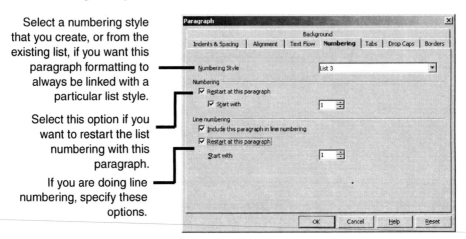

## Paragraph Formatting Window: Tabs Tab

I've got a procedure coming up that walks you through how to do tabs. You can set them up here or just click on the ruler to quickly create left-aligned ones. Here, however, is where you specify dot leaders, and can even pick your own character for a jazzier dot leader style.

Specify the position where you want the tab.

Specify the tab alignment.

Specify whether you want a fill character in the area covered by the tab.

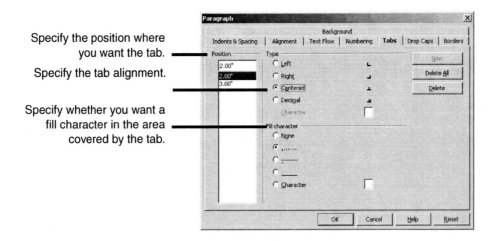

## Paragraph Formatting Window: Drop Caps Tab

You might think this would be in the character formatting window, but it's here. It's a good way to make your doc to look like an old manuscript or just have a distinctive look.

Select Display Drop Caps to have the first character or word in drop caps, as shown. Select Whole Word to use the whole word rather than the first character only.

If you want to apply a character style to the drop cap or drop word, select it here.

The preview area shows the effect of your selections.

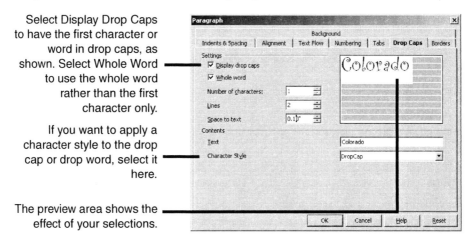

Here's an example of a drop cap, with a character style applied, as well.

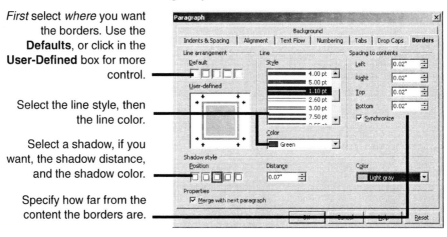

continually challenges and inspires. Whether you're a weekend warrior or extreme adventurer, you'll find the call of Mother Nature too strong to resist. And with so much to do, why would you want to? Outdoor recreation comes in all forms in Colorado: fishing, golfing, ballooning, skiing, rock climbing, mountain biking, backpacking, snowmobiling, camping, horseback riding,

## Paragraph Formatting Window: Borders Tab

You do have the option of using the paragraph formatting icons on the toolbar, though these need to be added sometimes. This window gives you more control.

*First* select *where* you want the borders. Use the **Defaults**, or click in the **User-Defined** box for more control.

Select the line style, then the line color.

Select a shadow, if you want, the shadow distance, and the shadow color.

Specify how far from the content the borders are.

## Paragraph Formatting Window: Background Tab

This gives you the same features as the paragraph background icon on the formatting toolbar. However (if you wanted to) you could also put in a graphic as the background of the paragraph.

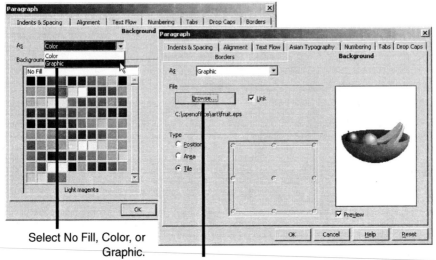

Select No Fill, Color, or Graphic.

Click Browse to find a graphic, then select Position and assign a position; Area to fill the area with the graphic, or Tile to repeat the graphic within the area.

## Indenting Paragraphs Using the Paragraph Window

We talked about indenting paragraphs by dragging and by indenting; see *Indenting Paragraphs by Dragging, and Using the Indent Icon* on page 76. Here's another way—just use the Paragraph formatting window.

**1**  Select the paragraph(s) to change spacing for. Right-click and choose Paragraph, or choose Format > Paragraph.

**2**  In the Paragraph window, select the Indents and Spacing tab. In the Before Text field, type the amount of space to indent, such as .75.

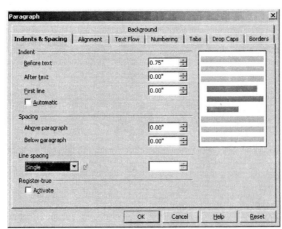

**3**   Look at the preview area; you'll see the effect.

**4**   Click OK to apply the formatting.

# Putting Space Below Each Paragraph Instead of Creating a Blank Line

You generally want to have some blank space between paragraphs and after headings—it just looks better that way. It should look something like this.

---

**On the Rocks**

In Colorado, there's nothing wrong with your vacation being on the rocks. With so many peaks, both small and large, mountaineering is accessible to nearly everyone. Spend a week climbing a Fourteener, one of the state's 54 peaks higher than 14,000 feet, or drive right to the top of one. Visitors can also scale canyon walls, overhanging crags and immense boulders.

Many of the state's best rock climbing sites are on public land. Shops sell or rent all the equipment you would need, and many provide instruction. For a different rocky experience, take an easy walk through some of the high country caves that are open to visitors. Or, for the more adventurous, there are longer tours of undeveloped caves and caverns.

---

But how do you do it? The simple approach is just to press Return and put in a blank line wherever you want space. However, that can cause a lot of problems, and it's not a very precise way of getting the spacing you want.

---

**On·the·Rocks¶**

¶

In·Colorado,·there's·nothing·wrong·with·your·vacation·being·on·the·rocks.·With·so·many peaks,·both·small·and·large,·mountaineering·is·accessible·to·nearly·everyone.·Spend·a week·climbing·a·Fourteener,·one·of·the·state's·54·peaks·higher·than·14,000·feet,·or·drive right·to·the·top·of·one.·Visitors·can·also·scale·canyon·walls,·overhanging·crags·and immense·boulders.·¶

¶

Many·of·the·state's·best·rock·climbing·sites·are·on·public·land.·Shops·sell·or·rent·all·the equipment·you·would·need,·and·many·provide·instruction.·For·a·different·rocky experience,·take·an·easy·walk·through·some·of·the·high·country·caves·that·are·open·to visitors.·Or,·for·the·more·adventurous,·there·are·longer·tours·of·undeveloped·caves·and caverns.¶

---

A better approach is to format the paragraph so it automatically has the spacing you want below each paragraph. It takes less effort each time, you can specify exactly the spacing you want, and it only takes a moment to set up.

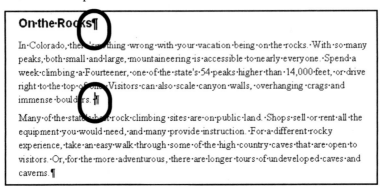

Here's a quick procedure to put spacing below paragraphs and headings.

For more tips on formatting, see *Guide to Good Layout and Formatting* on page 141.

**1**    Select the paragraph(s) to change spacing for.

**2**    Right-click and choose Paragraph, or click on the Format menu and choose Paragraph.

**3**    In the Paragraph window, select the Indents and Spacing tab.

**4**    In the Below Paragraph field, specify roughly .08 to .12 inches. To change the unit of measure displayed here from inches to another unit such as points, choose Tools > Options > OpenOffice.org Writer > General and set a different unit of measure.

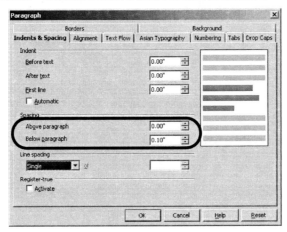

**5**    Click OK to close the window and save changes.

# Setting and Formatting Tabs

You can set tabs by clicking at the point you want them on the ruler, then dragging each tab. You can also right-click on an applied tab to change the options.

## About Tabs

There are default tabs, and standard tabs you apply manually. Tabs are good for some situations, but you should steer clear unless you absolutely need to use them.

### When to Use Tabs

Tabs are good for something like this, where you have one item, then across from it something else. The tabs are the –> characters.

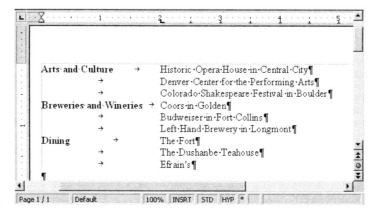

Don't use tabs if you've got more than one line of text on the left. This will drive you crazy; use tables instead. See *Using Tables* on page 178.

This is a good way to drive yourself crazy. Use tables instead of tabs when you have two or more lines of text on the left. Or just use columns—more on that in the page setup chapter.

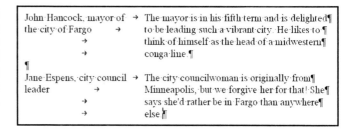

### Default Tabs Versus Created Tabs

There are default tabs and tabs you set. Default tabs are just how far you indent when you press Tab, without saying how far in. You can see them on the ruler. If that's not what you need, though, or if you need special characters like dots to fill in the tab space, use the Paragraph Formatting window.

---

**Note –** The default tabs are overridden by tabs that you specifically set.

---

### Dot Leaders

To help readers see what information goes together, you might want to use dot leaders. They fill in the space covered by the tab, as in this example.

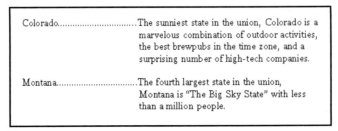

> Colorado................................The sunniest state in the union, Colorado is a marvelous combination of outdoor activities, the best brewpubs in the time zone, and a surprising number of high-tech companies.
>
> Montana................................The fourth largest state in the union, Montana is "The Big Sky State" with less than a million people.

**Note** – To indent a whole paragraph, don't use tabs. Indent the paragraph using one of the ways covered earlier. Tabs will get you in a whole mess o'trouble if you add text or change the formatting.

## Setting up Default Tabs

Look at the ruler. You'll see small tabs, typically every half inch.

If this isn't where you want tabs, use this procedure to change them.

**1**    Choose Tools > Options > OpenOffice.org Writer > General.

**2**    Specify how far apart the tabs should be. Use the arrows to set the value.

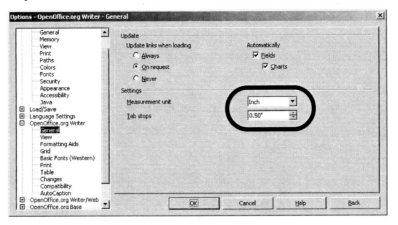

**3**    Click OK.

## Setting up Your Own Tabs

This procedure will show you how to set up tabs with more control.

**1**    Choose View > Nonprinting Characters to see the tabs when you use them.

**2**    Select the text where you want the tabs. It's best to type all the text and tabs, then select it and apply the correct tabs..

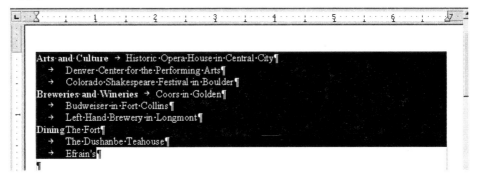

**3**    Choose Format > Paragraph.

**4**    Click the Tabs tab.

**5**    In the Position field, specify how far in you want the first tab to be. This is how far in from the left margin of the paragraph, not the page. So if your whole paragraph is indented an inch, then a 2 inch tab will be indented 3 inches from the left page margin.

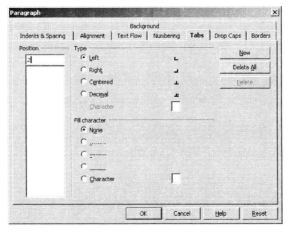

**6**    In the Type list, specify whether the tab should be left, centered, right, or decimal (the decimal of a number is aligned at the tab mark). For decimal, specify a period, comma, or another character you use for decimals.

**7**    If you want a dot leader for the tab, then either select a preexisting fill character or type one in the Character box.

**8**   Click New to add the tab to the Position list.

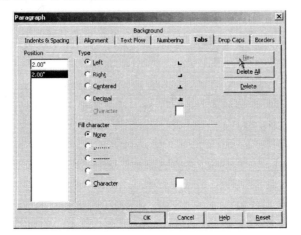

**9**   Add any additional tabs in the same manner.

**10**  Click OK to save changes and close the window.

**11**  The text will reflect the change you made.

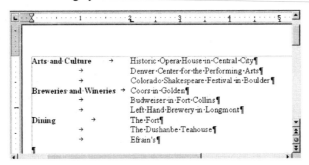

## Modifying Existing Tabs You've Created

If you want to modify tabs, you need to select all text with the same tab settings, not text with mixed tab settings. That means you can't select all the text in the document and go back and modify them to be all the same. This process is easier with styles.

## Setting Up Tabs and Paragraph Alignments for Indented Wrapping

A common format is something like this, if you have a heading and a lot of text you want to associate with it There's text on one side and the first line is flush left, but the other lines wrap back even with the tab, which is in farther. Here, it's at two inches.

| Colorado | → | The sunniest state in the union, Colorado is a marvelous combination of outdoor activities, the best brewpubs in the time zone, and a surprising number of high-tech companies.¶ |
| Montana | → | The fourth largest state in the union, Montana is "The Big Sky State" with less than a million people.¶ |

> **Note** – Another way to do this would be to use tables, and remove the borders. See *Creating and Formatting Tables* on page 177.

Here's how to set up tabs for the example.

**1**    Select the appropriate paragraphs.

**2**    Choose Format > Paragraph.

**3**    Make the indicated settings in the Indents & Spacing, and Tab, tabs. In this example, the main text is two inches farther in from the left text margin. If you wanted to have the main text 1.25 inches farther in, you would change the settings to 1.25, 1.25, and -1.25.

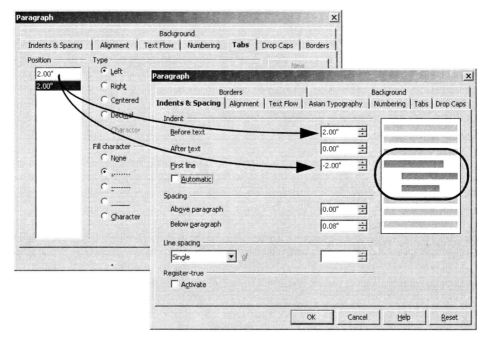

**4**    Click OK to save changes and close the window.

# Viewing Carriage Returns and Other Formatting Markups

If you're used to WordPerfect, you had reveal codes, which told you what formatting was actually applied to text.

In Writer, you pretty much know by looking at the tools you used to format the text, and at the nonprinting characters. These are valuable tools that will help you when you have problems, and help prevent them in the first place.

## Keep the Nonprinting Characters Turned On

Choose View > Nonprinting Characters. When these are on, you can tell that there's a tab, or an unexpected carriage return, an empty table, or extra spaces, and that's what's making your formatting weird.

Something weird is going on here, but what?

In Colorado, there's nothing wrong with your vacation being on the rocks. With so many peaks, both small and large, mountaineering is accessible to nearly everyone.      Spend a week climbing a       Fourteener, one       of the state's 54 peaks higher than 14,000 feet, or drive right to the top of one.

Visitors can also scale canyon walls, overhanging crags and immense boulders.

There's a carriage return at the end of each line. There are tabs to delete, extra spaces, and the two paragraph returns on the same line indicate a table.

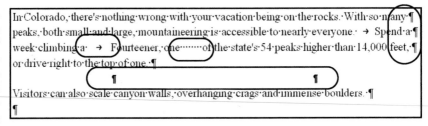

## Field Shadings

Fields that have automatic data in them like dates, dot leaders for tabs, etc. have gray shadings to show they're not just ordinary text. Keep these on to remind yourself—choose View > Field Shadings. (This is not View > Field Names; keep that turned off.)

The shading won't print; it's just a helpful indicator.

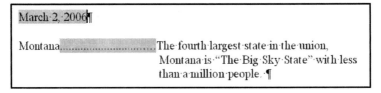

## Look at the Icons and Ruler

You can tell what's going on with text by looking at the icons and the ruler.

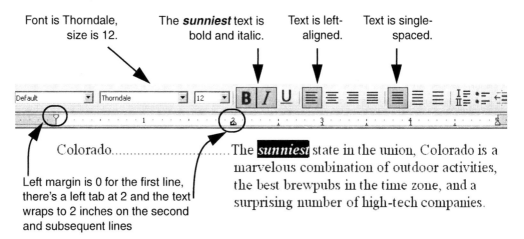

Font is Thorndale, size is 12.

The **sunniest** text is bold and italic.

Text is left-aligned.

Text is single-spaced.

Colorado..........................The **sunniest** state in the union, Colorado is a marvelous combination of outdoor activities, the best brewpubs in the time zone, and a surprising number of high-tech companies.

Left margin is 0 for the first line, there's a left tab at 2 and the text wraps to 2 inches on the second and subsequent lines

# Spellchecking, Search and Replace, and Word Count

These are a few of the most commonly used tools.

## Spellchecking

Use the curly-red-underlining feature if you've got a short document and if the curly red underline doesn't bug you. Use the spellcheck window for longer documents.

### Using the Red Underline Spellcheck Feature

**1**    To underline the misspelled words with a red line, find the red-underline spellcheck icon.

**2**    The words that OpenOffice.org thinks are misspelled will be underlined in red.

**Fines**
Fines are $ 50 per day per item.

**Time Per Checkout**
You can check out an item for *two weeks* and renew it *once*.

**Online Resources**
Online renewal: www.douglaslibrary.com
New books: www.douglasnewbooks.com
Activities: www.douglasactivities.com

**Dropoff Locations for Books**
120th and Lincoln
4th and Main
7th and Oak

**3**   Correct each word that needs correcting; right-click on a misspelled word for suggestions.

## Using the Spellcheck Window

This approach is better for longer documents, or if the red wavy line drives you crazy.

**1**   Click the blue checkmark spellcheck icon for the spellcheck window. You can also choose Tools > Spellcheck.

**2**   In the spellcheck window, the first misspelled word will be displayed as shown. Choose to ignore, or replace with one of the suggestions.

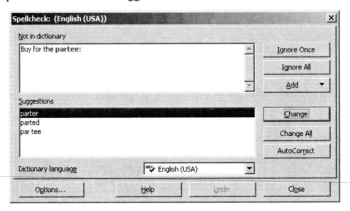

**3**   If the suggestions aren't right, type over the misspelled word and click Change.

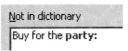

**4**   After you click a button for ignoring or changing, spellchecking will continue.

**5**   If you want to set options such as whether to ignore capitalization, click the Options button and make selections in the options window Click Close when you're done.

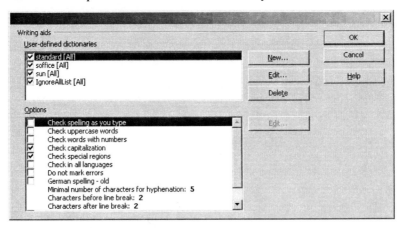

**Note** – You can set these up under Tools > Options > Language Settings > Writing Aids.

## Troubleshooting and Language

If you find the spellchecker skipping obviously misspelled words, look at the language that the text is formatted as. Select the text and choose Format > Character, and click the Font tab. Select the language to match your spellchecker.

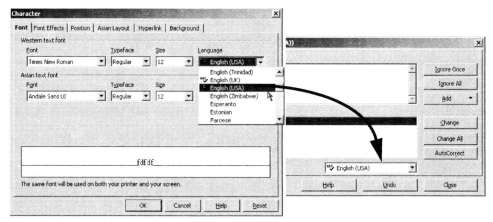

# Searching and Replacing

Perhaps there's been a reorganization in your company and you need to change all instances of your old department name in all documents, Research and Development, to the new name, Developmental Research. Or perhaps you're just looking for a particular word or phrase to be sure it's right. In any case, automatic search and replace is the feature to use. You can also search for things like carriage returns, and replace them with blanks, tabs, spaces, etc.

## Standard Search and Replace

1   Open the document you want to search.

2   Choose Edit > Find and Replace, or press Ctrl + F.

3   In the Find and Replace window, type the word you want to find in the Search For field. If you want to replace it with something, type that in the Replace With field.

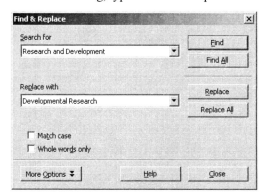

**4**  Click Find. At the first instance, choose whether to replace. Very rarely should you use the Replace All option unless you are absolutely positive you want that.

## Searching for Carriage Returns and Other Regular Expressions

**1**  Open the document to search. Choose Edit > Find and Replace, or press Ctrl + F.

**2**  In the Search For field, type what you're looking for. You can see the online help for a list of items you can search for; press F1 in this window and click the link for the "List of Regular Expressions." Here's a list of commonly used ones.

 ◆ Regular carriage returns are **$**

 ◆ Soft returns inserted with a Shift Return, are **\n**

 ◆ Just an empty paragraph, i.e. a carriage return but with no text on that line, is represented by **^$**

 ◆ Tabs are **\t**

  If you're using a mix of regular expressions and normal characters, you might need to use a **\** in front of anything you want evaluated normally. For instance, if you really are looking for the symbol **$** but you want to replace it with a carriage return **\n**, then you need to actually search for **\$** in the Search field and replace it with **\n** because **$** is a special character.

**3**  In the Replace With field, type what you want to replace the item with, if anything.

 ◆ If you want to replace something with a carriage return, put **\n** in the Replace field.

 ◆ If you want to replace one carriage return with two, put **\n\n** in the Replace field.

 ◆ You can't replace something with soft returns. As you see, a **\n** in the Replace field turns into a normal hard return.

 ◆ Just use **\t** normally, in both the Search and the Replace fields, for a tab.

**4**  Click More Options and mark the Regular Expressions checkbox.

**5**  Click Find, and find and replace as usual.

## Searching and Replacing Styles

You can search for a particular style and replace with another. (See *Saving Enormous Time and Effort With Styles* on page 147 for more information.)

**1**  Start the search and replace, then click the More Options button.

**2**  Select Search for Styles.

**3**    Select the style you want to search for in the Search For list, and the style to replace it with from the Replace With list.

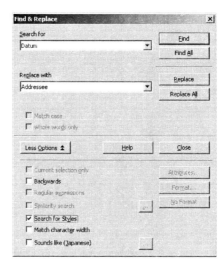

# Doing a Word Count

**1**    Choose File > Properties.

**2**    Click the Statistics tab. The number of words will be displayed.

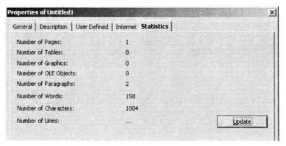

**3**    If the word count seems incorrect, click Update to see the correct wordcount.

**4**    Click OK or Cancel.

# Inserting and Printing Notes

To insert a note, choose Insert > Note and type the note. When you're done, click OK.

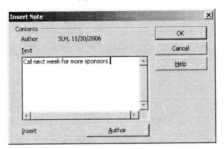

A yellow mark will indicate the note has been inserted. To delete the note, delete the mark.

## On the Road

In Colorado, the road is so much more

To print notes, choose File > Print, then click Options and select the printing option you want.

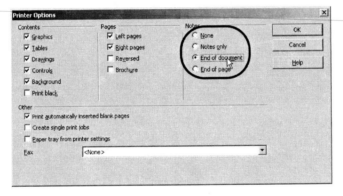

# Margins, Page Numbers, Page Layout, and More

# Introduction to Page Layout

To make a simple document, you don't *need* to know about page layout: margins, footers, page numbers, or background graphics. But if you want to do something a little more interesting, control how much text goes on a page, print multi-page documents with page number, and do other cool things that can really make your documents more valuable, then you'll follow the instructions in this chapter. Luckily, most of the things you'll do in this chapter will be in one powerful window: the Page Styles window.

One common task is combining two different page styles in one document—a landscape page within a portrait document, a background graphic on just the first page, etc. That's covered in *Saving Enormous Time and Effort With Styles* on page 147, since you need to use page styles.

# Page Layout

This section covers the basics of page layout: the margins, whether it's sideways or vertical, and anything else you want to modify.

## Changing Page Orientation

1   Choose Format > Page.

2   In the Page Style window, click the Page tab.

3   Select the Landscape or Portrait option.

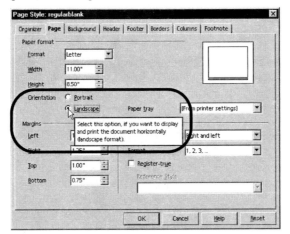

4   Look at the preview area; it will show the effect of your changes.

5   Click OK.

6   The layout of the document will change.

## Changing Margins

Let's say you're going to create a template for employee announcements, which have to be all on one page since no one will ever look to see what's on the second page. This means you want all four margins as narrow as possible so that you can get as much text and pictures on the page as possible.

Or perhaps you're putting together a 600-page book that will be published in a three-ring binder; in that case, you'll want a wide inner margin so that all the text will be visible. In any case, you'll want to change the page margins to accomplish what you want.

There are two ways to change the margins—using the page setup window that you've seen so far in this chapter, or just dragging.

## Using the Page Setup Window to Change Margins

**1**    Choose Format > Page.

**2**    In the Page Style window, click the Page tab.

**3**    Type the margins you want in the Margins area.

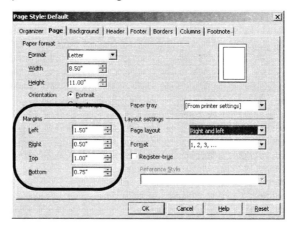

**4**    Look at the preview area; it will show the effect of your changes. Click OK.

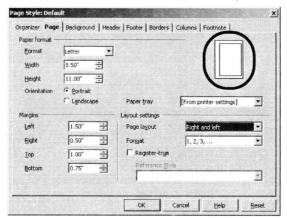

## Dragging Page Margins

This is a bit tricky. Make sure that your mouse looks exactly like the picture.

**1**    Open the document. Click somewhere in the page.

**2**  Find the left-hand margin line on the ruler, circled here. You're actually looking for the change from white to shaded, not the little hourglass thing, but they usually hang out in the same place.

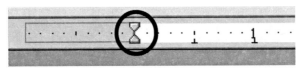

**3**  Put your mouse over that spot and wait for the cursor to turn into a left-right double-sided arrow as shown.

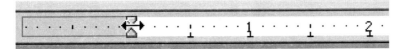

**4**  Drag the margin left or right to give yourself more or less space on the page. A line will show you where the margin is being changed to.

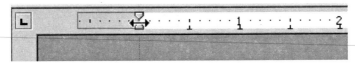

**5**  Repeat the steps for the right side, if necessary.

**6**  Move your mouse over the vertical ruler and drag so that the top and bottom margins change, as well.

## Page Size

Usually you just want Letter or A4 size document size; that's what normal documents are. However, you can pick anything—legal, tabloid for really big documents like book covers, envelope, or specify your own user-defined dimensions.

**1**  Choose Format > Page and click the Page tab.

**2**  Specify the page size using either of the following methods.

◆ Select an option from the Format list

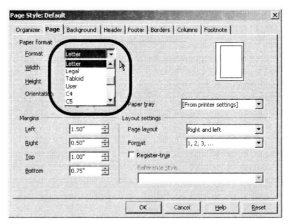

◆ Or in the Width and Height fields, type the dimensions you want. When you do this, remember that the margins will subtract from the overall size. If you have a 4x6 page size and .5 inch margins, you have a 3x5 area for content.

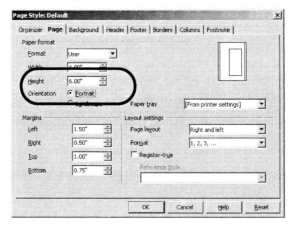

**3**   Click OK.

## Setting Up Columns

You can easily set up a document to have two or more columns. You also have the option of how far to separate them and whether to have a line between columns. This is a nice feature for newsletters, brochures, etc.

**1**   Choose Format > Page and click the Columns tab.

**2** Select the number of columns you want from one of the preset options, or type the number of columns you want in the Columns tab.

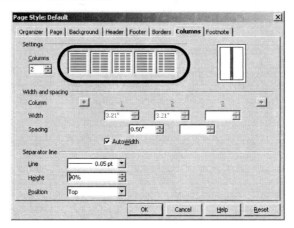

**3** In the Width and Spacing area, specify the width for each column if you want to change the default values, and how far apart they should be. Unmark the AutoWidth checkbox to make changes.

**4** In the Separator Line area, select a line if you want one to be displayed between your columns, and the line width, position, and height.

**5** Click OK.

# Inserting a Page Break

**1** Click where you want the new page to begin.

**2** Choose Insert > Manual Break. Leave all selections as is.

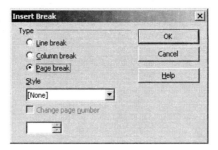

**3** Click OK. You'll see a dark line indicating a manual break.

### On the Road

To remove the manual break, just click to the left of the text below the line and press Backspace.

## Fitting More Content Into a Page

There isn't a feature that says "Force all this onto one page." However, you can do it yourself.

◆ Change the margins, and make the spacing between the header and footer, and the main content, smaller. (See *Changing Margins* on page 102 and *Turning on Headers and Footers* on page 107.)

◆ Change the font size.

◆ Change the spacing above and below the paragraphs. See *Putting Space Below Each Paragraph Instead of Creating a Blank Line* on page 87.

# Headers, Footers, and Page Numbers

Once you've got the page set up with the dimensions and text flow you want, it's time to help the reader find her way more easily through your document. For this, you use headers and footers; they're simply text boxes at the top and bottom of your document that repeat the information you put in them on every page.

## Turning on Headers and Footers

You can turn on text boxes at the top and bottom of each page, headers and footers, in the page format window. You're going to create a standard document with a header and footer, with the date in the header and the page number in the footer.

**1** Choose Format > Page. In the Page Style window, click the Header tab.

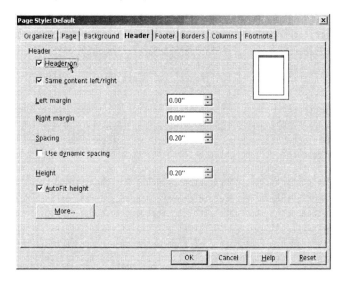

**2** Mark the Header option.

**3** If you want different content on the left than on the right, like a header with the date on the left side and the title on the right side, unmark the Same Content Left/Right option.

4    You can change how much space is between the header and the main text by changing the measurement in the Height field. The preview area shows the effect.

5    Click the Footer tab.

6    Click the Footer option.

7    Apply the same spacing and left-right options as for headers, if you want.

8    Click OK.

---

**Note** – You can also do this by choosing Insert > Footer > Default or Insert > Header > Default. Default is the page style; once you do more page styles you will see other options like CoverPage or MainBody.

---

## Adding Page Numbers, Text, and Date Content to Headers and Footers

You can add an automatically increasing page number to headers and footers, as well as automatic fields like dates.

1    To make sure you can see your headers and footers, choose View and be sure that there's a check mark by Text Boundaries and Nonprinting Characters. If there isn't, select each.

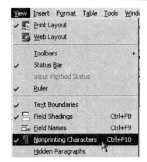

2    In a document where you've turned on the header or the footer, scroll to the area where you want to add content and click in the header or footer.

3    Choose Insert > Fields and select the information to insert. These are common choices.

  ◆    Choose Insert > Fields > Date to insert the date.

  ◆    Choose Insert > Fields > Page Number for the page number.

  ◆    Choose Insert > Fields > Page Count for the total number of pages.

4    The field will appear in the header or footer.

**5**   The page number will appear. If you want to type any words like Page or Date, you can do that in the footer, as well.

**6**   Use the text alignment icons in the toolbar to center or right-justify the word page and the page number, or create tabs under Format > Paragraph to specify exactly where you want the page number and any additional parts of the footer to appear.

**7**   Format the header or footer content as you would normal text.

## Changing the Date or Page Number Format

If you don't like how the date or page number field is displayed, double-click it and you'll see this window. Select the format you want and click OK. In this window you can also make the date fixed, or updated every time you open the document to the current date. The window shows dates; for pages, you can select Arabic, Roman, alphabetic, and other formats.

**Date (fixed)** is the default and means the date will always stay the same as when you inserted it. **Date** is the current date and each time you open the document, the current date will be used.

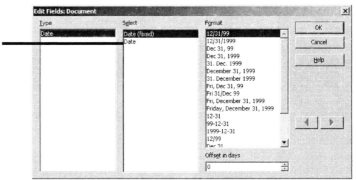

## Making a Header or Footer Say "Page X of Y"

There's no prefab way of inserting that all at once. But it's easy to do in steps.

**1**   Choose Format > Page, click the Header or Footer tab, and turn on the header or footer.

**1**   Click OK.

**2**   Click in the header or footer and type the word page.

**3**   Type a space, then choose Insert > Fields > Page Number.

Page 1

**4**   Type of.

**5**  Type a space, then choose Insert > Fields > Page Count.

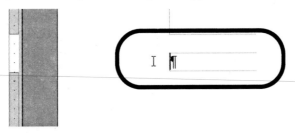

## Printing the File Name and Location of a Document in the Footer or Header

It's convenient to have the location of the document, i.e. where the Writer file is stored on your computer or the network, printed on documents. If you have a document you use infrequently, the path is a handy reminder to where the actual file is when you need to find it.

**1**  Open the document you want to add the information to and turn on the footer or header. (You could also just put the path anywhere in the document, such as at the top or bottom of the first page.)

**2**  Click in the footer, or wherever you want the path to appear.

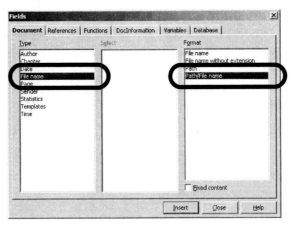

**3**  Choose Insert > Fields > Other.

**4**  Click on the Document tab.

**5**  In the Type list, select File Name, and in the Format list, select Path/File Name.

**6**  Click Insert.

**7**  Click Close.

**8**    The path and file name will appear in the footer. (Your path will be different.)

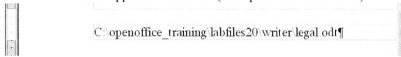

C:\openoffice_training\labfiles20\writer\legal.odt¶

## Using the Fields Window

Choose Insert > Fields > Other and you'll get this window.

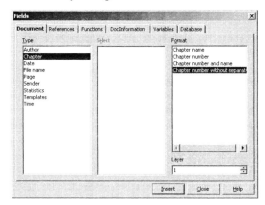

This is a very complicated, very powerful window. I'm not covering it in this book because I could spend 1000 pages on it. However, I'd recommend that you play around with it a bit, read the online help, and see how you think you might take advantage of the features. Try the Number Range field if you want to experiment with numbering systems.

# Decorative Page Formatting

Margins, headers, and page numbers are the important stuff. But the fun stuff comes with designing how the page looks. Maybe you want a fancy cover page with a colored border, or just a gray background for a left-facing page following the cover in a book. Here's how to jazz up the pages a bit.

---

**Note** – These procedures will apply to all pages in the document, unless you're using styles to separate page styles. See *Saving Enormous Time and Effort With Styles* on page 147 for more information. If you don't want to bother with styles at this point, you might want to make your fancy page a separate document, then combine it with the main document when you print.

---

## Giving a Document a Background Color

A colored background can set off a cover or the beginning of a new chapter.

**1**    Choose Format > Page. Click the Background tab.

**2**    Select Color from the dropdown list, then select a color you want.

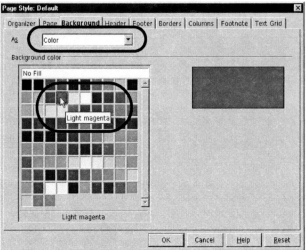

**3**    Click OK. The color be applied to the margins of the document, for every page in the document (or every page of that page style).

# Giving a Document a Background Graphic

This is similar to applying a background color, but you have a few more options. Note that the graphic will appear in the background of every page where you apply this page style.

**1**    Choose Format > Page.

**2**    Click the Background tab.

**3**    Click in the **As** list that says Color and select Graphic.

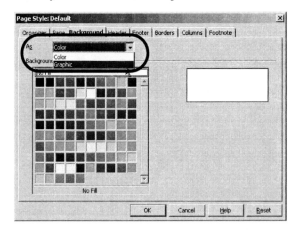

**4**    The window will change. Usually you want to select Position and specify the center dot, though you can also choose to tile.

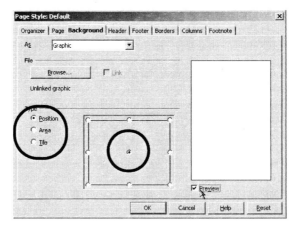

**5**    Select the Preview checkbox.

**6**    Click Browse. Find the graphic on your computer that you want to use.

**7**    Click Open.

**8**    The picture will appear in the Page Style window.

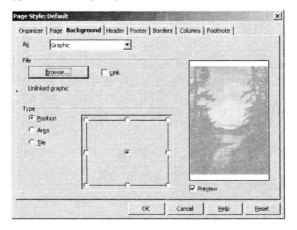

**9**    Click OK.

**10**  Here's what a sample document looks like with a background graphic.

**Note –** Go to the last line of text on the current page and press Return until you get a second page. You'll see the graphic in that page, as well; it applies to the whole document.

## Giving a Document Borders

**1**  Choose Format > Page,

**2**  Click the Borders tab.

**3**  Scroll down and select a line style and a color.

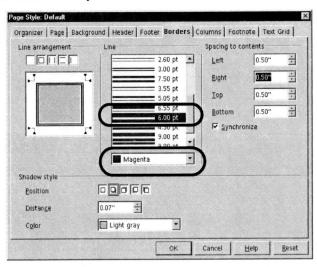

**4**  You don't want the text to be too crowded, so specify a space, something like .5 inch for the left, between the border and any text.

**5**    The Synchronize option is marked by default so all the other fields will default to the same thing; unmark Synchronize if you want different spacing on each side.

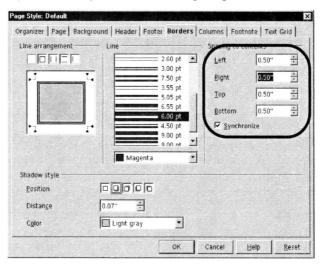

**6**    You'd think you'd be done with the borders by now, but you have to also tell OpenOffice.org *where* you want the borders. Click on one of the icons in the Line Presets area. You generally want them on all four sides. However, you can use the other preset icons for border placement, as well, to put borders only on the top and bottom.

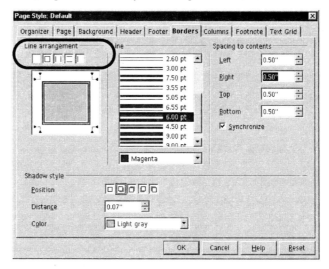

**7**    Click OK.

# Sections

Sections and frames (see *Frames* on page 214) are two ways to offset one or more paragraphs of text within a column. They're good for:

◆ Inserting a few paragraphs that are in column format, or are wider or narrower than the rest of the page, without having to use page styles

◆ Inserting a note that is distinct from the rest of the page, such as an advertisement within a brochure

◆ Inserting linked text into a document; for instance you could insert a section or frame whose contents are composed of a different document. You can also choose whether to protect this content from changes with a password

◆ Sections are better for existing text that's part of the document flow; frames are better for text that you want to be separate from the flow. The following illustration shows how they look.

This **section** is a linked section, bringing in the data from a **clothing.odt** file. When the contents of that file change, this document will be updated, as well.

This **frame** is separate from the other text, which wraps around it. It has a colored border and the text inside it is formatted differently.

### How·to·Dress ¶

Clothing ·isn't·much·of·a·problem·either. ·Dry, ·comfortable ·hiking·boots·(preferably·water proof)·work·fine·for·recreational·jaunts. ·Just·about·any·warm·clothing·will·suffice. ·The trick·is·to·match·apparel·to·the·conditions, ·which·means·layering·--pulling·off·and·putting on·as·weather·and·degree·of·activity·dictate. ·You'll·also·want·to·bring·along·a·backpack·to hold·extra·clothes, ·plenty·of·liquid·and·high-energy·food. ·Don't·forget·your·sunscreen·and sunglasses. ·¶

The·listings·below·will·tell·you·where·trailheads·within·the·county·are·located; ·the·length of·the·trail·is·listed·in parentheses. ·For·additional information·on·the·trails, ·you may·want·to·purchase·a·specific map·for·the·area·that·you·are going·to·explore. ·These·maps can·be·obtained·at·the·Clear Creek·Ranger·District·Office, located·at·Exit·240·on·I-70. ·As with·every·snow-related·activity outside·ski·area·boundaries, ·be acutely·aware·of·avalanche danger·and·approaching storms. ·To·obtain·the·most·up- to-date·information, ·call·303- 275-5360·or·303-567-2901 before·you·go. ·Red·Feather Snowshoes, ·Winter·Park·Resort:

To·get·a·discount·on trail·maps·at·state parks·throughout Colorado, ·mention this·Colorado·and You·brochure!¶

Tours·include·snowshoes, ·poles, ·a·one-time·lift·pass·on·Gemini·Express·and·a knowledgeable·tour·guide·leading·the·way. ·Tours·are·offered·daily, ·November·through April. ·Call·800-729-7907·or·visit·www.skiwinterpark.com·for·reservations·and information. ¶

## Inserting a Section

1   If you want to make the section linked to another file, choose Insert > Section. If you just want to make existing text be treated differently, select the text, then choose Insert > Section.

**2**    Make the appropriate selections.

To make the content come from
another file, select Link and
browse to the file in the File
Name field.

To protect the contents from
being changed, select Protect.
Select With Password and type
the password. You'll need to type
this again to unprotect the
section.

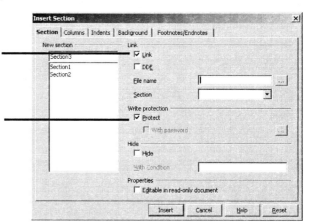

**3**    Click the Background tab and Column tab, if necessary, and make additional selections.

In the Settings area, specify the
number of columns you want, then i
the Width and Spacing area, specify
how far apart they should be.

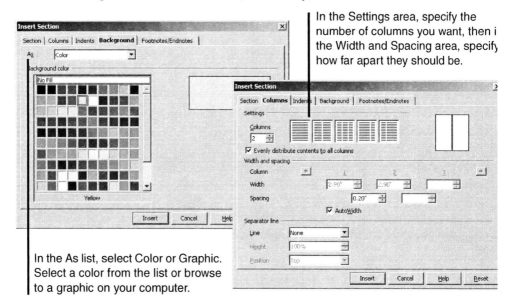

In the As list, select Color or Graphic.
Select a color from the list or browse
to a graphic on your computer.

**4**    Click Insert.

To modify the section later, select it and choose Format > Section.

## Inserting a Frame

See *Offsetting Text From the Main Flow* on page 216.

# Power Tip: Creating a Trifold Brochure

If you choose File > Print and click the Options button, you'll see an option for Brochure printing. However, I find this option extremely difficult to deal with. Instead, use linked frames (see *Making Nonconsecutive Text Flow Together* on page 216). You can download a template for the brochure from the Templates section of the Book Resources blog, **http://openoffice.blogs.com/ bookresources**.

To create your own, follow these steps.

**1**    Create a new Writer document and set it up as landscape, with quarter inch margins.

**2**    Press Return to create two pages.

**3**    Insert a borderless frame, approximately 3.33 inches wide by 8 inches high.

**4**    Paste the frame five more times, arranging them as shown with space between.

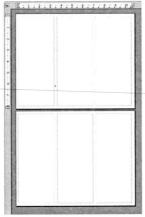

**5**    Link the frames in order. See *Making Nonconsecutive Text Flow Together* on page 216.

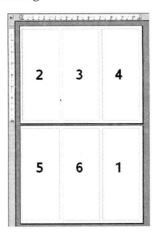

**6**    Type your content, then print or photocopy so that the pages line up correctly.

# Creating and Formatting Lists

# How Lists and List Formatting Tools Make Life Easier

Lists aren't that complicated. You type 1, type the text, press Return, type 2, and so on. Why would you even need help from the software to make your lists?

> Presenters at the Awards Ceremony
> 1. Jane Espens
> 2. Charisma Butcher
> 3. Angelus Masterson
> 4. Jude Whelder

# You Need List Formatting Because Everything Changes

You might not need automatic list formatting initially, but sooner or later, your simple lists will change. You'll need to renumber the list, possibly even daily or hourly. Or perhaps instead of reordering the items, you'll need to change the numbering style from **1 2 3** to **A B C**. You might even decide you don't want it numbered at all.

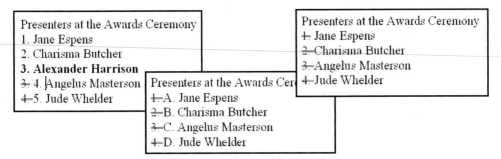

OpenOffice.org provides list formatting features because things change, and an office suite should make change as painless as possible. You'll save yourself enormous time with the list tools in Writer.

# Standard List Formatting Versus List Styles

Let's say you've got this text in your list.

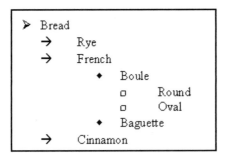

What a formatting task! You have to tell OpenOffice.org each time you encounter a new list that *level 1* has the arrowhead bullet, *level 2* has the regular arrow bullet, *level 3* has the diamond bullet, *level 4* has the square bullet, and so on. You also have to specify each time, for each level, how much each *bullet* is indented from the *left margin*, and how much the *text* is indented from the *bullet*.

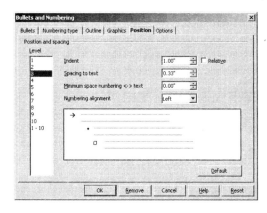

*And* let's say you have 439 other multi-level lists that have to be formatted that way, in your document. Even if you apply the formatting with the list formatting window each time, you're going to get very sick of lists very quickly. You'll be in for carpal tunnel surgery before you can say "my fingers are about to fall off."

If you have any kind of complexity in your lists, especially if you have many multi-level lists like this with different formatting at each level, *use list styles*.

List styles are just like regular styles—they "freeze" complex formatting and save it under a name you give it, so that you can apply the formatting again and again just by selecting the style name. Applying the list formatting again means you just click the style name in the style list, rather than specifying the same formatting repeatedly.

**I cannot overemphasize the importance of using list styles.** Just as styles save huge time and effort for paragraph formatting, styles save *enormous* amounts of time and effort for lists.

You don't need to use list styles all the time. Just use them for complex lists, or if you have a lot of lists.

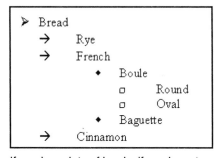

If you don't have lots of levels, if you don't have to have different bullets or numbers at the different levels, and if you don't care much what the indent is for each level, go ahead and just use the list formatting tools in this chapter for your list.

If you have lots of levels, if you have to have different bullets or numbers at the different levels, and if you have requirements for what the indent is for each level, you need extra formatting power. Use the list formatting tools in this chapter and the styles in the styles chapter to "freeze" your style formatting into styles.

To make a list style, you just use the same tools you would to apply normal list formatting, but then you click a New Style icon to say "make me a style just like this."

Everything you need to know about styles is in *Saving Enormous Time and Effort With Styles* on page 147; specifics about lists styles are in *List Styles* on page 156.

## What to Do Next

Regardless of whether you need to preserve your list formatting in styles, you'll need to know everything in this chapter. So continue through the chapter and learn how to apply the formatting to your lists according to the steps. If you need to, then go to *Saving Enormous Time and Effort With Styles* on page 147 to learn about applying and creating styles. Then you'll be able to create styles by just setting up the formatting once as described in this chapter, and "freezing" that formatting to create a style.

# Basic Lists

Here's how to format a series of items as a list, with bullets and numbers, and turn it off again.

## Creating Numbered Lists

**1**     Open a document and select the items in the list that you want to number.

> **Time Per Checkout**
> You can check out an item for *two weeks* and renew it *once.*
>
> **Online Resources**
> Online renewal: www.douglaslibrary.com
> New books: www.douglasnewbooks.com
> Activities: www.douglasactivities.com
>
> Note that you do not have to select the whole line, just part of it. This is because numbering and bullet formatting automatically apply to the whole paragraph.

**2**     Click the numbered list icon at the top of the window.

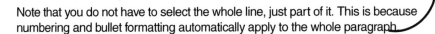

**3**     The list will become numbered.

> **Online Resources**
> 1.  Online renewal: www.douglaslibrary.com
> 2.  New books: www.douglasnewbooks.com
> 3.  Activities: www.douglasactivities.com

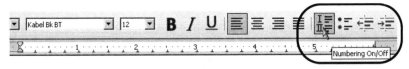

## Creating Bulleted Lists

**1**    Open a document and select the text you want to bullet.

**2**    Click the bulleting icon.

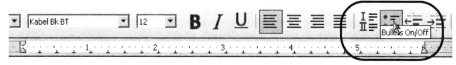

**3**    The list is now bulleted.

## Getting Rid of Numbers or Bullets

Let's say you don't want text to be numbered or bulleted anymore. Or suppose you've got something like this where one or two of the lines need to have the list attributes taken off.

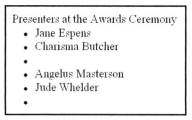

The best way is to just *turn off* the "listness" for those lines.

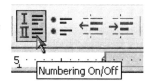

You know that the icons don't say Number This or Bullet This. They say **Numbering On/Off** and **Bullets On/Off**. That means the icons work like light switches. Click once to turn on list formatting; click again to turn it off.

Click on the line where the unwanted list formatting is, and just click the same icon you used to put it there in the first place. Then just delete the extra lines, or leave them there and fill in non-numbered text.

Presenters at the Awards Ceremony
- Jane Espens
- Charisma Butcher
- 
- Angelus Masterson
- Jude Whelder
- |

# Formatting Lists

It's easy to turn numbered and bulleted lists on and off. Those default list formats, however, aren't that interesting and don't offer anything like roman or ABC numbering. Here's how to make your list look exactly how you want it.

## Applying Different Types of Numbers

1   Select the list and choose Formatting > Bullets and Numbering. (Or right-click on the list and choose Numbering > Bullets.) The Bullets and Numbering window appears.

2   Click the Numbering Type tab, to apply a specific type of numbering, or click the Outline tab, to apply prefab outline types.

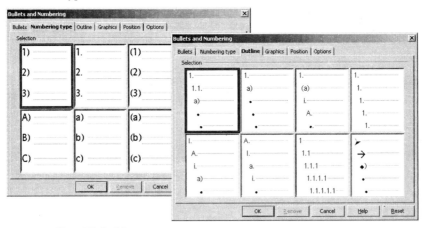

3   Select a list type you like. Click OK.

**Note** – To make the different levels for the outline numbering apply correctly, see *Indenting Items* on page 136.

# Applying Different Types of Bullets

**Note** – For more bullets, see *Applying Different List Attributes at Different Levels* on page 162.

**1** Select the list and choose Format > Bullets and Numbering. The Bullets and Numbering window will appear.

**2** Click the Bullets tab, for interesting black bullets, or click the Graphics tab.

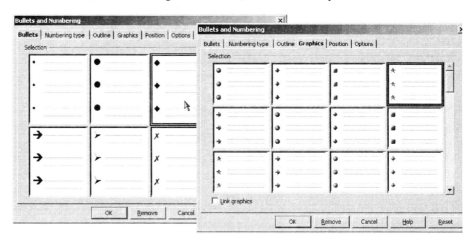

**3** Select the bullet style you want.

**4** Click OK.

# Creating and Formatting Your Own List Prefix

You can create lists that go way beyond just **1 2 3** or **A B C**. You can list items as **Resident 1**, **Resident 2**, and so on, or any other text prefix you want. An example of a user-defined prefix, with a number and with formatting, is shown at right.

**1** Select the entire list and choose Format > Bullets and Numbering.

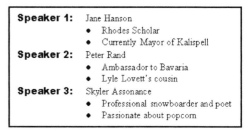

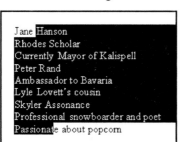

**2** The Bullets and Numbering window will appear.

**3**   Click the Options tab.

**4**   Click the 1 item in the Level list, or the level that you want the prefix at.

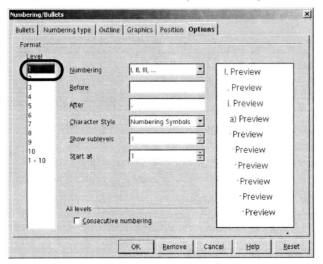

**5**   In the Numbering list, select the number, if you want a list like **Speaker 1, Speaker 1**, or else select None if you only want your prefix to appear.

**6**   Delete anything that's in the Before field, then type the text you want for the prefix, followed by a space. Look at the preview area to see how the list will look.

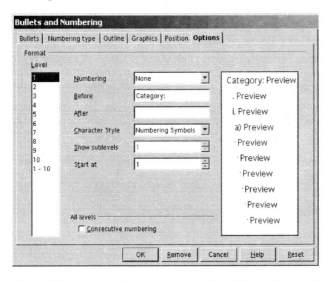

**7**   If you want something different after the prefix or number, like a colon or dash, type it in the After field.

**8**    If you have a character style you want to apply to the prefix, like **BoldItalforLists** or **BrightRed**, select it from the list. If you don't have one now but want to use one, you can create it and come back to this window later. See *Creating a New Style* on page 152.

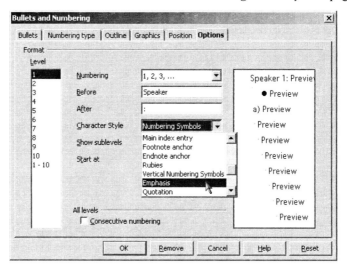

**9**    If you want to continue and create your own prefix at level 2 or beyond, select the 2 item in the Level list and repeat the steps.

**10**    Since words take up a lot more space, you'll need to adjust the indent, as well. Click the Position tab.

**11**    Click the 1 in the Level list. Increase the value in the Spacing to Text field until the preview area at the bottom of the window looks right. The second line that wraps back should be left aligned with the first part of the top line. Usually the preview area will make it look like you need more space than you actually do, so expect to tweak this once you're done. You probably don't need more than an inch or an inch and a half for even the longest prefixes.

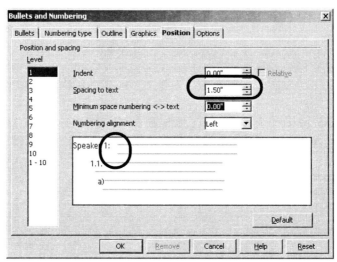

**12** If you're going to have sub-items in this list, click the 2 in the Level list. Set the **Indent** to the same value you set in the **Spacing to Text** field for level 1. If you have a prefix at this level, as well, you'll need to increase the Spacing to Text in this field, as well, to something that allows space for the word you're using.

This makes subitems align correctly under the wrapped text for the main level.

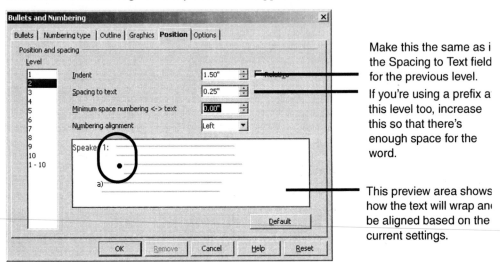

Make this the same as i the Spacing to Text field for the previous level.

If you're using a prefix a this level too, increase this so that there's enough space for the word.

This preview area shows how the text will wrap an be aligned based on the current settings.

**13** Click OK.

**14** Indent any subitems by clicking to the left of each and pressing Tab.

**15** You'll see your prefix or prefixes.

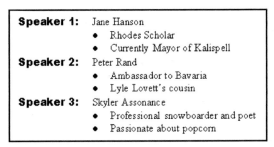

# Formatting the Numbers, Prefixes, or Bullets in Lists

So far, I've talked about how to select a different numbering scheme. But there's much more you can do. For instance, maybe for the document you're doing, you'd like the numbers for your lists to be bold, green, highlighted, and 12-point size.

You can make them look like that, or apply any other formatting you want.

> Presenters at the Awards Ceremony
> 1. Jane Espens
> 2. Charisma Butcher
> 3. Angelus Masterson
> 4. Jude Whelder

Here's how. You need to create a *character style* first, so if you haven't hit styles yet, you'll want to read up on that first. See *Creating a New Style* on page 152. Once you've got the style, the process is pretty simple.

**1**    Create the character style or styles that have the formatting you want for the numbers or characters preceding each list item. See *Creating a New Style* on page 152.

**2**    Open the document and select the list to format.

**3**    Choose Format > Numbering/Bullets.

**4**    Click the Options tab.

**5**    Be sure that the formatting for that level is a **character or a standard bullet** by choosing actual numbers or text such as 1 2 3 or A B C. This won't work with graphical bullet, since a character style can only affect numbers or letters. However, it will work if you just select Bullet, since those bullets are based on characters that can be formatted.

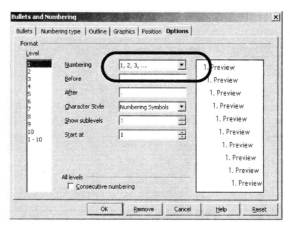

**6**    Select one level in the Level list, or select 1-10 in the Level list to apply the character formatting to all levels.

**7**   Select the character style you want to use from the Character Style dropdown list.

**8**   Click OK.

**9**   The numbers in the list will look like the style you created.

Presenters at the Awards Ceremony
1. Jane Espens
2. Charisma Butcher
3. Angelus Masterson
4. Jude Whelder

# Advanced Reference to the List Tools

The Numbering and Bullets formatting window has cropped up in quite a few of these procedures, and I've talked about the most commonly used features. You'll learn more about them in *Creating List Styles* on page 159.

For now, though, here's a quick reference. You can also use the online help to learn more about these windows.

## Outline Tab

Use this tab to apply commonly used outline formats.

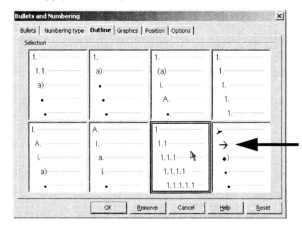

Select the format you want. You can modify it by using the options in the Position and Options tabs.

To indent items in your list, so that the formatting at each sublevel will apply, click to the left of each item and press Tab once for each indent you want.

The window as shown results in a list formatted as shown.

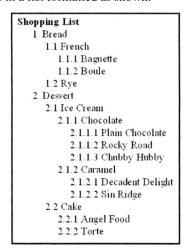

To apply the level so that the text matches the specifications in this window, you still need to indent the items. Click to the left of each item and press Tab, or use the instructions in *Indenting Items* on page 136.

## Position Tab

Use this tab to control how far to the right each item at each level is, and how far the text is from the list formatting item.

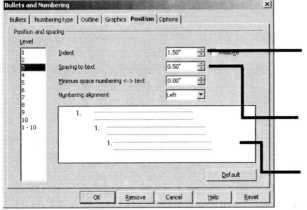

This value is the space to the left of the number or bullet. On levels 2 and below, it should be the sum of the Indent, and Spacing to Text values, for the level immediately above it.

This value is the space between the number or bullet and the text in the list.

Use the preview area to see how the list will look.

The window as shown results in a list formatted as shown.

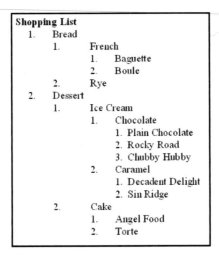

To apply the level so that the text matches the specifications in this window, you still need to indent the items. Click to the left of each item and press Tab, or use the instructions in *Indenting Items* on page 136.

## Options Tab

Use this tab to specify by level what list formatting item should be used at each level, the text formatting for numbered lists, and more. This window has a huge number of options; one is the ability to specify the type of numbering for each level such as Roman, Arabic, etc.

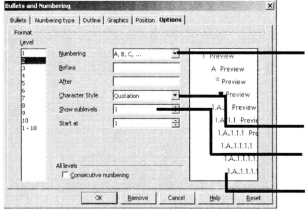

Select the type of number or bullet here. The subsequent options change based on the selection here.

Use the Before and After fields if you want a prefix for the list like **Speaker 1:**

Use a Character style to format the number or prefix.

Use the maximum value for Show Sublevels for outlines.

Use the preview area to see how the list will look.

The window as shown results in a list formatted as shown.

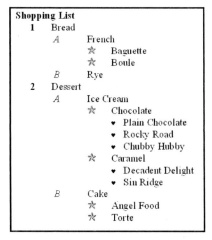

To apply the level so that the text matches the specifications in this window, you still need to indent the items. Click to the left of each item and press Tab, or use the instructions in *Indenting Items* on page 136.

# Indenting and List Management

Let's talk about *indenting* and *levels* and how they relate lists. This is really important; you'll save yourself screaming and hair pulling if you get levels and indenting down.

## The Most Important List Concept: Levels

If you read nothing else about lists, read this section.

### Levels Are Powerful, Important, and Useful Features

Here's a plain list with *no levels*, and a more complex one, with three *levels*.

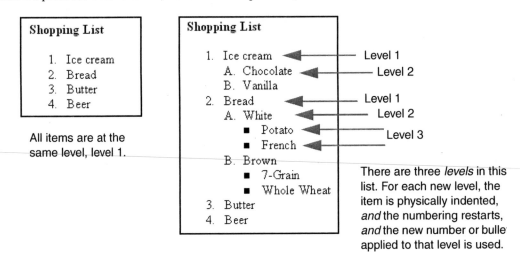

When a topic has subtopics, just as the topic Ice Cream has the subtopics Vanilla and Chocolate, you *indent* those subtopics to a different *level*. You usually just do this to physically and visually separate them, to indicate that they all belong together. You do this when you're just writing by hand, and when you're using Impress or Powerpoint.

That's just the surface of what levels mean in Writer lists, however.

### What You Get With Levels: Physical Indenting and Much More

It's nice to visually indent text, sure, to show how topics are related and that some are subtopics of other. But when you indent items in lists, you get other useful stuff.

- There's the **physical indenting**, of course.
- But also the concept of a **level**. When you indent an item correctly, **it knows that it is level 2**, or level 3, It carries that knowledge with it.

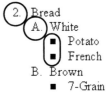

- When an item knows its level, it can apply the right formatting for its level, and **the formatting for every level can be different**. This means that for the top level items you can have certain formatting, and for the next level down you can have entirely different formatting. This lets you do outline numbering, or numbering at the top level and bullets at the next level, or pretty much anything you want.

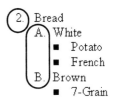

- In addition, when you indent correctly, the **numbering for any numbered lists restarts automatically**.

- Any item with levels, that has subpoints, keeps track of its subpoints. In the example at right, **Bread** knows that the rest of the list are its subpoints, and **Brown** knows that **7-Grain** and **Whole Wheat** are its subpoints. This is useful when you want to move items up and down in a list, or indent or promote them.

## Two Ways to Indent List Items Correctly

You can do this two ways.

- Press Tab – Click to the left of an item, press Tab, and it's indented. A level 1 item is now level 2. Press again and it's at level 3.

- Use the Bullets and Numbering toolbar – Use the icons on the Bullets and Numbering toolbar. Select a list, or choose View > Toolbars > Bullets and Numbering, to view it. This is better when you have many items to indent, since you can select them all and indent them at once.

The icons are Up One Level, Down One Level, Move Up With Subpoints, and Move Down With Subpoints. Click the icon you want.

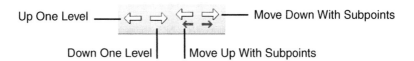

You can get more into these icons in *Indenting Items* on page 136.

### How to Avoid Hating Lists: Stay Away From the Standard Indent Icon on the Formatting Toolbar

I talked about how you indent an item to put it at a certain level, by pressing Tab. That's an excellent way to do it. Using the Promote and Demote icons works too.

But why not indent the way you do it with paragraphs? There's this Indent icon sitting there on the toolbar.

**Never use this toolbar! It will cause a lot of problems with *levels*.**

Indenting with the Indent icon does not give the items in the list the concept of levels. It is physical indentation, nothing more. So with this icon:

◆ Your list numbering won't restart at a new level.

◆ You won't be able to do different formatting at each level.

◆ List styles won't work correctly.

◆ Main items won't be associated with their subitems.

> Shopping List
>
> 1.  Ice cream
>        2.  Chocolate
>        3.  Vanilla
> 4.  Bread
>        5.  White
>               6.  Potato
>               7.  French
>        8.  Brown
>               9.  7-Grain
>               10. Whole Wheat
> 11. Butter
> 12. Beer

**What you get with lists when using the Standard Indent icon**

In fact, you might want to just take it off the toolbar. See *Choosing the Icons That Are Displayed on Your Toolbars* on page 33.

---

**Note –** If you find a lot of automatic formatting going on with lists, turn off automatic formatting using the instructions in *Turning Off Other Automatic Formatting* on page 8.

---

## Indenting Items

Let's say you've got a shopping list: things to buy at a few different stores. It would be nice to be able to have the main level of the list be the stores, and then have the sub-item under each be the items you need to buy. If you have just one item to indent, you can click to the left of it and press Tab. If you have more, or if you just prefer this approach, follow these steps.

**1**   Open the document with the items you need to indent.

**2**   Select the items to indent. If necessary, apply the bullet or numbering formatting.

**3** The list object bar will appear. It might be floating in the middle of the work area as shown in the previous illustration, or it might be with the other object bars. If it doesn't appear, choose View > Toolbars > Bullets and Numbering.

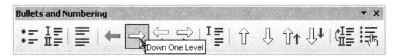

If the toolbar is floating, move it to the bottom of the work area, or out of the way by docking it.

**4** Select items to indent and click the Down One Level icon on the object bar.

**5** The items will be indented.

# Indenting Items and Their Subpoints, Using Icons

Here's how the basic icons, **Move Up** and **Move Down**, work. They simply affect the item or items selected when you click the icon.

**Before**                              **After**

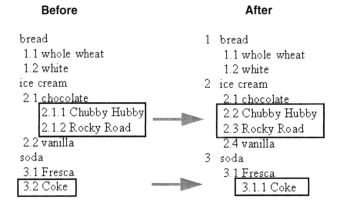

Two items were selected and **moved up a level** with the Up One Level icon.

One item was selected and **moved down a level** with the Down One Level icon.

Here's how the **Move Up With Subpoints** and **Move Down With Subpoints** icons, work. They affect not only the item selected when you click the icon, but all of that item's subpoints, if any.

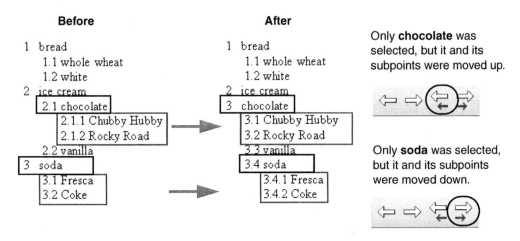

Only **chocolate** was selected, but it and its subpoints were moved up.

Only **soda** was selected, but it and its subpoints were moved down.

# Reference to Advanced Features in the Bullets and Numbering Toolbar

Here's a quick guide to two less frequently used, but still valuable, list management features.

## Restarting a List at 1

To restart any list at one, just select the item you want to be restarted at one, and click the Restart Numbering icon.

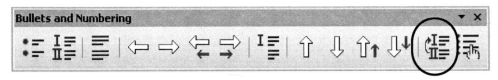

## Inserting Unnumbered Text in the Middle of a List

To insert an unnumbered piece of text in the middle of a list, just click *above* where you want the text, and click the Insert Unnumbered Entry icon.

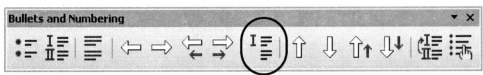

# List Power Tip: Using Fields for More Control

The information in this chapter and in *List Styles* on page 156 will give you a lot of power. I want to mention one more item: using the numbering fields in the Fields window. See also the More Information link at **http://openoffice.blogs.com/bookresources**.

The problem is that restarting numbering must be done manually; this is especially a problem if you have lists in multiple documents you combine in master documents.

To have more control, use an entirely different approach.

**1**     Choose Insert > Fields > Other.

**2**     Click the Variables tab. For Type, select Number Range and for Format select the type of numbering you want. Then type the name for the numbering, like Roman, and if you want this to be a number restarting field, type 1 in the Value field.

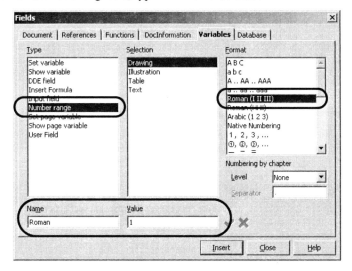

**3**     Click Insert. The number will appear. Type a tab and the content. You'll need to set up the tabs and wrap correctly yourself; see *Setting and Formatting Tabs* on page 89.

**4**     In the Fields window in the same tab, make the same selections and type the **same name** for the field, like Roman. However, this time to make a continuation field, leave the Value field blank. Click Insert.

**5**     The field will appear. Type a tab and your content.

Move your mouse over a field to see its value.

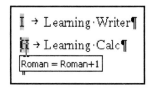

**6**     Now you can copy and paste the continuation field and the restart field wherever you need them. You can also set them up as AutoTexts so that you can just type **RR F3**, for instance, to put in your Roman Restart field. See *AutoText* on page 47.

# Guide to Good Layout and Formatting

# What This Chapter Is About

I've been talking for the past several chapters about how to do things: how to make tables, how to set up page layout, how to format text, and so on.

I haven't talked much about what you *should* do.

That's what this chapter is about. There's a whole world of formatting choices you can make to create documents that are:

- More professional-looking: more space between lines of text but with slightly less than a full blank line between paragraphs is a more professional look

- Easier to format and update: updating formatting is easier than changing carriage returns and tabs or spaces

- Easier to convert between Microsoft Word and OpenOffice.org: formatting is more easily handled between the programs than manual markup

# The Old Way of Formatting

When you type on a typewriter, you don't need to do anything complicated. You press Tab or the spacebar if you want to indent. You press Return twice to make a blank line.

**Introduction·to·Bread¶**
¶
→    Bread·is·a·good·food.·It·is·inexpensive,·nutritious,·and·provides¶
→    ·energy.¶
¶
→    Bread·comes·in·a·variety·of·flavors,·such·as·rye,·white,·whole·¶
→    wheat,·potato,·and·dill.¶
¶

When you switch from a typewriter to a computer, you learn to use the software to create a new document, print, and all those other features.

But there isn't a lot of emphasis on the fact that when you're using software to produce documents, there are some fundamental differences in the way you make the document look the way you want to.

With word-processing software, you can and should:

- Create spaces below text differently

- Indent text from the left or right differently

- Arrange text in parallel columns differently

- Position the text body differently within the page

# Use Spacing Below the Line Rather Than an Extra Carriage Return

This is a good example of a bad way to do formatting.

| | |
|---|---|
| Don't press Return if you want a blank line to create a space between paragraphs. | Bread·is·a·good·food. ·It·is·inexpensive, ·nutritious, ·and·provides·energy. ¶<br>¶<br>Bread·comes·in·a·variety·of·flavors, ·such·as·rye, ·white, ·whole·wheat, potato, ·and·dill. ¶<br>¶<br>One·way·to·use·bread·is ·in ·sandwiches. ¶<br>¶ |

Using Return for spacing between paragraphs is quick, but it's bad because:

♦ Pasting the text into another document can give you too much spacing below each paragraph.

♦ It gives you an unprofessional look; most professional books and documents have a little less spacing between paragraphs.

♦ It's an extra step you don't need.

Instead, add the space using the Paragraph formatting window. Select the text, choose Format > Paragraph, and specify roughly .08 or .10 of an inch below the paragraph.

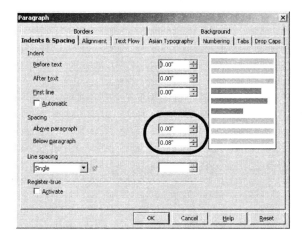

With that formatting, and without the carriage returns, your document looks like this.

Bread·is·a·good·food. ·It·is·inexpensive, ·nutritious, ·and·provides·energy. ¶

Bread·comes·in·a·variety·of·flavors, ·such·as·rye, ·white, ·whole·wheat, potato, ·and·dill. ¶

One·way·to·use·bread·is ·in ·sandwiches. ¶

To get this automatically, use the built-in Text Body style in Writer. Select the text, then from the dropdown list shown, select Text Body.

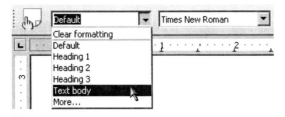

You generally want to use less space below each line for your bulleted lists, and more space below your bigger headings.

# Use Indenting Instead of Tabs or Spaces

One of the best ways to drive yourself crazy, and cause problems going between Word and Writer, is to use Tab or the space bar to indent.

Here's what it looks like when you use Tab, with a carriage return at the end as in typing, to indent from the left.

> → Bread·is·a·good·food.·It·is·inexpensive,·nutritious,·and·provides·¶
> → energy.¶
> ¶
> → Bread·comes·in·a·variety·of·flavors,·such·as·rye,·white,·whole·¶
> → wheat,·potato,·and·dill.¶
> ¶
> → One·way·to·use·bread·is·in·sandwiches.¶
> ¶

And here's what it looks like if your font, page size, default tabs, or pretty much anything else changes even the slightest. To do this example, all I did was to add one manual tab and everything went crazy.

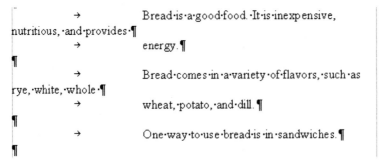

Plus, what if you need to change some of the content? Then you need to change all the placement of the tabs or spaces. And again, if you paste this content into another document with different settings of any kind, it'll probably look terrible.

> **Note –** Another reason not to press the space bar to indent is that the width of a space varies depending on the font. If you change the font, or give the document to someone who doesn't have that font, the spacing will change.

Here's what you do. Just *format* the paragraph as indented. There are a few different ways to do this.

Select all the text you want to indent and do one of the following:

◆   Grab the hourglass-looking icon by the *bottom* and drag it to the right.

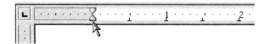

◆   Or use the Indent icon.

◆   Or choose Format > Paragraph and specify the indent in the Paragraph window. This is the best approach. For more on this, see *Indenting Paragraphs Using the Paragraph Window* on page 86.

# Using Tables, Not Tabs, for Parallel Columns of Text

Let's say you need text to look like this.

| John Hancock, mayor of Fargo and candidate for governor | John has been mayor of Fargo since 1966, and has seen a lot: the big flood of 1997, the big flood of 1992, and the big flood of 1989. He likes snowmobiling and playing cards. |
|---|---|
| Hannah Mercer, city council member | Hannah used to live in Williston and considers Fargo the brightest light on the North Dakota landscape! She enjoys canning fruit and gardening. |
| Dan Jaxtman, former Badger quarterback | Dan loves nothing more than to hear the roar of "Badgers! Badgers! Fighting Badgers!" in his ears. When not attending games as the official Badgers mascot, he smokes ham. |

There's not just one line of text at the left; there are two or more. You *could* do it with tabs. However, you will drive yourself crazy for the reasons mentioned previously. Use tables; just remove the borders when you're done if you don't want borders around the text. See *Creating and Formatting Tables* on page 177.

> **Note –** If you simply want text in columns, but you don't need to control exactly where the text is, use column formatting. See *Setting Up Columns* on page 105.

# Capture Your Formatting in Styles

Following these guidelines will give you a great-looking document that converts better between office suites. To bring it on home and create a great, maintainable, elegantly structured document, capture your formatting in styles. See *Saving Enormous Time and Effort With Styles* on page 147.

# 10

# Saving Enormous Time and Effort With Styles

# Understanding How Useful Styles Are

Styles are your one-stop shop for making documents consistent, and easy to update. A day without styles is like a day without sunshine.

## What's a Style?

Styles are just sets of formatting, captured under one title, like Heading1 or Signature or List. You could have a style called Heading 1 that's 18-point, using Helvetica font, bold, and centered. You'd apply it to any text that is a top-level heading in your document.

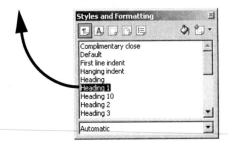

## And You Care About Styles Because?

There are many, many reasons to fall desperately in love with styles.

### Styles Making Applying Formatting Easier

Instead of having to apply the same four formatting characteristics again and again when you want that heading, you just apply your Heading 1 style and bam, it's formatted. When you have a 10-page document, that's nice. When you have a 1000-page document, it's essential.

### Styles Make Consistency Easier

You're good, but are you perfect? I'm not. I don't always remember how I want my headings formatted. (Was it 18 point of 16 point, and how much space below?) However, my Heading 1 style remembers for me. Use styles and you'll never have to go back to make changes because you forgot how to format.

### Styles Make Changes So Much Easier

This is where you really see how effective styles are. Sooner or later you'll need to change your formatting. After 200 pages and 75 headings, let's say you find out the font for all your headings needs to change and you need 8 points of space under each line. If you did all that manually, you are going to have a *lot* of work to do. If you used styles, it takes about 30 seconds to change the formatting. *If* you use styles.

# Types of Styles

There are several kinds of styles. We'll look at *paragraph styles*, which affect things like indentation and spacing as well as font and font size, and apply to the entire paragraph you're in when you apply the style. You generally use paragraph styles for headings, and for body text like normal body text, notes and hints that should stand out, captions, etc.

---

**Austin's in Old Town**

This reasonably priced downtown staple with a big sidewalk patio that wraps around two sides of the building is perfect for a casual summer lunch or dinner. Don't miss the sandwiches, soups and steaks. Light summer fare includes grilled vegetables, smoked salmon and Caesar salads that seem to taste that much better on the patio.

---

There are *character styles*, which affect things like how wide or narrow individual characters are and what color they are, and which apply only to the characters you've selected when you apply the style. Character styles are very useful for other formatting features like the numbering in captions and lists, and any part of a table of contents.

---

See their web site at **www.austinsoldtown.com** ‹

---

There are frame styles, which control objects like graphics, frames, and so on. Frame styles can control object size, borders, wrapping, spacing to the text, and so on.

Canon·City/Royal·Gorge·on·Day·Seven¶
Take·off·for·a·full·day·trip·to·Canon·City and·the·Royal·Gorge·Canyon.·Take·the morning·train·on·the·Royal·Gorge·Route Railroad·(two·hours·roundtrip)·which offers·spectacular·views·from·along·the Arkansas·River·at·the·bottom·of·the canyon.·The·canyonŽÖs·walls·rise·304 meters·above·the·train.·This·historic railway·also·offers·a·"Twilight·Dinner"·in the·historic·Theodore·Roosevelt·car
Watch·river·rafters·from·outdoor·boxcars,·then·travel·to·the·top·of·the·canyon·to·the Royal·Gorge·Bridge·&·Park·home·to·the·world's·highest·suspension·bridge,·aerial·tram and·incline·railway.·Or,·hike·in·the·Dinosaur·Fossil·Quarry·and·view·the·Jurassic·dinosaur graveyard·or·add·a·half-day,·whitewater·rafting·trip·on·the·Arkansas·River.·¶

There are *list styles*, which affect only list-specific things like what type of number or bullet to use and how far indented the text is from the number or bullet. List styles don't affect font.

---

Other jazz venues to consider:

➢ Pierre's Supper Club: 2157 Downing St.

➢ Burnsley Hotel: 1000 Grant St.

➢ Capitol Bar: 1550 Court Pl.

➢ Trios Enoteca: 1730 Wynkoop St.

---

There are *page styles*, which affect page margins, orientation, footers, etc., and apply to the page you're in, up to and down to either the beginning or end of the document, or the next page break (well, the next specially inserted page break).

**Note** – Page styles are a bit different: somewhat in how you apply them, but mostly how you switch from one to another. We'll get into that in a separate section in this chapter.

## Your Tool for Creating and Applying Styles

You will soon become very familiar with the Styles and Formatting window. That's where all the styles action takes place; choose Format > Styles and Formatting to open it. Take a look at it here to understand how to display styles.

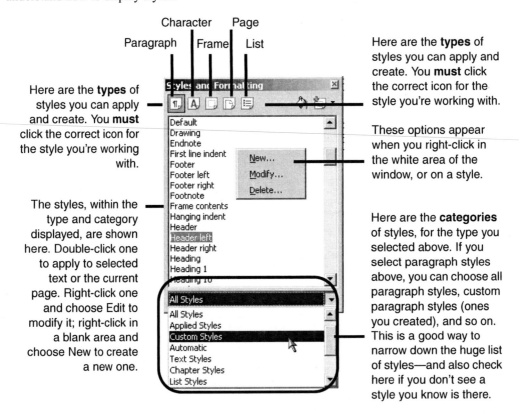

Paragraph    Character    Page
            Frame    List

Here are the **types** of styles you can apply and create. You **must** click the correct icon for the style you're working with.

Here are the **types** of styles you can apply and create. You **must** click the correct icon for the style you're working with.

These options appear when you right-click in the white area of the window, or on a style.

The styles, within the type and category displayed, are shown here. Double-click one to apply to selected text or the current page. Right-click one and choose Edit to modify it; right-click in a blank area and choose New to create a new one.

Here are the **categories** of styles, for the type you selected above. If you select paragraph styles above, you can choose all paragraph styles, custom paragraph styles (ones you created), and so on. This is a good way to narrow down the huge list of styles—and also check here if you don't see a style you know is there.

**Note** – See *Guide to Good Layout and Formatting* on page 141 for guidelines on how to create great-looking, easily updatable documents.

## Where Styles Are Stored

Styles stay in the document where you create them. If you create a paragraph style called Green Heading in your **2007brochure.odt** document, it's only in that document. However, there are easy ways to get styles into other documents.

◆   Create the styles in a document and save that document as a template, then create a new
    document based on that template. See *Saving Time With Templates and More* on page 37.

◆   In the document where you need a style, just load it from the document where the style is.
    See *Getting Styles Into Your Document* on page 174.

# Applying, Creating, and Modifying Styles

Complete the procedures in this section to use styles.

## Applying a Style

You can apply any style using the Styles and Formatting window.

### Applying Any Style

1   Choose Format > Styles and Formatting.

2   Select an icon at the top—Paragraph, Character, Page, Frame, or List.

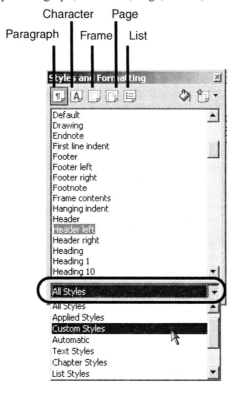

3   Find the style you want to apply. If you don't see it, be sure the right category is selected in
    the list at the bottom. Select All Styles to see all the styles.

4   Select what you want to apply the style to.

◆   Paragraph styles – Just click somewhere in the paragraph.

◆   Character styles – Select all the characters.

◆   List styles – Select at least part of each line in the list

◆   Page styles – The style will apply to the entire document, unless you're using the
    instructions in *Using Multiple Page Layouts in the Same Document* on page 169. You
    don't have to do anything to just apply a page style to the whole document.

5    Double-click the style in the Styles and Formatting window. The style will be applied. .

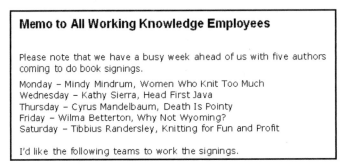

## Applying Any Currently Used Page Style

You can apply any currently applied paragraph style to another paragraph. Click in the paragraph,
then select the style to apply from this list on the Formatting toolbar.

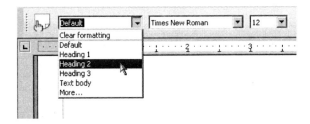

# Creating a New Style

Creating styles is just doing the formatting, within the Styles and Formatting window. Refer to the
formatting information in *Formatting Using the Paragraph and Character Windows* on page 78,
*Margins, Page Numbers, Page Layout, and More* on page 101, and *Formatting Lists* on page 124
for more information on how to do the formatting itself.

For heading styles, table heading styles, caption styles, or other styles that are applied
automatically in OpenOffice.org, I recommend just modifying them rather than creating new ones.
See *Modifying A Style* on page 155.

## One Approach: Do the Formatting, Then Base a Style on It

1    Choose Format > Styles and Formatting to display the Styles and Formatting window.

**2**    Click the appropriate icon at the top for the type of style you're creating.

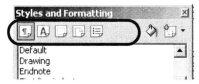

**3**    Select the paragraph, character, frame, or list, and format it how you want it. Or for a page, just do the page setup and add header and footer content.

**4**    With the text still selected, or in the newly formatted page if you're doing page styles, then click and hold down the black arrow in the Styles and Formatting window. Select New Style From Selection.

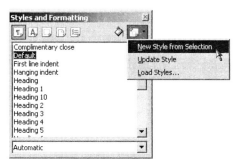

**5**    In the window that appears, type the style name and click OK.

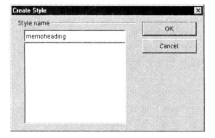

## Another Approach: Create a New Style, and Define Its Formatting Attributes

**1**    Choose Format > Styles and Formatting to display the Styles and Formatting window.

**2**    Click the appropriate icon at the top for the type of style you're creating.

**3**    Right-click in the blank part of the window and choose New.

**4**    In the style window, name the style, and specify the other options.

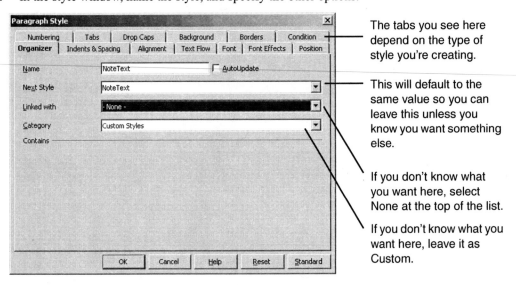

The tabs you see here depend on the type of style you're creating.

This will default to the same value so you can leave this unless you know you want something else.

If you don't know what you want here, select None at the top of the list.

If you don't know what you want here, leave it as Custom.

**5**    Use the other tabs to format the style.

**6**    Click OK to close the window and save the style.

---

**Note –** With page styles, if you want header and footer content to be part of the style, you'll need another step. Apply the style to a page, add the header or footer content, and save the document.

---

**Note –** For list styles, if you want different attributes at different levels, you must use the Outline, Position, or Options tab. Don't use the Graphics, Numbering, or Bullets tabs.

---

# Modifying A Style

Everything you learned in *Creating a New Style* on page 152 applies here, too. There are two ways to modify: modify, then update the style; or find the style and choose to modify it.

## One Approach: Do the Modification, Then Update the Style

**1**   Choose Format > Styles and Formatting to display the Styles and Formatting window.

**2**   Click the appropriate icon at the top for the type of style you're creating.

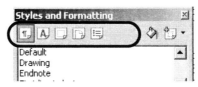

**3**   Select some text in your document, and be sure that the style you want to modify is applied to it. Or for page styles, be sure you're on the page that has the style to modify. The style you're modifying should be highlighted in the Styles and Formatting window.

**4**   Make the modifications you need to make. If you rename a style, all items with that style currently applied will be updated appropriately; the newly renamed style will be applied to them.

**5**   In the Styles and Formatting window, click and hold down on the black arrow and select Update Style.

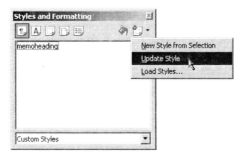

**6**   Everywhere the style was applied, the modification will take effect.

## Another Approach: Find the Style and Modify Its Attributes

**1**   Choose Format > Styles and Formatting to display the Styles and Formatting window.

**2**   Click the appropriate icon at the top for the type of style you're creating.

**3**    Right-click on the style and choose Modify.

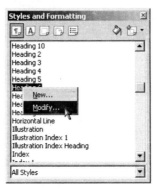

**4**    In the style window, make the necessary modifications.

**5**    Click OK.

# List Styles

Lists are just a little more complicated than paragraph styles. More complicated, but powerful.

---

**Note** – Technically, you can make and use list styles without reading this section at all. The previous sections, *Applying a Style*, *Applying a Style*, and *Applying a Style* tell you correctly what to do. But you'll understand lists a whole lot better once you read this section.

---

## What List Styles Are and How to Use Them

List styles are just list formatting, captured in a style.

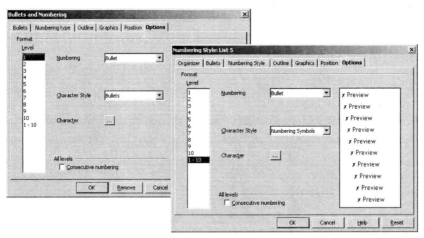

The formatting capabilities are the same, regardless of whether you apply the formatting manually each time (left) or whether you create the formatting in the Styles window and apply the style each subsequent time (right).

This is the same as paragraph formatting and styles; character formatting and styles; and page formatting and styles.

## What List Formatting Can and Can't Do

List formatting can provide the following attributes of a list. There are also attributes that a list style cannot provide.

The number or bullet, for each level; here it's italic Roman.

The formatting and size for the number or bullet, for each level.

The amount of space each number or bullet is indented from the left margin, for each level.

The amount of space the text is indented from each number or bullet, for each level.

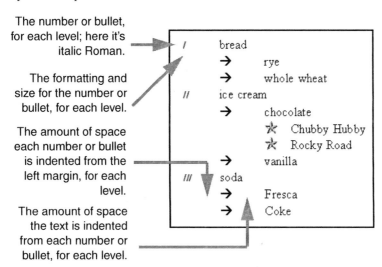

List styles do not provide any character formatting for the list content itself. You cannot, for instance, make "Chubby Hubby" bold and italic using any aspect of list styles. Use paragraph styles to format the list content.

**What list formatting, and list styles, do and don't provide**

## Using List Styles and Paragraph Styles Together

List styles provide everything inherent to a list. But to apply formatting to the text in your list, you need to use paragraph styles. You can use the same paragraph style for each level (this is simpler), or apply a different paragraph style to each level.

The list style **Silly Demo List** provides the indentation, the roman numeral at the top level, and other list attributes.

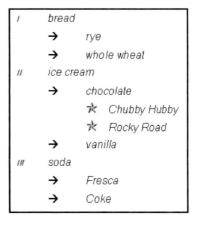

The paragraph style **List Formatting** provides the formatting for the contents. It makes the text italic and Arial, and with .06 inch below each line.

## Applying a List Style and a Paragraph Style to a List

You can do this in two ways.

**The manual way** You can do this the same way you'd apply styles normally. Just select the list, then apply the styles as you would normally. In the Styles and Formatting window, find the List Styles category, then double-click the list style of your choice. With the list still selected, switch to the Paragraph Styles category, then double-click the paragraph style of your choice.

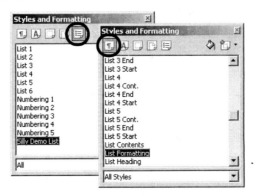

**The slick way** Set up the paragraph style to always be linked with the corresponding list style. Modify the paragraph style and go to the Numbering tab. Select the numbering style to use with that paragraph style, and click OK. Now when you use this paragraph style, that numbering style will always be applied automatically.

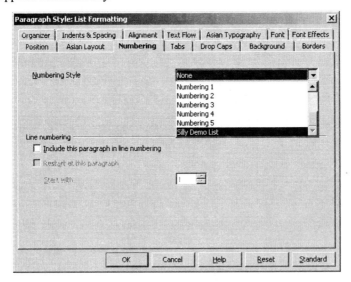

From now on, whenever you apply that paragraph style, the selected numbering style will be automatically applied, as well.

# Creating List Styles

Here's the detail for creating list styles.

## Creating a Simple List Style

Follow these steps to create a simple list style with the same list formatting on each level.

**1**   Choose Format > Styles and Formatting.

**2**   Click the List Styles icon.

**3**   Right-click in the white space and choose New.

**4**   Name the style.

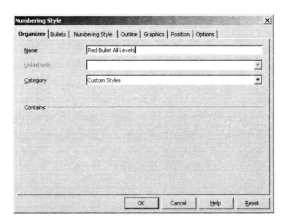

**5**   Click the Bullets, Graphics, or Numbers tab, and select the design you want.

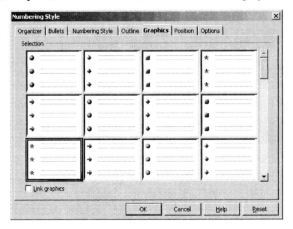

**6**   Click OK. The style name will appear in the window.

**7**   Select the list, and double-click the new style, to apply the style.

## Creating an Outline List Style

There are many prefab outline formats in the Bullets and Numbering window.

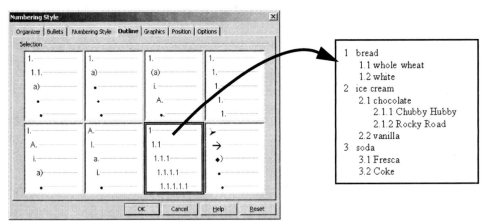

However, if you use them regularly, it's best to create a style based on one so that you have more control over the formatting so you can tweak aspects of the list formatting.

**1**    Choose Format > Styles and Formatting.

**2**    Click the List Styles icon.

**3**    Right-click in the white space and choose New.

**4**    In the Organizer tab of the styles window that appears, name the style.

**5**    Click the Outline tab and select the design you want.

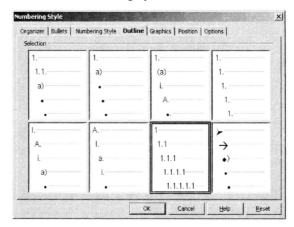

**6** If you want to tweak it, click the Options tab. Select the level in the Level list to change the numbering for, and select a different option from the Numbering list.

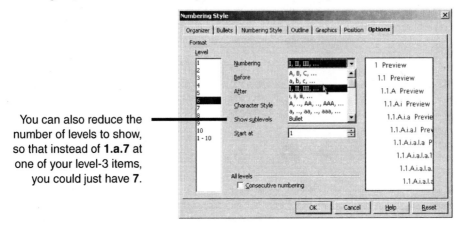

You can also reduce the number of levels to show, so that instead of **1.a.7** at one of your level-3 items, you could just have **7**.

**7** Click OK. The style will appear in your styles window.

## Applying Different List Attributes at Different Levels

With list styles you can specify different list formatting attributes for each level. This means you can have, for instance, a roman numeral at level 1 indented a quarter inch, a red star bullet for level 2 that's indented .35 inches, and so on.

**1** Choose Format > Styles and Formatting.

**2** Click the List Styles icon.

**3** Right-click in the white space and choose New.

**4** Name the style.

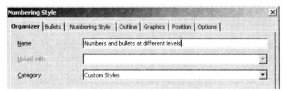

**5** The next part is very important. **You must use the Options and Position tabs to do this.** If you click on one of the prefab designs in the other tabs, then just click OK, you'll get the same formatting at every level.

**6** Click the Position tab. Select the first level.

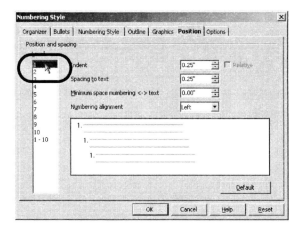

**7** Set your indenting formatting in the **Indent** and **Spacing to Text** fields. You typically want to have 0 indent on the first level, if you want the bullet or number to be flush left with the other text.

Then specify .25 or more as the distance from the number or bullet to the text.

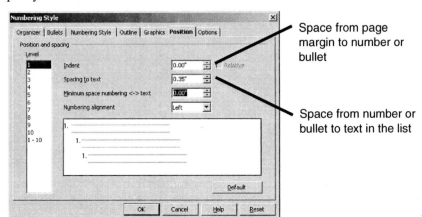

Space from page margin to number or bullet

Space from number or bullet to text in the list

**8**   Select the next level, and repeat the previous steps. You want the **Indent** here to be farther in than the previous level.

♦   To do this easily, just mark the Relative checkbox and specify the indent.

♦   To do this manually, you have to do a little math. You want the **Indent** to be the **sum of the Indent and the Spacing to Text** from the previous level, for the levels to align correctly. Since those values were 0 and .35 respectively at level 1, you enter .35 for the Indent for level 2. The Spacing to Text can be anything, though .25 to .5 of an inch is normal

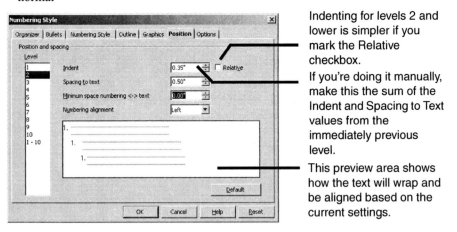

Indenting for levels 2 and lower is simpler if you mark the Relative checkbox.

If you're doing it manually, make this the sum of the Indent and Spacing to Text values from the immediately previous level.

This preview area shows how the text will wrap and be aligned based on the current settings.

As you go through the levels, keep an eye on the preview area at the bottom of the window to see how the alignment works.

**9**   Repeat the previous step for every level to set indenting for.

**10**   Click the Options tab and select the first level.

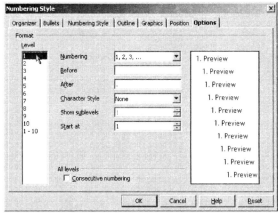

**11**   Select the type of number or bullet in the Numbering list. The options you get after that change drastically depending on what you select. Complete the instructions in step 12, 13, or 14 depending on what you choose.

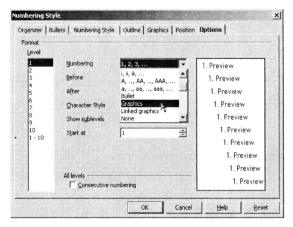

**12**   **Set options for numbers:**

- From the Numbering list, select the type of number.

- In the Before and After fields, specify whether you want a word like **Candidate** or **Item** before the number, as well as something like a colon or dash that you want after the number. You typically want to include a space in anything in the Before field

◆ Choose a character style if you want to use one to format the number and any text before or after.

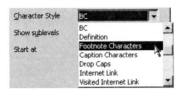

◆ For levels 2 and down, specify in the Show Sublevels field how many levels to show. If you're doing an outline, you probably want the maximum levels; for all others, stick to just one.

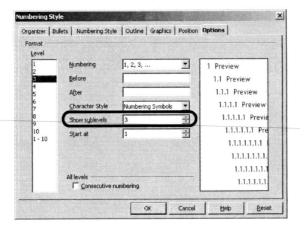

**13** **Set options for graphical bullets:**

◆ From the Numbering list, select Graphics.

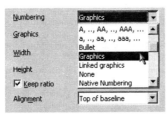

◆ Click on the Select dropdown list and choose From File or Gallery. If you choose From File you'll get a standard dialog box where you can choose a picture of your own. If you choose Gallery you'll get a list where you can choose things like red stars, blue diamonds, etc.

- You can change the size in the Width and Height area, Click the Keep Ratio option, then increase either the Width or the Height.

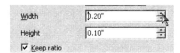

**14   Set options for standard bullets:**

- In the Numbering list, select Bullets.

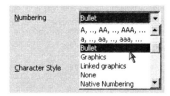

- Click the browse button by Character.

- You'll see the big window of bullet choices. Make a selection and click OK,

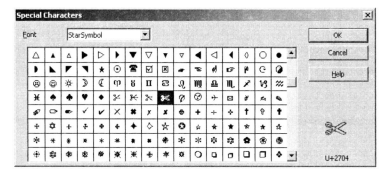

- Select a character style if you want to apply a specific color or other character format to the bullet.

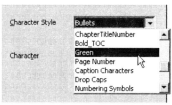

**15**   Click OK to save changes and close the styles window. You'll see the style in the Styles and Formatting window.

# The Styles That Come With OpenOffice.org

Choose Format > Styles and Formatting, and click the List Styles icon.

Here's what you get when you apply a style to a single-level list.

A one-level list formatted by
simply clicking the **Bullets
icon** on the toolbar

A one-level list formatted by
applying the **List 4 style**

Here's what you get when you apply a style to a multi-level list. As you can see, the style contains
formatting for all the levels of the list.

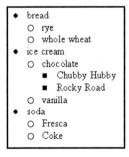

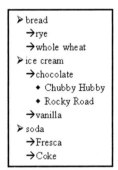

A multi-level list formatted
by simply clicking the
**Bullets icon** on the toolbar

A multi-level list
formatted by applying the
**List 4 style**

---

**Note –** The List 3 style in some versions is created incorrectly; the indenting for level 3 restarts
flush left, instead of continuing in.

---

# Using Multiple Page Layouts in the Same Document

Sooner or later you'll need a document where every page doesn't look alike.

You might want the whole document to be the same except that you don't want a page number on the first page. You might need a few pages that are landscape, or maybe you're making a user's guide and need lots of different page layouts.

**CoverPage** page style with no headers or footers, and a gray background.

**Contents** page style with a header and footer, and a wide right margin.

**FirstPage** page style with a centered footer and page number.

To define the page layout, you create page styles. Cover Page page style with a gray background for a cover page before the lowercase roman numeral TOC page, and so on.

That's the first step. The second step is, how do you tell Writer where to put the page styles? How do you apply the Cover Page page style to just the first page, and the Table of Contents With Header page style to just the second page, and the main body page style to all the rest?

You might think you just insert a page break. That's part of the story. But it's not the whole story. You have to apply your page style, then insert a page break *and* at the same time tell Writer what the next page style should be. It's reasonably straightforward once you learn it.

---

**Note –** You can switch page styles two other ways; these are more advanced and I'll mention how to get started with them at the end of this section.

---

## Creating a Document With Two or More Page Styles

In this procedure, I'm using a sample document with a cover page and several pages of normal content. However, this applies anytime you want two or more different page styles in a document.

1    Create or load the page styles you want to use.

2    Go to the first page of the document.

3    Choose Format > Styles and Formatting.

**4**    Click the Page Styles icon.

**5**    Find the page style to use on that page and double-click it.

**6**    The style will be applied to the entire document.

**7**    Scroll to the line where you want the next page style to be applied. This is the line that should be at the top of the new page.

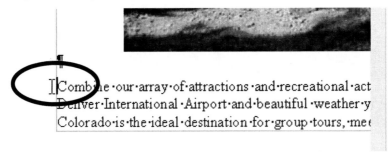

**8**    Choose Insert > Manual Break. The Manual Break window will appear.

**9** In the Style list, select the page style to switch to. By doing this, you're saying that after the page break you want to switch to this page style.

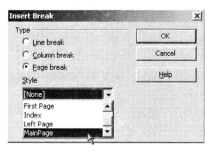

**10** Click OK.

**11** Keep switching to other page styles if you need to, the same way.

**12** Here's what the first and second pages look like in this example.

# Headers and Footers, Page Numbering, and Page Styles

Follow the directions in *Creating a New Style* on page 152 to create a page style. However, page styles have a little something extra not covered in that section: the option for headers and footers, and page numbers and other content. That information is saved as part of the style but you need to add it in the document, not in the style definition window. Here are some tips and procedures for header and footer content, and page numbering.

## Adding Content to Headers and Footers for Page Styles

You can turn on the header and footer, but you need to add the content for the headers and footers after the fact.

**1** When defining the page style, turn on headers and/or footers.

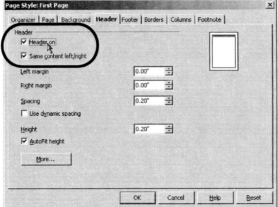

**2** Apply the page style by double-clicking the page style in the Styles and Formatting window.

**3** Add content to the headers and/or footers. For more information on page numbers, see *Adding Page Numbers, Text, and Date Content to Headers and Footers* on page 108.

page ii

**4** Save the document. All the content in the headers and/or footers is part of the style definition.

## Controlling What Type of Page Numbering Is Used

You might usually want Arabic numbering, 1 2 3, but upper and lowercase Roman numerals are useful in front matter of books. How do you set the type of numbering?

You can set it manually by double-clicking an inserted page field and selecting a style as shown.

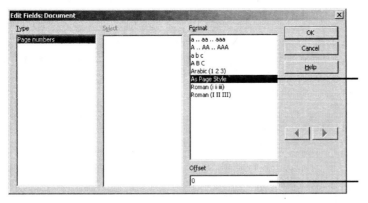

You can select a different page numbering style here but it's a really good idea to leave **As Page Style** as the selection.

The Offset field here doesn't work correctly; there's another offset feature you can use.

However, it's more flexible and better to control it through the page style.

**1** When defining the page style, click the Page tab.

**2**    In the Format field, specify the numbering style.

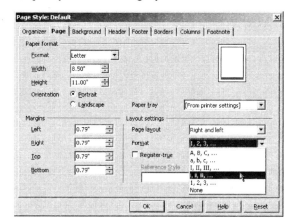

**3**    When you insert the page number, choose Insert > Fields > Page Number, as usual. The page number will be inserted to adapt to the page style.

**4**    When you want to change the page numbering type for that page style, just change it in the style definition.

## Starting a Page With a Specific Page Number

If you have a cover page on the first page, that page number is 1. The next page is page 2. However, that's the first page of your actual content. That means it would be nice if the page number displayed 1, even though it's technically page 2.

This is simple. You just specify the page number you want using the same Insert Break window you use when switching page styles.

This opens up a question—do you have to change to a different page style when all you want to do is restart or change the page numbering? No. But you do have to select the page style to use, even if it's the *same one.*

You have these options in this window.

◆    You can *just switch page styles* in this window

◆    You can switch page styles, *and* specify a different page number, in this window

◆    And you can just specify a *different* page number, and stick with the *same* page style, in this window

The following illustration demonstrates this.

You have to insert a manual break and specify a page style. The page style you select in the Page Style list can be different, or the same one on the previous page—you don't need to switch to a different style.

Leave this unmarked, or you can type a specific page number to use after the page break.

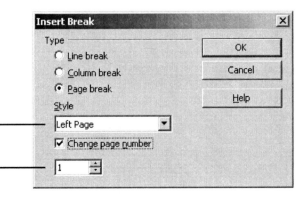

To switch page numbers on page 2 or subsequent pages in the document, just complete the steps in *Creating a Document With Two or More Page Styles* on page 169. But before you click OK, select **Change Page Number** and type the page number you want on that page.

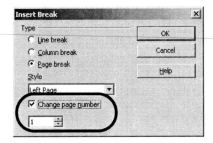

# Getting Styles Into Your Document

The styles that come with OpenOffice.org are always available from the Styles and Formatting window no matter what document you're in, *but* the styles you create and any modifications you make are only in the document you're in when you make them.

Until you load them into another document, that is. So how do you get them into another document? You can just open a document, and bring in the styles from another document. Or, if you want to plan ahead and/or if you're the Template God for your department, you can load the styles you want into a template.

## Bringing Styles into a Document

**1**  Open the document where you need the styles.

**2**  Choose Format > Styles and Formatting.

**3**  In the Styles and Formatting window, click and hold down on the black arrow and select Load Styles.

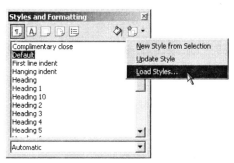

**4**  The Load Styles window will appear. Select all the checkboxes at the bottom if you want all styles, or select just the ones you need. (Text Styles are both character and paragraph.)

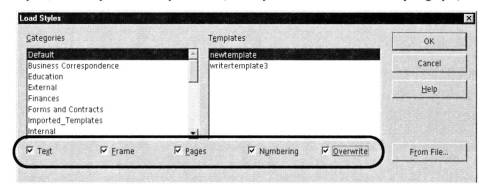

**5**  Select Overwrite, as well, if you want the imported styles to overwrite any in your current document with the same name. (You almost always want this.)

**6**  Click From File and locate the file containing the styles.

**7**  Click Open.

**8**  The styles will be imported into the document and will show up in the appropriate categories in the Styles and Formatting Window.

## Creating a Template With Specific Styles

1   Create a new document, and create or load the styles you need. See the previous procedure to load the styles, *Bringing Styles into a Document* on page 175. Put in whatever else you want, too: canned text, graphics, etc.

2   Delete any styles you don't want—you can delete any you've created, but many that are built into OpenOffice.org can't be deleted since they're used in the program. To do so, right-click on the style in the Styles and Formatting window, and choose Delete.

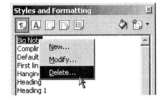

3   Make the document into a template. See *Creating a New Template* on page 41.

4   If you need to make sure that other people use this template, email the template to everyone who needs to use it. Alternately, you can put the template in a central location (how you do this depends on how OpenOffice.org was installed and where the users' installations point to). Tell them to use the template and styles or you will become very angry (and they wouldn't like you when you're angry). All they need to do to create a document based on your template is follow the instructions in *Creating a Document Based on a Template* on page 42; to apply styles, they just follow the instructions in *Applying a Style* on page 151.

# Creating and Formatting Tables

# Using Tables

Sometimes you just need a document with standard text and pictures, one after another. You have a paragraph, a list, a picture, and so on.

That ends pretty quickly when you get anything remotely complicated, or if you need to cram a lot of information onto a page. It's also time for a new approach if you want to be able to easily compare information side by side.

Anytime you want to control visually where pieces of text go, when you've got lots of data to present in one spot, or if want to be able to do a little math with your numeric data, tables are a great idea. It's also a good idea to use tables when you have two columns of information that need to be side by side, and there are two or more rows in the first column.

| Salesperson | 1999-2000 | 2001-2002 | 2003-2004 | 2005-2006 |
|---|---|---|---|---|
| Jensenson | $29,088.00 | $48,990.00 | $38,447.00 | $48,866.00 |
| Halvorsen | $49,909.00 | $39,881.00 | $23,321.00 | $48,011.00 |
| Sanfordenson | $44,098.00 | $34,331.00 | $12,090.00 | $22,900.00 |
| Sixfingeredmansen | $49,800.00 | $43,510.00 | $43,000.00 | $48,220.00 |

Tables are good for straight-up financial figures, since you can easily compare the data, and you can apply automatic currency formatting.

| Organizer | Task | Notes |
|---|---|---|
| Jane | Design party invitations | Use kung fu or pulp fiction theme. |
| Larry | Organize games | Killer Bunnies is one option. |
| Judd | Organize games | Bring strategy guide for Twister. |
| Kathy | Desserts | Anything home-baked is fine. |
| Bert | Host | Greet guests, take care of coats, stear unsigned authors away from the signed authors. |

Tables let you arrange different pieces of information for particular topics, as shown. In this and the above example, you also see some options for shading and border formatting.

| John Hancock, mayor of Fargo and candidate for governor | John has been mayor of Fargo since 1966, and has seen a lot: the big flood of 1997, the big flood of 1992, and the big flood of 1989. He likes snowmobiling and playing cards. |
|---|---|
| Hannah Mercer, city council member | Hannah used to live in Williston and considers Fargo the brightest light on the North Dakota landscape! She enjoys canning fruit and gardening. |
| Dan Jaxtman, former Badger quarterback | Dan loves nothing more than to hear the roar of "Badgers! Badgers! Fighting Badgers!" in his ears. When not attending games as the official Badgers mascot, he smokes ham. |

Tables are an excellent approach for information like the example at left. Just use a table, and take off the borders. You will drive yourself crazy if you try to do this with tabs or wrapping text.

# Creating Writer Tables

Tables are pretty easy to insert and fiddle with. Use the Table menu, and all the features are right there. You get a special formatting bar for the table that has pretty much everything you need, and a toolbar that pops up to give other ways to access the features.

# Inserting a Table

There are a couple approaches to inserting a table.

## Creating a Table Using the Table Menu

**1**    Choose Insert > Table.

**2**    In the Insert Table window, specify the number of columns and rows. (This includes the header row.) If you don't want a header, unmark it.

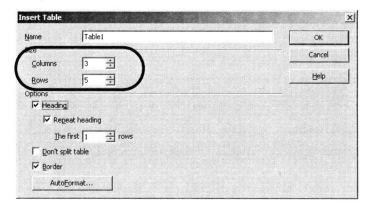

**3**    If you want to apply an Autoformat, click the Autoformat button and make your selection. (For more information, see *Creating and Applying AutoFormats: The Table Formatting Timesaver* on page 193.)

**4**    Click OK.

**5**    The table will appear in the document.

**6**    Fill in the table as needed. You can press Tab to move from cell to cell (Shift + Tab to move back).

| *Person* | *Task* | *Notes* |
|----------|--------|---------|
| Elaine | Balloons | Helium |
| John | Cake | Chocolate |
| Kathy | Decorations | Blue |
| Mark | Gift | Book |

## Creating a Table Using the Insert Menu or the Insert Table Icon

You can also insert a table by choosing Insert > Table. Another option is to display the Insert toolbar. Click and hold down on the Insert Table icon and select the number of rows and columns.

## Creating a Table With Multiple or No Heading Rows

1   Choose Insert > Table.

2   In the Insert Table window, select or unmark the Heading option.

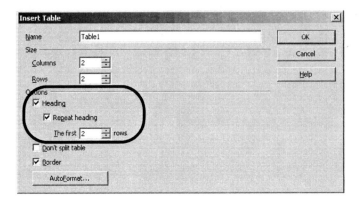

3   To have multiple heading rows, specify the number of heading rows; these rows will repeat on each page.

4   Specify the number of standard rows and other options, as usual.

5   Click OK.

# Table Management Tips

Some aspects of tables are a bit tricky; here's how to do the basics.

### Inserting a Blank Line at the Top of a Page Above a Table

You've inserted a table at the top of a page, and now you want regular text above the table. To do this, click in the top left cell of the table, and press Return.

| *Organizer* | *Task* | *Notes* |
|---|---|---|
| Jane | Design party invitations | Use kung fu or pulp fiction theme. |

### Separating Two Tables

You've got two tables, one immediately on top of the other. You want regular text between them; what do you do?

It's the same as inserting a blank line above a table. Click in the top left cell of the second table, and press Return.

### Deleting Just the Contents of a Table

Select the table and press Delete. Only the content will disappear.

## Deleting a Table

Here's one approach.

**1**   Select the first line above the table, as well as the entire table.

**2**   Press the Delete key on your keyboard. The table disappears.

Another approach is to select the whole table and click either the Delete Row or Delete Column icon.

## Deleting Rows or Columns

Click in the row(s) or column(s) you want to delete. Then use the Delete Row or Delete Column icons shown previously, or right-click and choose Row > Delete or Column > Delete. And in yet another approach, you can choose Table > Delete > Rows or Table > Delete > Columns.

# Skip the Tables—Use a Spreadsheet

Spreadsheets are easier to use. Create the spreadsheet, then paste into Writer.

The spreadsheet looks like this when you paste it into Writer

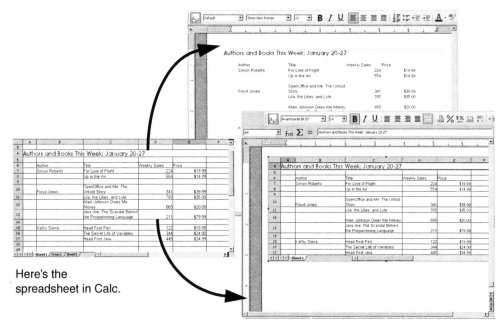

Here's the spreadsheet in Calc.

The spreadsheet looks like this when you paste it into Writer, then double-click it.

If you've got a lot of numeric data, or things that would be better done in a spreadsheet, then just do it in a spreadsheet. Then copy and paste the data into the Writer document. You can copy some or all of a spreadsheet.

When you paste it into Writer, it looks just like plain data; any borders you apply will come over, but if there aren't any borders, you don't see any. When you double-click in the spreadsheet data in Writer, then it looks like a spreadsheet.

### Plain Pasting

Copy the part of the spreadsheet you want to copy, then go to the other document and choose Edit > Paste to simply paste the spreadsheet.

### Linking to the Spreadsheet, for Automatic Updates

Copy the part of the spreadsheet you want, go to the other document, and choose Edit > Paste Special. In the Paste Special window, select DDE Link. Click OK.

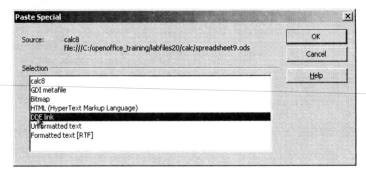

That means the pasted information will be updated every time you change the data in the spreadsheet. This is particularly nice if you need data from a spreadsheet to be included in several different documents. This works when you paste from a spreadsheet into a Writer document, and when you paste from a spreadsheet into another spreadsheet.

# Formatting Tables

You can format many aspects of a table—the background, borders, border styles, and so on. There's a specific toolbar, the Table toolbar, that helps you do much of that.

## Viewing the Table Formatting Bar

When you create a table, there are a bunch of table-specific things you'll want to do: apply borders, add and remove rows and columns, etc. To help you do these things more easily, OpenOffice.org provides a specialized table toolbar with these tools.

1    Click in a table.

2    Be sure that the Table toolbar appears. If it doesn't, choose View > Toolbars > Table.

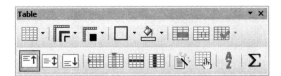

# Adding or Removing Table Borders

Table borders are good for making tables more legible. You can also remove table borders using these steps, if you want to use the approach described in *Using Tables, Not Tabs, for Parallel Columns of Text* on page 145.

**1** Open the table to apply borders to.

**2** Be sure you can see the table formatting toolbar. Refer to *Viewing the Table Formatting Bar on page 182* if you don't see it.

**3** Click on the borders icon and hold your mouse down on it. **Select the blank option, to clear the current borders, before you apply other borders**.

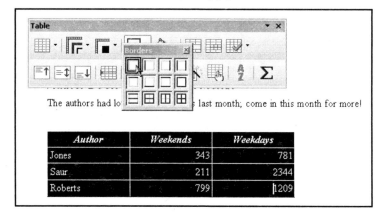

Whenever you switch where the borders are placed, you have to **clear the old borders first** by selecting the blank option. Then select a new border placement option.

**4**    With the table still selected, click and hold down the mouse again on the borders icon and select the icon for the formatting you want.

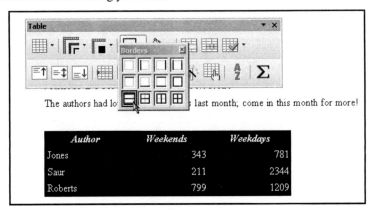

**5**    The table will show the new border placement.

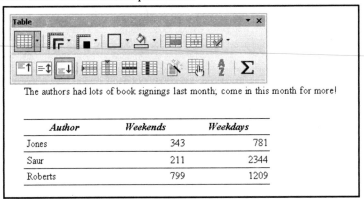

# Applying Different Border Styles

You can set off or distinguish certain lines, such as the heading row, in your table using different types of borders, such as double lines or single lines.

| Salesperson | 1999-2000 | 2001-2002 | 2003-2004 | 2005-2006 |
|---|---|---|---|---|
| Jensenson | $29,088.00 | $48,990.00 | $38,447.00 | $48,866.00 |
| Halvorsen | $49,909.00 | $39,881.00 | $23,321.00 | $48,011.00 |
| Sanfordenson | $44,098.00 | $34,331.00 | $12,090.00 | $22,900.00 |
| Sixfingeredmansen | $49,800.00 | $43,510.00 | $43,000.00 | $48,220.00 |

**1**    Select the table to change line styles for.

**2**    Be sure the table toolbar is displayed.

**3**   Click and hold down your mouse on the Border Style icon.

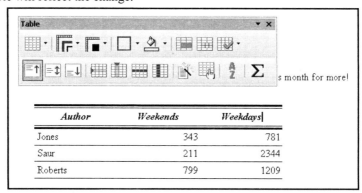

**4**   Select a border type you want.

**5**   The table will reflect the change.

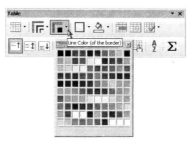

## Changing the Border Color

This is very similar to the other procedures. Just select the table and use the line color icon on the table toolbar.

## Applying Background Shading

Background shading is another good way to highlight information in a table or make a table with lots of columns or rows more readable.

| Organizer | Task | Notes |
|-----------|------|-------|
| Jane | Design party invitations | Use kung fu or pulp fiction theme. |
| Larry | Organize games | Killer Bunnies is one option. |
| Judd | Organize games | Bring strategy guide for Twister. |
| Kathy | Desserts | Anything home-baked is fine. |
| Bert | Host | Greet guests, take care of coats, stear unsigned authors away from the signed authors. |

**1**    Select the table, and be sure you can see the table formatting bar.

**2**    Click and hold down the mouse on the Background icon.

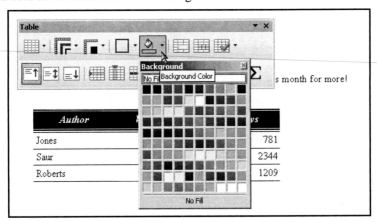

**3**    Select a color.

**4**    The table will reflect the change.

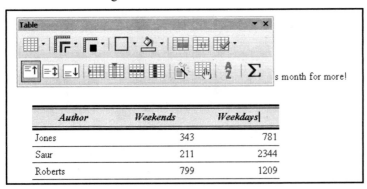

# Advanced Reference to Borders and Shading

Let's say you want a table that looks like this. There are different border widths, border styles, and though it doesn't show in the printed version of the book, different colors, on various lines within the table.

| *Organizer* | *Task* | *Notes* |
|---|---|---|
| Jane | Design party invitations | Use kung fu or pulp fiction theme. |
| Larry | Organize games | Killer Bunnies is one option. |
| Judd | Organize games | Bring strategy guide for Twister. |
| Kathy | Desserts | Anything home-baked is fine. |
| Bert | Host | Greet guests, take care of coats, stear unsigned authors away from the signed authors. |

Very few people would, of course, since it's not that attractive. But the point is, how do you apply specific border formatting to each border in a table? To have more control over border formatting, you'll want to use the Table Format window. Select the table and choose Table > Table Properties.

## Borders Tab

You can use the presets but you can also click on each line in the border area. Clicking on a line in the User-Defined border area will switch it from selected to deselected

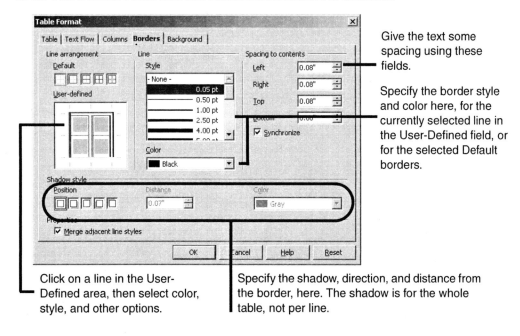

Give the text some spacing using these fields.

Specify the border style and color here, for the currently selected line in the User-Defined field, or for the selected Default borders.

Click on a line in the User-Defined area, then select color, style, and other options.

Specify the shadow, direction, and distance from the border, here. The shadow is for the whole table, not per line.

When you select a line in the User-Defined area, or when you choose a preset Default pattern, here's what it translates into in a table.

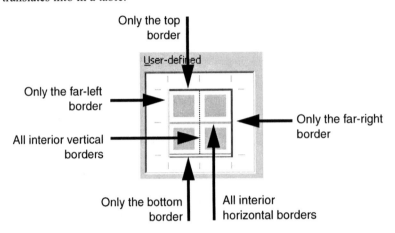

**What about Merge Adjacent Line Styles?**  This option in the Borders tab merges two different border styles of adjacent cells in a Writer table into one border style. This property is valid for a whole table in a Writer document.

The rules can be condensed to the statement that the stronger attribute wins. If, for example, one cell has a red border of 2 point width, and the adjacent cell has a blue border of 3 point width, then the common border between these two cells will be blue with 3 point width.

## Background Tab

This doesn't provide all that much additional value, but you can apply the formatting to the cell, row, or whole table. You can also choose a background color or background graphic for the cell, row, or table

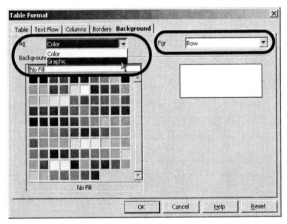

# Adding and Managing Rows and Columns

Once you've got the formatting down and you start entering information in the table, you'll probably find that you don't have enough rows, or you have too many columns here's how to hand that—and as usual, the Table toolbar has the tools you need.

## Adding and Deleting Rows and Columns

**1**   Be sure you can see table toolbar; if you can't, choose View > Toolbars > Table.

**2**   Click in the row above where you want a new row.

| Person | Task | Notes |
|--------|------|-------|
| Elaine | Balloons | Helium |
| John | Cake | Chocolate |
| Kathy | Decorations | Blue |
| Mark | Gift | Book |

**3**   Click the Insert Row icon

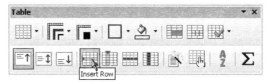

**4**   Click in the row you want to delete, or select rows to delete, and click the horizontal icon.

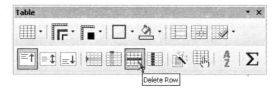

## Changing Column Width

You can use the Table Format window to change column width, or drag the borders.

### Dragging the Column Borders

**1**   Select the entire table and position your cursor over the line on the ruler where you want to change the width of a column. Make sure the cursor turns into a two-ended arrow, as shown.

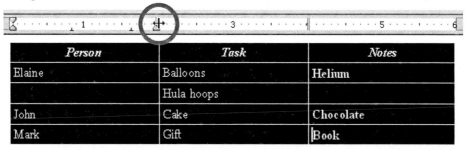

**2**   Drag the column separator to the left or right to change the width.

This will also work if you move your mouse over the table itself; when the icon looks like this, drag the border left or right.

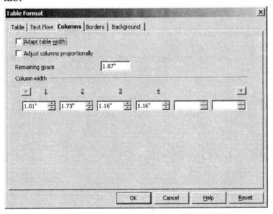

## Using the Table Format Window to Change Column Width

**1**   Select the table.

**2**   Choose Table > Table Properties.

**3**   Click the Columns tab.

**4**   Specify the column widths.

**5**   Click OK.

## Resizing Columns Using the Optimization Icons

Use these tools to automatically make all columns equal in width, or make them all the right width for their content (optimal width).

**1**    Select the table.

| Person | Task | Notes |
|---|---|---|
| Elaine | Balloons | Helium |
| | Hula hoops | |
| John | Cake | Chocolate |
| Mark | Gift | Book |

**2**    Be sure you can see the table toolbar; if you can't, choose View > Toolbars > Table. You'll be using the Optimize icon in this procedure, and the options available when you long-click on it.

**3**    You can distribute the columns evenly, or simply optimally for the content.

♦    To make columns equal, click and hold down on the Optimize icon and select the Distribute Columns Evenly icon. The columns will be resized equally.

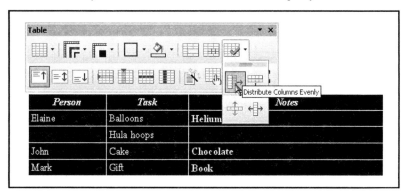

♦    In the table toolbar, click and hold down on the Optimize icon and select the Optimize Width icon. The column widths adjust to the minimum width the need to display all text on one line.

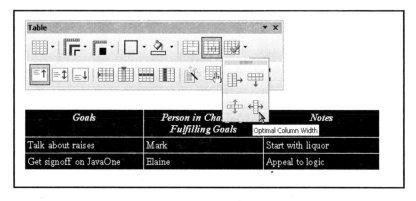

# Splitting and Merging Cells

**1** Select the cells you want to merge.

| Books Sold This Week | | | |
|---|---|---|---|
| Fiction | | Nonfiction | |
| Title | Author | Title | Author |
| Hakunah Mywhatah? | Randall marks | Feminism is a Fat Issue | Gerard Gemini |
| Twelve Blue Plates | Mira Munos | My Golden Calves | Sonja Jones |

**2** Click the Merge Cells icon on the table toolbar.

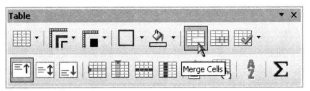

**3** The results will look like this.

| Books Sold This Week | | | |
|---|---|---|---|
| Fiction | | Nonfiction | |
| Title | Author | Title | Author |
| Hakunah Mywhatah? | Randall marks | Feminism is a Fat Issue | Gerard Gemini |
| Twelve Blue Plates | Mira Munos | My Golden Calves | Sonja Jones |

**4** To split cells, click in a row where you've already merged cells.

| Books Sold This Week | | | |
|---|---|---|---|
| Fiction | | Nonfiction | |
| Title | Author | Title | Author |
| Hakunah Mywhatah? | Randall marks | Feminism is a Fat Issue | Gerard Gemini |
| Twelve Blue Plates | Mira Munos | My Golden Calves | Sonja Jones |

**5** Click the Split Cells icon in the table formatting toolbar.

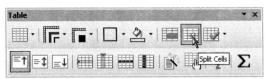

**6**    In the resulting window, select the correct number of cells and specify vertical split. Don't just accept the default; it's usually incorrect

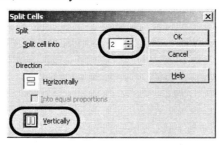

**7**    Click OK.

# Creating and Applying AutoFormats: The Table Formatting Timesaver

Once you've formatted a few complex tables, you realize that it is a huge time sink. Just applying the formatting once can take a long time; how long would it take you to apply all the formatting at right, to twenty tables? Longer than you want to spend. Luckily, you can save time with *AutoFormats*. AutoFormats are like styles for tables: you "freeze" the formatting settings for a table the way you want it, and then just apply it quickly to any other table. AutoFormats don't just retain table formatting; they retain things like font and font size, as well.

AutoFormats come with you from one document to another. They also work the same way in Calc spreadsheets.

**StandardTable Formatting**

Borders on horizontal lines only

Borders are 2 pts wide and light gray

Dark gray-shaded top line

Black Arial 12 point text in heading

Black Times New Roman 10 point text in body

Numbers have $ and two decimal places

## Creating an AutoFormat

**1**    Format a table the way you want it to appear.

**2**    Select the entire table. (In Calc, select at least three cells across and two down.)

**3**    Choose Table > AutoFormat. (In Calc, choose Format > Autoformat.)

**4** The AutoFormat window will appear. In that window, click Add.

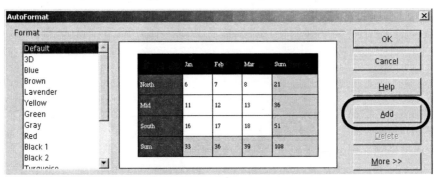

**5** In the Add AutoFormat window, type a name for the format. Click OK.

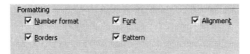

**6** Click More. Specify any additional options like number formatting.

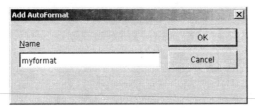

**7** You'll see a preview of the autoformat in the AutoFormat window.

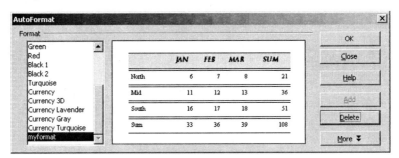

**8** Click OK.

## Applying an AutoFormat to a Table

Once you've created your AutoFormat, you're ready to apply it to other tables you want to format. (You can also, of course, apply any of the existing AutoFormats.) You can also apply an AutoFormat when you create a table in the first place; see *Creating a Table Using the Table Menu* on page 179.

**1** Open a document and select a table that you want to format.

**2**   Choose Tables > Autoformat. The AutoFormat window will appear.

**3**   In the Format list, scroll down and select the AutoFormat you want.

**4**   Click the More button at the right side.

**5**   Unmark or mark any options you want to change.

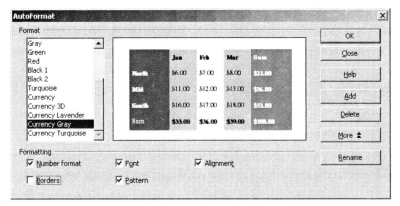

**6**   Click OK.

**7**   The table will reflect the AutoFormat.

| Author | Weekends | Weekdays |
|--------|----------|----------|
| Jones | $343.00 | $781.00 |
| Saur | $211.00 | $2,344.00 |
| Roberts | $799.00 | $1,209.00 |

# Converting Between Text and Tables

You can do more than create a table; you can convert it from text, or from a spreadsheet.

## Converting Text to a Table

The approach we've shown so far is to create the table structure, then put in the text. That's fine but what if you've already got some text, and you just want it in table format? Luckily, there's the text-to-table conversion feature.

**1** Select the text. The text needs to be separated with tabs or another separator so that Writer can tell where the columns will go.

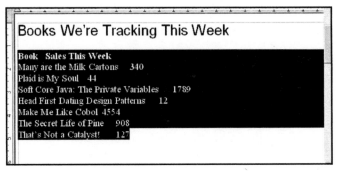

**2** Choose Table > Convert > Text to Table.

**3** The conversion window will appear.

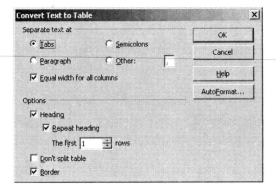

**4** Select the item that separates the columns, such as a tab, and set other options such as whether you want a heading row.

**5** Click OK.

**6** The text will be converted to a table.

| Books We're Tracking This Week | |
| --- | --- |
| Book | Sales This Week |
| Many are the Milk Cartons | 340 |
| Plaid is My Soul | 44 |
| Soft Core Java: The Private Variables | 1789 |
| Head First Dating Design Patterns | 12 |
| Make Me Like Cobol | 4554 |
| The Secret Life of Pine | 908 |
| That's Not a Catalyst! | 127 |

## Converting a Table to Text

This is just the opposite of the previous procedure. Let's say you've got a table full of data and you just want it in paragraphs instead.

**1**   Select the entire table.

**2**   Choose Format > Convert > Table to Text.

**3**   The conversion window will appear. Leave the values as is, or change the separator item.

**4**   Click OK.

## Converting a Table to a Spreadsheet

Copy the table, switch to a spreadsheet, click in one cell of the spreadsheet, and paste.

## Converting a Spreadsheet to a Table

This is simple, in a way. You need to paste the spreadsheet into a Writer document as formatted text, then just convert that text to a table.

**1**   Copy the portion of the spreadsheet that you want to turn into a table.

**2**   Move to a Writer document.

**3**   Choose Edit > Paste Special and select Formatted Text. Click OK.

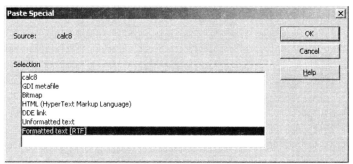

You can also click and hold down on the Paste icon and paste as Formatted Text.

**4**   The text will appear as a table, but without borders. Select all the text and the table toolbar will appear. Apply a border if you want one on the table. See *Adding or Removing Table Borders* on page 183.

# Automatic Number Formatting

When you've got a big table full of sales figures or prices, it's a pain to type all those currency symbols in by hand. Fortunately, OpenOffice.org will do it for you.

**1**   Open the document with the table containing numbers.

**2**   Select the numbers (not the heading) in the numbers column and right-click on that column. Choose Number Format.

**3**   In the Number Format window, in the Category list, select the number format you want such as Currency. Then in the Format list, select the variant that you want.

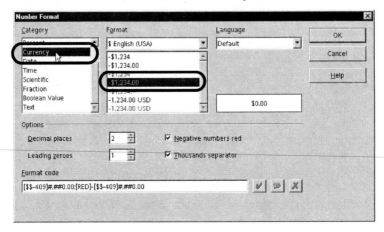

**4**   In the Options area, specify the number of decimal places, if you want to change the default settings, and how negatives are displayed.

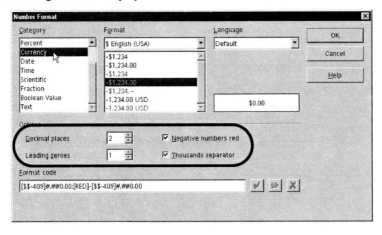

**5**   Click OK.

**6**   The table will reflect the changes.

# Sorting Data in a Table

This process works with plain text lists, as well; however you can only sort by the first word in the list.

**1**   Open the document and select the table, **without** the headings.

| Person | Task | Price |
|--------|------|-------|
| Elaine | Balloons | $20.00 |
| John | Cake | $25.00 |
| Elaine | Decorations | $15.00 |
| Anne | Gift | $30.00 |
| Anne | Invitations | $7.00 |
| John | Sandwiches | $65.00 |
| Anne | Entertainment | $80.00 |

**2**   Choose Tables > Sort. The Sort window will appear.

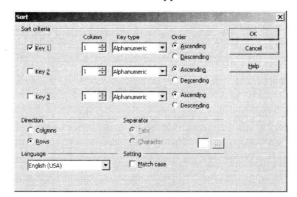

**3**   Be sure that in the Direction area, Rows is selected. You typically want to sort the rows of data, so that the *rows* are re-ordered, so this is correct.

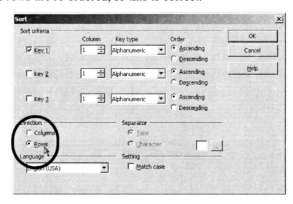

**4**   Be sure the Key 1 item is selected. Key 1 just means the first thing to sort by. Then in the
Column list, type the number of the column you want to sort by. In the example shown earlier,
if you wanted to sort by price, you would select Column 3.

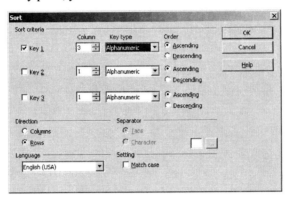

**5**   Then choose whether to sort by Alphanumeric or Numeric, and Ascending or Descending.
You must choose Numeric to sort numbers.

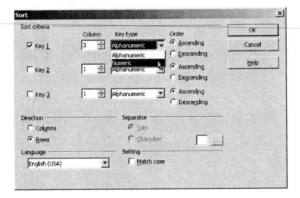

**6**   If you want to sort by another column now, select Key 2, and select the column and options for
that sort.

**7**   Click OK. The data will be sorted.

| Person | Task | Price |
|---|---|---|
| Anne | Entertainment | $80.00 |
| Anne | Gift | $30.00 |
| Anne | Invitations | $7.00 |
| Elaine | Balloons | $20.00 |
| Elaine | Decorations | $15.00 |
| John | Sandwiches | $65.00 |
| John | Cake | $25.00 |

If you have problems sorting numbers, select all the number cells, right-click, choose Number Format, and be sure that they're a number or currency format rather than Text. If your numbers are left-aligned in the table, they're not the right format. See *Automatic Number Formatting* on page 198 for more information

# Doing Calculations in Tables

In general, I recommend doing calculations in spreadsheets, then pasting them into your Writer document. However, you can also do some calculations in tables.

**1**   If you want to apply number formatting, see *Automatic Number Formatting* on page 198.

**2**   Click in the table, where you want the calculation result to appear.

| ¶ | Monthly·Utilities¶ | Monthly·Rent¶ | Total¶ |
|---|---|---|---|
| 2006¶ | $220.00 | $1,200.00 | |
| 2007¶ | $189.00 | $1,300.00 | |
| Total¶ | | | |

¶

**3**   Choose Table > Formula. The formula toolbar will appear.

**4**   Type the calculation. Use <> around the cell references. The first cell in the first row and column is A1, and so on.

| D2 | $f_{(x)}$ · ✖ ✔ | =(<B2> * 12) + (<C2> * 12) |
|---|---|---|

**5**   Click the check mark icon.

**6**   The calculation result will appear in the table cell.

| ¶ | Monthly·Utilities¶ | Monthly·Rent¶ | Total¶ |
|---|---|---|---|
| 2006¶ | $220.00 | $1,200.00 | $17,040.00 |
| 2007¶ | $189.00 | $1,300.00 | |
| Total¶ | | | |

¶

# Using Graphics in Documents

# Adding Graphics

Inserting graphics in Writer is pretty simple. You just have to know where the graphic file is located.

## Inserting a Graphic

1    Click where you want the graphic to appear.

2    Choose Insert > Picture > From File.

3    Select a graphic.

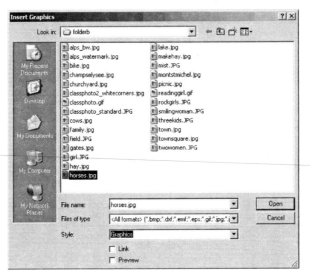

4    Click Open.

5    The graphic will appear in your document.

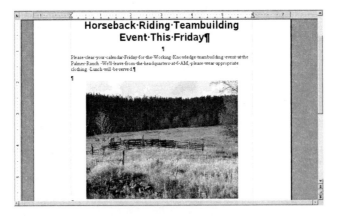

# Resizing a Graphic

The graphic will come into your document the size that it is (up to the width of your document). If you want to change its size, you have two options.

## Resizing by Dragging the Graphic Handle

1    Click on the graphic; handles will appear as shown.

2    Move your mouse over one of the corner handles until it looks similar to the illustration. This will vary by operating system and computer but it should like a two-ended arrow.

3    Hold down the Shift key; this will maintain the correct proportions.

4    Drag the handle toward the center of the graphic to reduce the size or out away from the center of the graphic to increase the size. A dotted line will indicate what size the graphic will be when you release the mouse.

5    Release the mouse and the Shift key.

## Resizing Using the Picture Window

**1** Click on the graphic; handles will appear as shown.

**2** Right-click on it and choose Picture.

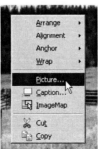

**3** Click the Type tab.

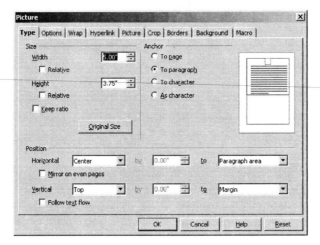

**4** Specify the size you want.

**5** Click OK.

# Positioning Graphics

Once you've got the graphic in, it's nice to be able to put the graphic where you want it.

## Moving a Graphic

Select the graphic, then move your mouse generally into the middle of the graphic. Your mouse should look like this. Then drag the graphic to where you want it.

## Aligning a Graphic

Pictures come into your document centered in the middle of the document by default. If you want it to end up at one side or the other, though, you can do that too.

Right-click on the graphic and choose Alignment > Left, Centered, or Right.

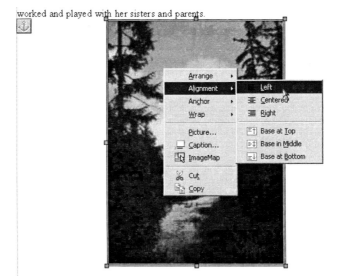

## Anchoring a Graphic to Paragraph

This is an important concept: where the picture is anchored. Anchoring refers to the text or part of the document that the graphic calls home. Does the myvacation.gif graphic just belong on that page, or does it belong·wherever the word "vacation" is positioned?

It matters because it affects where the picture is positioned. When you add or remove content from the document, this shifts where pictures and text are positioned. If you want your picture to always be next to the paragraph about your vacation, for instance, you want to be sure that the picture stays with the paragraph. That means you anchor the picture *to paragraph* and then specify *which paragraph*. If you always want your picture to be on the first page your document, regardless of what text is on the page, then *anchor to page*, and position the graphic on the *correct page*.

If this sounds a little complicated, don't worry—generally, you want the graphic to be anchored to the paragraph. It's usually done that way by default but it's good to know how to control the anchoring yourself.

**1**   Click on your graphic.

**2**   You'll see an Anchor icon. If you want the picture to stay with a particular paragraph, then just drag that anchor icon to the top of the paragraph the picture goes with.

In this illustration, for example, you might want to drag the anchor icon down to the top of the second paragraph.

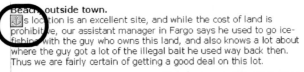

Beach outside town.
s location is an excellent site, and while the cost of land is prohibitive, our assistant manager in Fargo says he used to go ice-fishing with the guy who owns this land, and also knows a lot about where the guy got a lot of the illegal bait he used way back then. Thus we are fairly certain of getting a good deal on this lot.

One advantage of the beach site is that it is near an old airport recently slated for renovation. We believe that direct flights can make our bookstore a destination site for family trips and weddings. Additionally, the direct flights allow us to do advertising not only in inflight magazines for a reduced rate but at all hotels on the island.

**3**   Right-click on the picture and choose Anchor. **Page**, **Paragraph**, **To Character**, and **As Character** are your options You want Paragraph most of the time.

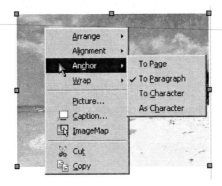

**4**   Here's when you'd want any of the other options.

♦   To Page: Use this if you want the picture to stay in a particular spot on the page, no matter what happens to the text.

♦   To Character: Use this if you have a particular character or word, not just a paragraph, that you want the picture to stay with.

♦   As Character: Use this if the graphic is small and you want to use it just like a word or character in a paragraph.

When you go visit, look for the little donut signs.  This is an indicator that you can get a cold drink and a pastry of some sort. You'll need it.

# Wrapping Text Around Graphics

Sometimes you'll want to make text appear to the left or right, or both, of the graphic you've inserted, rather than just above or below. It just looks better that way for many documents.

**1**   Click on the graphic.

**2**   Right-click on the graphic and choose Wrap > Page Wrap.

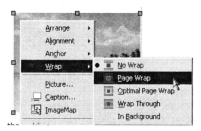

**3**   The graphic will wrap with the text.

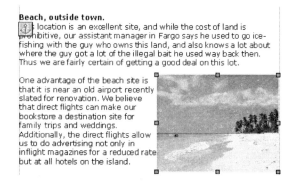

## Controlling Spacing Around Graphics

**1**   When you wrap text around a graphic it's often too close. To adjust the spacing, right click on the graphic and choose Picture.

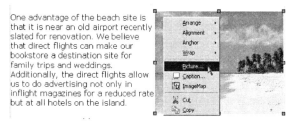

**2**   In the Picture window, click the Wrap tab.

**3**  In the Spacing fields, specify the amount of space around the text.

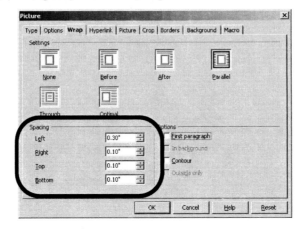

**4**  Click OK.

# Adding a Border

**1**  Select the picture in your document.

**2**  Right-click on it and choose Picture.

**3**  In the Picture window, click the Border tab.

**4**  Click on the indicated icon to put a border on all four sides.

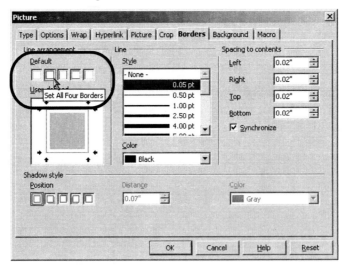

**5**   Select the type of line you want for the border, and select the color for the border.

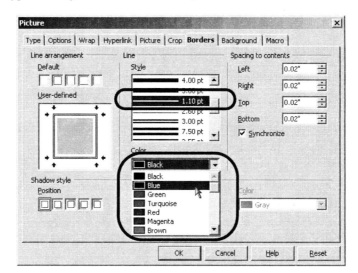

**6**   Click OK. The graphic will have the border you specified.

# Creating a Watermark

If you want a watermark graphic in back of your document, you can do it with a background graphics. See *Giving a Document a Background Graphic* on page 112. However, unless you're using page styles, the graphic will appear on every page of your document. A more straightforward way is to follow these steps.

**1**   Open your text document and go to where you want the watermark.

**2**   Choose Insert > Picture > From File and bring in the graphic you want.

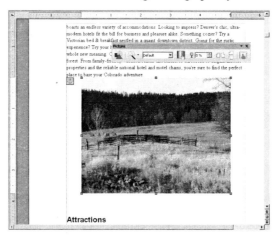

**3**   The next step depends on what the graphic looks like. If you're ready to put the graphic in the background, skip to step 7. If the graphic is too dark or colorful to be suitable, select the graphic. The Picture toolbar will appear. (If it doesn't, choose View > Toolbars > Picture.)

**4**   Select the Watermark effect.

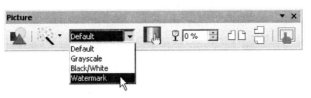

**5**   The effect will be applied. If it's what you want, leave the graphic as is; if the effect is too light, select Default from the same list or press Ctrl Z to go back to the original look.

**6**   You can lighten the graphic another way by clicking on the Color icon, increasing brightness, and decreasing contrast.

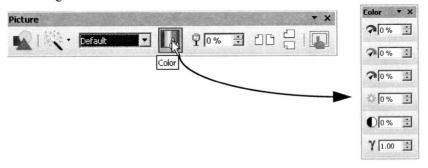

This is what +40 lightness and -30 contrast looks like for the example graphic.

**7**    Once the graphic is the way you want it, right-click on it and choose Wrap > In Background.

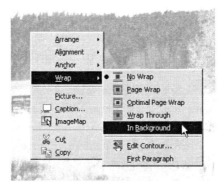

**8**    The graphic will appear in the background. Drag it as necessary to reposition it.

### Attractions

Colorado's attractions are as diverse as its landscape. Amusement parks, zoos and sightseeing trains guarantee fun for the younger set, while the state's homegrown wineries and breweries present tempting adult diversions. Ghost towns, archaeological sites and monuments offer the promise of discovery to history and heritage buffs while modern art museums and a lively theater scene satisfy the arts and culture clique. Relaxing hot springs and dramatic canyons and waterfalls beckon the outdoor enthusiast with adventures both mild and wild, while Colorado's exciting casinos offer action of an entirely different variety. Opt for a taste of it all with an organized sightseeing tour or pick and choose to create your own Colorado experience.

### Outdoors and Nature

From rugged, snow-crested peaks to dramatic canyons, towering sand dunes to endless expanses of rolling prairies, Colorado's picturesque landscapes are more than just breathtaking. Thousands of miles of trails are your passageway to pristine forests, glaciated valleys and roaring rivers. Climb toward the heavens on a Fourteener, drift over the landscape in a hot air balloon or cast your fly in a pristine mountain stream. Whether you're a veteran backcountry camper, an avid mountain biker or just a weekend warrior

# Editing Inserted Graphics

You can change lightness and contrast, RGB values, and other aspects of graphics with the Picture menu. For more information, see *Editing Graphics* on page 430.

# Making Your Own Graphics in OpenOffice.org Draw

If you choose File > New > Drawing, you'll have a wonderful set of tools for creating graphics. When you complete the drawing, you can create a graphic file like the ones inserted in these exercises, and insert it in a Writer document if you want. This is the best way to put a design that's at least a little complicated into your Writer document.

Making the design and exporting it to a JPG or other file that you can insert in a document, is covered in later in this book in *Exporting a Drawing to a JPG or Other Graphic Format* on page 556.

# Using the Drawing Tools

The drawing tools like rectangle, circle, and 3D are available throughout OpenOffice.org. I've covered them in the Impress/Draw section, in *Using Text, Objects, and 3D* on page 403.

# Frames

Frames are just what it seems like they are. A border within which you can put text, graphics, and columns, and that text flows around.

**On the Road**

In Colorado, the road is so much more than a way to get from point A to point B. Our highways, country roads and backcountry byways offer a chance to experience the grandeur of the Centennial State without ever leaving your car. Not that you need a car. Touring by motorcycle or even by bicycle presents the same opportunity for sightseeing. Whatever your mode of transportation, the scenery is guaranteed to inspire. Climb winding mountain passes, skirting raging rivers and deep canyons. Pass lush green meadows dotted with spring wildflowers or bask in the Aspens' gold glow in the fall. Take a break for a short hike or a picnic lunch next to a cascading waterfall. In Colorado, the journey really is half the fun.

> The best way around Colorado is on a bike! Visit Fred's Bikes to get your rental today!

## Making and Formatting Frames

To insert a frame, just choose Insert > Frame and enter information in the window that appears and click OK. It's fine to not fill in any information, and adjust the frame once it appears.

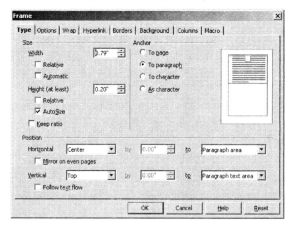

Click on a frame and you get the same Frames toolbar I mentioned. Double-click the frame and you get the big Frame configuration window above. You can wrap, border, and arrange frames the same way you do graphics.

**Typing in frames**  Clicking in frames is a little tricky. If you're trying to click in the frame to type or insert a graphic and it won't work, just click outside in some normal text, then click inside the frame again.

Frames have many uses. Here's an overview of a few.

## Using a Frame to Group Items

If you have text and graphics that you want to keep together, or any other graphical elements that need to stay together, use a frame to keep them together. Without a frame, it's possible that, depending on anchoring, your graphical elements might go shooting off to different parts of the document

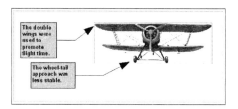

Insert the frame, then either create the graphical items in the frame, or cut and paste them into the frame.

## Offsetting Text From the Main Flow

The text inside a frame is separate so that other text flows around it You can use columns, shading, and other formatting inside the frame.

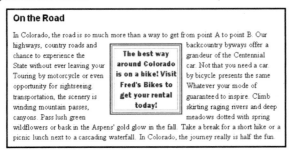

Just insert the frame, then click in the frame and type the text you want.

## Making Nonconsecutive Text Flow Together

This is especially nice for brochures, magazines, etc.

**1**   Insert two empty frames somewhere in the document.

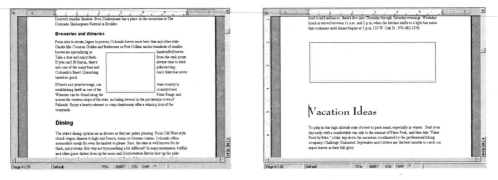

**2**   Click on the first frame, then click on the Link Frames icon on the Frame toolbar.

**3**    Move your mouse over the second frame; your mouse will look like this. Click on the second one.

**4**    A line appears linking the two frames.

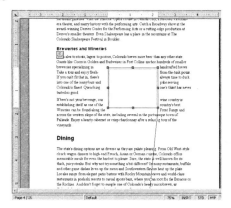

**5**    Now when you type in the first frame, the text will flow to the next frame.

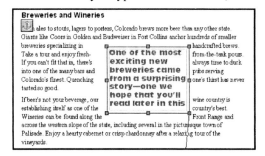

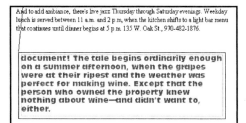

**6**    Move, or cut and paste, the frames anywhere you want. You can link many frames together; just be sure they're all *completely empty* when you link.

# Reference: Formatting and Managing Graphics and Frames

Here's a reference guide to the options you have for managing frames and graphics. See the online help for more information on each.

## Using The Frame Toolbar

When you click on a picture, the Frame toolbar appears. (If it doesn't, choose View > Toolbars > Frame.) You can use the Frame toolbar icons to align the graphic differently and apply other features like alignment and borders.

## Frame and Picture Formatting Windows

When you right-click, you get the Frame or Picture options.

When you choose each, you get a window with a huge number of formatting options. You've already seen some of them. I encourage you to spend a little time fiddling with these windows and all the tabs so you know what your options are.

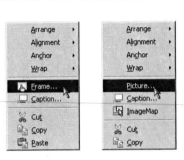

## Frame Formatting Window

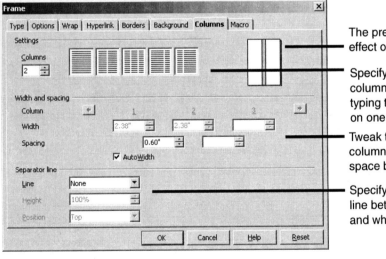

The preview area shows the effect of your current choices.

Specify the number of columns in the frame here, by typing the number or clicking on one of the preset options.

Tweak the width of each column here, and specify the space between columns.

Specify whether you want a line between the columns, and what it should look like.

## Picture Formatting Window

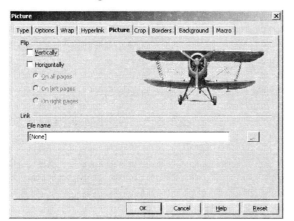

Use this window to flip a graphic.

# Captions

It's always nice to have captions for your pictures, if you want to clearly identify them. You can have captions for pictures, tables, and even just chunks of text. The captions are numbered automatically so you don't have to, and if you have pictures and table captions, for instance, the table captions are numbered independently of the picture captions.

You can add them one by one, manually, or set them up to be added automatically.

## Manually Adding Captions

Here's how to add them one by one.

**1**    Click on the graphic. (For tables, click in the top row.)

**2**    Choose Insert > Caption.

**3**    The Caption window will appear. Select the type of item the caption is for, such as Illustration. This word will appear in the caption; if you don't want anything, select None.

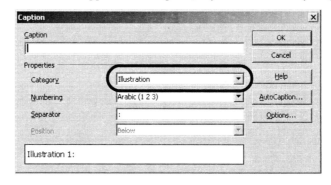

**4**     Type the caption.

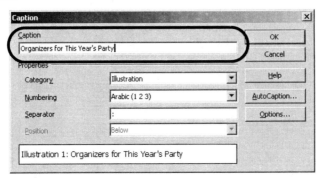

**5**     Select the type of numbering from the Numbering list: Arabic, Roman, etc.

**6**     If you want a different separator than a colon after the word "Illustration" or "Table," change that in the Separator field. If you understand character styles, you can specify a character style for the number and prefix. See *Creating a New Style* on page 152.

**7**     For tables, you can specify where you want the caption, above or below.

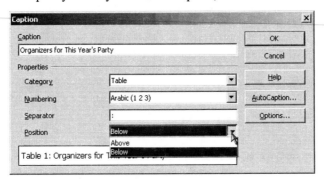

**8**     Click OK; the caption will appear. The caption for pictures is text, grouped with the picture in a frame. The frame is added when you apply the caption. Click in the caption text to format it.

# Automatically Adding Captions

Anytime you add a table, picture, or any other type of object that you apply autocaptioning to, an automatic caption just appears. The identifying text itself doesn't appear, but the prefix, the "Table 1" part of it and, for pictures, the frame around the caption and prefix. You add the text of the caption once the structure of the caption automatically appears.

**1**    Choose Tools > Options > OpenOffice.org Writer > AutoCaption, or from the Captions window in the previous procedure, click the AutoCaption button.

**2**    For each caption type, specify the options you want. Unless you're doing chapter numbering you don't need to worry about the level numbering options.

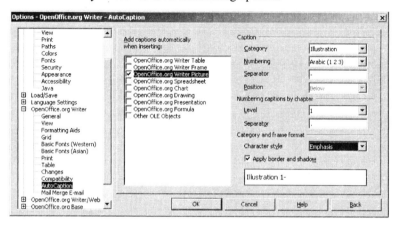

**3**    Click OK.

When you insert an item, the caption appears. Click to the right of the separator to add the caption text.

# Printing in Writer

# Printing in Writer

This section covers the printing options within OpenOffice.org, print preview, and other features common among all platforms.

## Printing the Whole Document to the Default Printer

If you always print to the same printer, and you just want a single copy of the whole document you're working with, printing is incredibly easy.

Click the Print icon at the top of the window; the document will be printed.

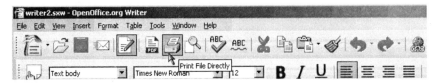

## Printing to a Specific Printer

1   Choose File > Print; you'll see the Print window. Select the printer that you want from the Name dropdown list at the top. This will depend on what printers your computer is set up with.

2   Choose other options such as whether to print the whole document, a page range, or just the selection; and how many copies to print and whether to collate.

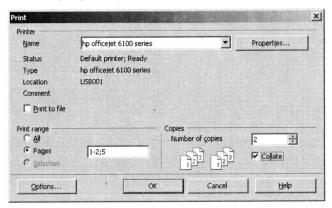

**3**    Click the Options button; you'll see additional options such as the ability to just print black (text is printed in black). Click OK to save options and close the window. You can also set these options under Tools > Options > OpenOffice.org Writer > Print.

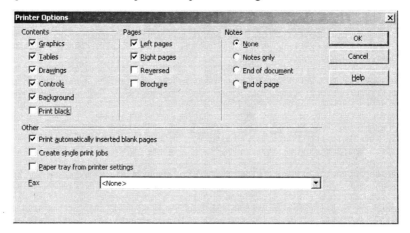

**4**    Click OK.

# Additional Printing Tips

If you want more than the basics of printing, here are some additional options.

## Printing Specific Pages in a Document

**1**    Choose File > Print. In the print window, look for the Print Range fields.

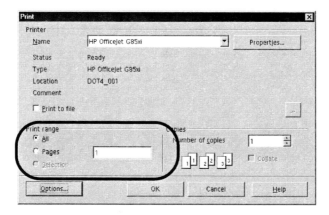

**2**    Select the Pages option. Type a dash between consecutive pages and a **semicolon** between nonconsecutive pages. For instance, to print page 1, and pages 4-7, you would type:

1;4-7.

**3**    Click OK.

# Using Page Preview

It's convenient to use Page Preview to ensure a document is going to look like you want it to.

**1**    Choose File > Page Preview.

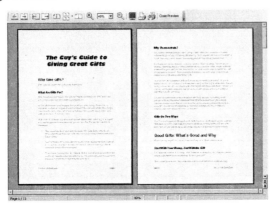

**2**    Click the Next Page icon to see each page.

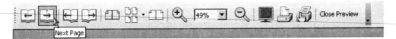

**3**    Click and hold down on the Page Preview: Multiple Pages icon and choose to show several pages at once, as shown.

**4**    The document will look like this.

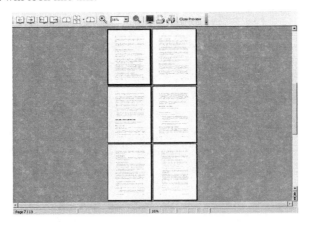

**5** Click Close Preview to exit the Preview view.

# Printing Several Pages on One Sheet of Paper

You don't always need to print full size. When you want to restrict the number of pages to print on, follow these steps.

**1** Choose File > Page Preview.

**2** You can quickly specify the number of pages per sheet by clicking and holding down on the Page Preview: Multiple Pages icon, and choosing the layout across and down.

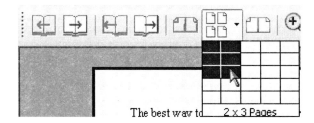

The preview will change to reflect your changes.

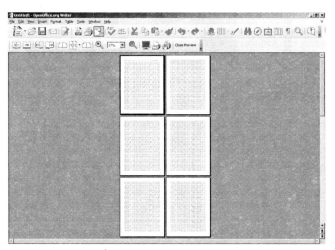

**3** If you want to specify additional options, or if you just prefer this way instead, click the Print Options Page View icon.

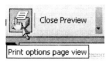

You'll see this window. Specify orientation, spacing, and margins. The margins are magnified in this view, so enter very small margins like .20 inches.

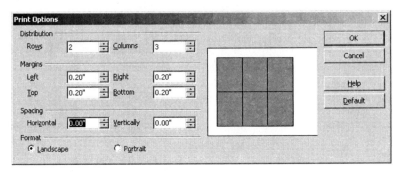

**4**   Click OK.

**5**   To print these settings, click the Print Page View icon.

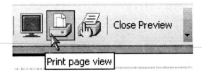

# Previewing Right-Left Pages for a Book

When you're printing a book, you need to see how the pages will look printed, and the first page always starts on the right. You can use the Book Preview icon in the preview.

**1**   Set up pages using the **Mirrored** setting under Format > Page, Page tab. Choose Format > Page, click the Page tab, and select the Mirrored layout as shown. Click OK.

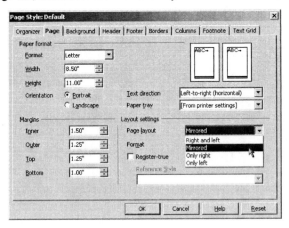

**2**   Choose File > Page Preview.

**3**   Click the Book Preview icon.

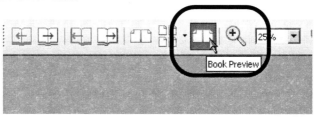

**4**   Click the Close Preview icon.

# Emailing Your Document in One Step

This is related to printing, though of course not quite the same thing. You can email your document to someone else in one step.

## Sending Your Document

Choose File > Send > and then pick the option you want. In Calc the options will include sending as Excel; in Impress the options will include sending as PowerPoint.

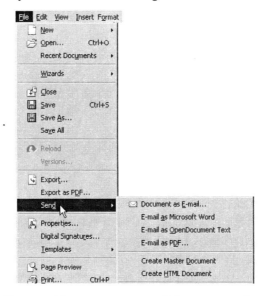

Your email program will start, with a new empty email document, and a copy of your current document, in the format you selected, will be attached.

## Setting the Default Email Program

Use your operating system tools to set the default email program. This will vary by your operating system but here are two examples.

In Windows XP, go to the Control Panel, choose Internet Properties, and set the default email program.

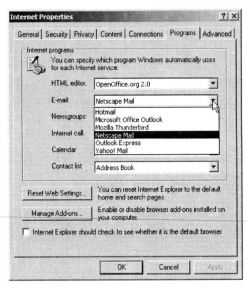

In Ubuntu Linux, choose System > Preferences > Preferred Applications.

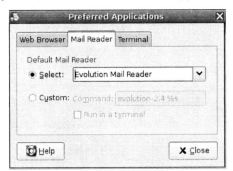

# Printing to PDF

Printing to PDF, Adobe's portable document format, is one of the very nice additions in OpenOffice.org. PDF "freezes" your document so that no one can change it, and everyone can read the PDF format using the Adobe Reader program on virtually every computer in the world. For more information and procedures, see *PDF, Publishing, and the Web* on page 51.

# 14

# Simple Envelopes and Labels

# How Envelopes and Labels Work

Envelopes and labels are pretty similar. You have to specify two things:

+ The text that you want: just type it in the big text boxes in the setup windows
+ The size of the label or envelope document: envelope size 10, label 8160, etc.

This is really just like creating normal documents, except that with normal documents you don't think as much about the size of the document because it's always just the default, letter size or A4.

There are other optional features like formatting, you might need to fiddle with your printer setup and give it some more information about in what position envelopes are inserted, and there's a very cool feature for automatically updating labels. But this is all you *have* to do.

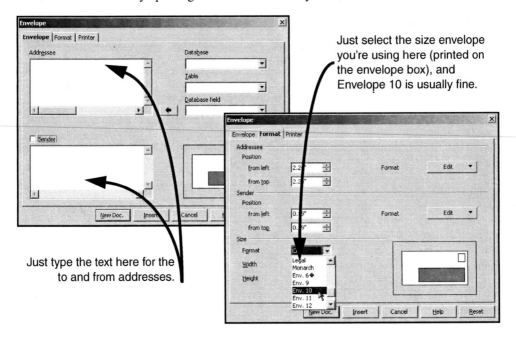

Just select the size envelope you're using here (printed on the envelope box), and Envelope 10 is usually fine.

Just type the text here for the to and from addresses.

**Two required features for envelopes**

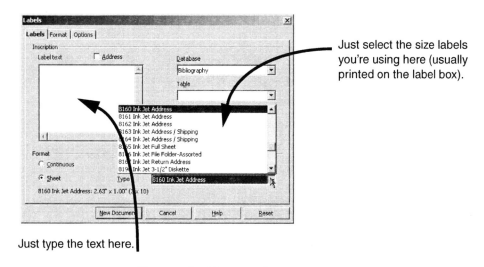

Just select the size labels you're using here (usually printed on the label box).

Just type the text here.

**Two required features for envelopes**

### If You Can, Just Use the Same Envelope or Label Document Over and Over

It's usually simplest with envelopes especially, just to create it right once, make it a template, then just change the content each time. See *Creating a New Template* on page 41 and *Creating a Document Based on a Template* on page 42.

### The First Envelope is the Hardest

Envelopes aren't standard paper and can be inserted lengthwise or crosswise. That means you might have to do some setup the first time. However, once that's done, it's done. See *Printer Setup for Envelopes* on page 236.

### This Chapter Doesn't Cover Mail Merge Envelopes and Labels

That's an advanced topic—not extraordinarily difficult, just one that involves additional steps. See *Creating Mail Merge Databases and Documents* on page 619.

# Envelopes

The steps for creating the envelope are simple. If it doesn't work perfectly the first time, then refine your document and printer setup following the instructions in *Printer Setup for Envelopes* on page 236. And of course, once you get an envelope you like, it's a good idea to just make a template out of it. See *Creating a New Template* on page 41 and *Creating a Document Based on a Template* on page 42.

## Creating an Envelope Document

This is how to create the document. There's the standard way, first, and then the roll-your-own way which just might work better, depending on your printer and your inclination toward do-it-yourself projects.

## Using the Envelope Creation Window

1   In a Writer document, choose Insert > Envelope.

2   In the window that appears, click the Envelope tab if it isn't already showing.

3   Type the name and address for where the envelope is going, and the return address, in the appropriate fields.

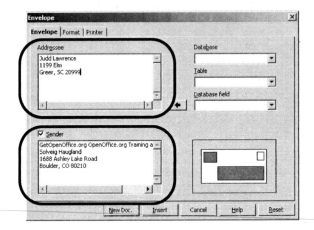

4   Click the Format tab.

5   At the bottom of the window, select Envelope 10, or the size you're using.

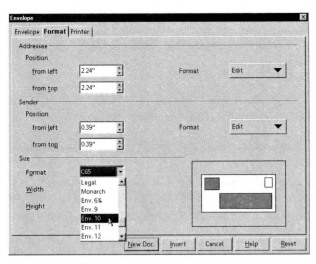

6   Click the Printer tab. At the top, you have the option of specifying how the envelope will be inserted. Make a note of what the current setting is and insert the envelope this way when you print.

Or if you know that your printer needs envelopes to be inserted a different way, change it here by selecting the appropriate icon.

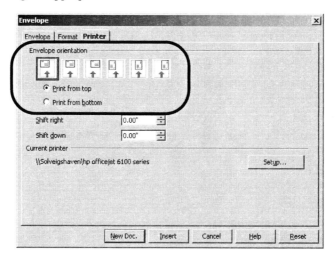

**7**    Click New Doc.

**8**    The envelope will appear.

**9**    The text is in frames. (See *Frames* on page 214.) Click inside each frame to format the text. If you have trouble clicking inside the frame. click somewhere else in the envelope document, then click in the frame again.

**10**    Print the envelope, feeding envelopes in manually.

## A Simple Do-It-Yourself Approach to Creating Envelopes

It's so simple. Just create a document and make it an envelope-sized document.

**1**    Create a new text document.

**2**    Choose Format > Page, click the Page tab, and in the Layout list select an envelope size like Envelope 10.

**3**    In the same window, specify Landscape.

**4**    Click OK.

**5**    Type your text in the document. Use tabs or just indent the paragraph to position the text where you want it. Change the margins as necessary. The illustration shows tabs, but you can indent the text, as well.

```
Solveig·Danesdweller¶
401·Behn¶
Boulder,·CO·80026¶
¶
¶
¶
¶
¶
¶
        →    →    →    →    →    →    →    →   Judd·Lawrence¶
        →    →    →    →    →    →    →    →   4201·Pearl¶
        →    →    →    →    →    →    →    →   Denver,·CO·80066¶
```

**6**    Print it on plain paper to see where it prints for your printer.

**7**    Print it on an envelope.

# Printer Setup for Envelopes

You need to change the printing preferences for the printer where you'll print envelopes. On many versions of Windows, to do this you choose Start > Settings > Control Panel and double-click the Printers and Faxes icon. Double-click the icon and find the printer where you'll print the envelope. Right-click the icon and choose Printing Preferences.

For paper preferences, set up the printer for Envelope 10, or whatever envelope you specified in the envelope document. If your printer provides information on how the envelopes are inserted, make a note of those so you can insert the envelope correctly.

Test it by printing your envelope document on a piece of regular paper to see where your printer prints envelopes. Then insert an envelope the same way and print your envelope.

## Creating a Special Printer Instance Just for Envelopes

If your computer allows you to create multiple instances of your printer, here's a tip. Create one just for regular printing, and set up the other to always be ready and waiting for envelopes. Then just print normal documents to your HP OfficeJet and your envelopes to HP OfficeJet Envelopes.

# Labels

Labels are easier than envelopes because labels are normal Letter or A4 sized pieces of paper. However, you have different options because there are many places on that sheet of labels to print. I'm covering this by giving you two different procedures.

Creating a sheet of labels where you want to print on every label, and you want to print the same thing on every label. This is *Creating a Sheet of Labels For One Address* on page 237.

Creating a document so that you can just print one or a few labels at a time. You want to just manually type the text in the label document, in the spots where you still have labels to use up on the actual label sheet. This is *Creating a Reusable Document to Print a Few Labels at a Time* on page 240.

## Creating a Sheet of Labels For One Address

**1** Choose File > New > Labels. Click the Labels tab if it isn't already showing.

**2** Type or paste the address that you want on the labels in the Label Text area.

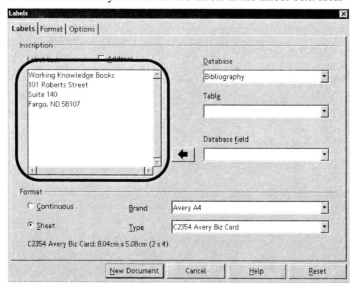

**3**   In the Brand dropdown list, select Avery Letter Size (or Avery A4).

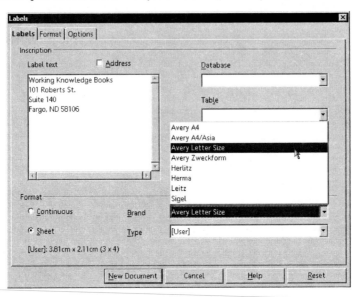

**4**   In the Type dropdown list, scroll through the labels. Select the label type you want from the box of labels you're using, such as 8160 Inkjet Address.

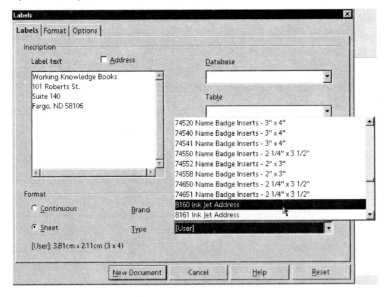

**5**   Click the Options tab.

**6**   Select the Synchronize Contents option. This will enable a feature that will be very convenient after you create the labels.

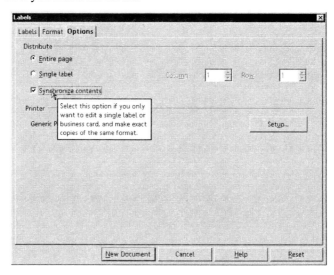

**7**   Click New Document.

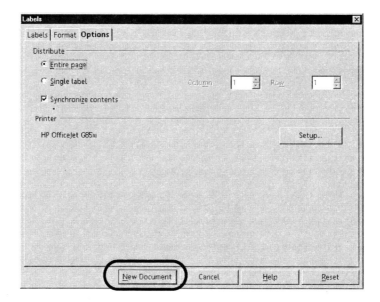

**8**    The labels will appear, with a floating Synchronize Labels button. The button is your friend, as you will see in a moment.

**9**    Let's say your boss comes by and yells at you for not making the address labels bold and italic. Sigh heavily.

**10**   Select the label in the upper left corner. Reformat the text as you like it.

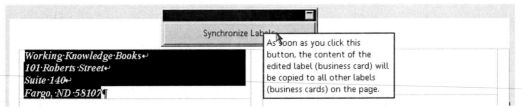

**11**   Click the Synchronize button.

**12**   All the labels will have the changes you made in the first label.

---

**Note –** If you're creating very small labels on which you'll need a small font, you're not going to be able to select all three lines of text. The bottom line might completely run off the bottom of the label. To fix this, select the first two lines of the label content and make it a small font, six points or so. Then you'll be able to select all the content, and apply the correct formatting.

---

## Creating a Reusable Document to Print a Few Labels at a Time

You'll reuse this document. Complete the steps in the previous procedure, but:

◆   Don't mark the Synchronize option

◆   Don't enter any content

◆   When you create the document, then just type the content you need in the labels corresponding to the labels that you have left on the label sheet.

To make it into a template, see *Creating a New Template* on page 41 and *Creating a Document Based on a Template* on page 42.

# 15

# Tables of Contents

# How Tables of Contents Work

A table of contents in Writer is an *automatically generated* list of the headings in your document. (The gray shading indicates it's a generated list, and doesn't print.)

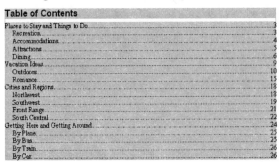

How does Writer know which headings to use? How does it know to use headings in the first place, anyway? It knows because of styles. Styles are used, as you saw in *Saving Enormous Time and Effort With Styles* on page 147, for formatting. But they're also used to describe or classify text, as in this case. Styles are why you don't have to go through manually and specify every individual heading you want in your table of contents. You just say "put all the text that I've formatted with the Heading1 and Heading2 paragraph styles into my table of contents."

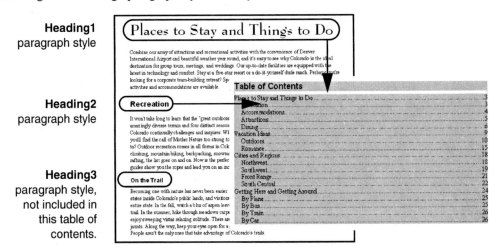

Of course, this means you need to apply styles in order to use tables of contents. But styles are so useful, you're using them anyway.

Writer uses the Heading1 through Heading10 styles by default for tables of contents. If you just use the Heading1 paragraph style for the top level, and so on, you won't ever have to specify your headings; just how many of the headings you want in the TOC.

**Note –** This is one reason why it's best to just modify the heading paragraph styles, rather than create new ones. You get all this automatic formatting still applied.

# Table of Contents Basics

Here's how to simply create the table of contents and other basics.

## Creating a Simple Table of Contents (TOC)

**1**　Be sure you've applied paragraph styles to the headings you want in the TOC. It's simplest to use the paragraph styles Heading1, Heading2, and so on.

**2**　Scroll to where you want the table of contents to begin.

**3**　Choose Insert > Indexes and Tables > Indexes and Tables.

**4**　In the Indexes and Tables window, be sure that Table of Contents is selected.

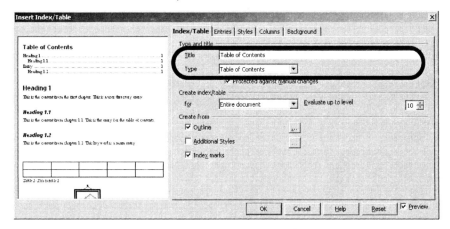

**5**　Specify how many levels of headings you want in the TOC; usually 2 or 3.

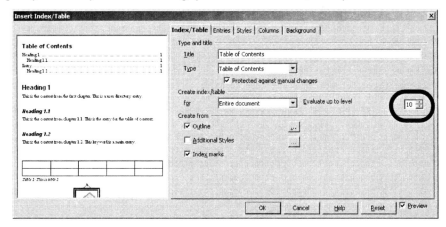

**6**　Be aware of which styles you want in the TOC.

◆　If you have used the paragraph styles Heading1 through Heading10 for your headings, you don't need to specify styles to use in the TOC.

♦    If you used different styles for your headings, set them up according to *Controlling What Is Listed in a TOC* on page 245.

**7**    Click OK.

**8**    The TOC will appear.

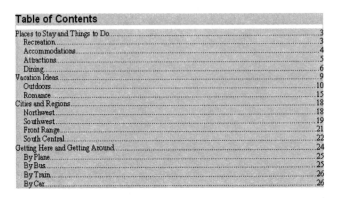

# Deleting, Editing, or Updating a TOC

Most of the TOCs you'll create will be protected from direct editing—you can't just type over them. This makes sense since you get the best TOC by automatically generating it based on what's in the document.

However, you still need to delete the TOC sometimes, or go back and change how it's set up, and of course update it when you change the headings.

## Deleting a TOC

**1**    Open the document containing the TOC.

**2**    Select a small part of the TOC.

**3**    Right-click in the selected portion and choose Delete Index/Table.

## Editing a TOC

Let's say you want to put different styles in the TOC, change the number of levels, or make other changes to how the TOC is set up. Here's how to get back to the TOC setup window.

**1**    Open the document containing the TOC.

**2**    Select a small part of the TOC.

**3**    Right-click in the selected portion and choose Edit Index/Table.

**4** The TOC setup window will appear; make your changes.

**5** Click OK.

### Updating a TOC

You must complete these steps when you've changed content in the document, to update the TOC to reflect those changes.

**1** Open the document containing the TOC.

**2** Select a small part of the TOC.

**3** Right-click in the selected portion and choose Update Index/Table.

**4** You'll see the TOC change to reflect the changes.

# Working With Advanced Table of Contents Features

One of the coolest features in Writer is the ability to make the TOC hyperlinked, so readers can click on a line and go to that heading. The links carry over to PDF when you export the document to PDF, as well. (Just be sure that you keep the Tagged PDF option marked when you choose File > Export as PDF. See *Making a PDF With More Control* on page 53.)

## Controlling What Is Listed in a TOC

You can make a good TOC just using the Heading styles. However, you can use other styles. For instance, if you forgot to use Heading styles and used your own styles, you could specify that you want to use Level styles only. Or you could specify that the first level is Heading 1 style, and the second level is your Topic2 style.

There are two ways to do it.

### Changing the Document Heading Structure in Outline Numbering

**1** Choose Tools > Outline Numbering.

**2** Select level 1.

**3** Specify the paragraph style you use for the top level in your document: ChapterTitle, TopLevel, HeadingMain, etc.

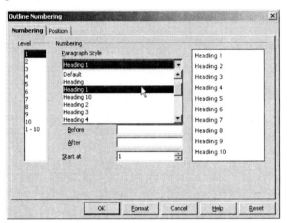

**4** Do the same for each additional level. You can skip the numbering options.

**5** Click OK.

**6** When you generate the table of contents, be sure that the Outline option is marked.

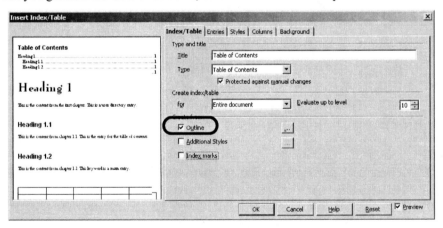

## Changing the Styles to Include in the TOC

**1** Open the document where you want to put the TOC.

**2** Click where you want the TOC and choose Insert > Indexes and Tables > Indexes and Tables.

**3** In the Create From area, select Additional Styles. Then deselect Outline and deselect Indexes.

**4**   Click the browse icon next to Additional Styles.

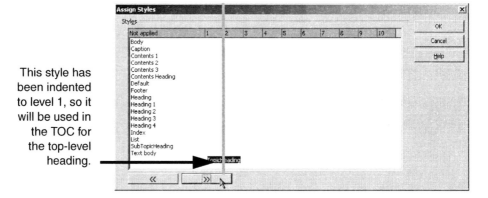

**5**   In the Assign Styles window, scroll to the top-level paragraph style you're using for headings. Click the right-facing arrow to move it to the first space.

This style has been indented to level 1, so it will be used in the TOC for the top-level heading. ➡

**6**   Repeat these steps for each additional heading you might want in the TOC, to specify the styles used for level 2, level 3, etc.

**7**   Click OK.

**8**   Click OK in the TOC setup window. The TOC will appear in the document.

# Controlling How the TOC Looks

Now that you've got the right elements in the TOC, here's how to format them.

### Specifying the Character Style to Format Each TOC Level

**1**   Open the document.

**2**   Choose Insert > Indexes and Tables > Indexes and Tables.

**3**    In the TOC window, click the Entries tab.

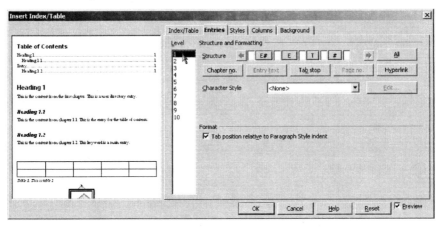

**4**    In the Level list, select the level you want to apply formatting options to.

**5**    Move your mouse over each item in the Structure field. You can select each one and options will appear below it, such as Character Style as shown. With the tabs, you can select the character for dot leaders.

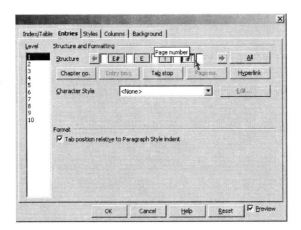

**6**    If you want to apply the options to all TOC levels, click All to apply settings to all TOC levels.

## Dot Leaders and Tables of Contents

To change the dot leaders for any level of the TOC, you need to either modify the currently applied style, or create a new style and apply it. See *Specifying the Formatting for Each TOC Level* on page 248 The dot leaders are set in the Tabs part of the paragraph formatting window; see *Setting and Formatting Tabs* on page 89 and *Paragraph Formatting Window: Tabs Tab* on page 84.

## Specifying the Formatting for Each TOC Level

If you want to apply different formatting to all the content in one or more heading levels, you can specify a style to use for each level.

### Modifying Styles

The simplest approach is actually to simply modify the currently applied style. Contents1 and subsequently numbered styles are applied to the top level, etc. Choose Format > Styles and Formatting, find the style, right-click and choose Modify, and change the formatting of the style. That's all you need to do.

### Creating and Applying Different Styles

You can also just create a new style and apply that style, instead of the currently applied style, to the appropriate level in the TOC. If you're going to do that, follow these steps.

**1**   Open the document.

**2**   Choose Insert > Indexes and Tables > Indexes and Tables.

**3**   In the TOC window, click the Styles tab of the Insert Index/Table window.

**4**   Select the level in the Levels list, and in the Paragraph Styles list, select the paragraph style to apply. Then click the arrow between the lists to assign the **Top Level TOC Heading Style** style to Level 1.

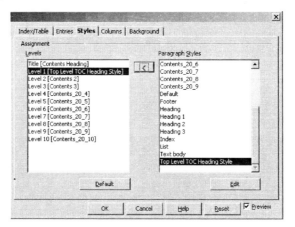

**5**   Repeat for each level that you're using in the TOC.

**6**   Click OK.

**7**   Click OK to insert the formatted TOC.

# Creating a Hyperlinked TOC

When you distribute a copy of a document with a TOC in it, your readers might like to be able to click on one of the items in the TOC and go straight to that part of the document. It's also just a nice navigational device for you.

Also note that you can export the document to PDF and links will come with. See *Making a PDF the Quickest Way* on page 53.

**1**   Open the document.

**2**   Select part of the TOC, right-click, and choose Edit Index/Table; or to create a new one choose Insert > Indexes and Tables > Indexes and Tables.

**3**   Click the Entries tab.

**4**    Let's say that you want to make every entry in the TOC hyperlinked so that clicking on it takes you to the corresponding heading in the document. You're going to put the hyperlink just around the heading part, not the page number.

To do this, click to the left of the **E** entry, which corresponds to the heading text.

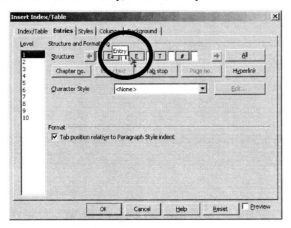

**5**    Click Hyperlink. An **LS** entry will be added at the beginning of the link.

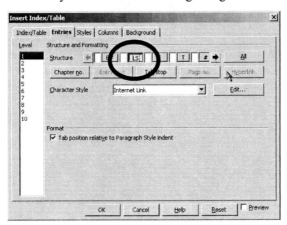

**6** Click immediately after the same **E** entry.

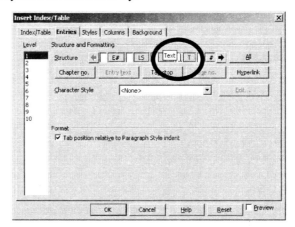

**7** Click Hyperlink again. An **LE** entry will be added where the cursor was.

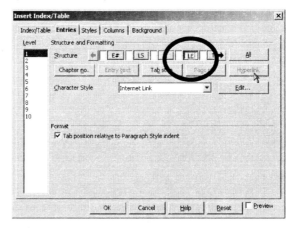

**8** To make all entries at all levels hyperlinked, click the All button.

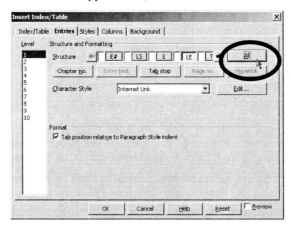

**9**    Click OK to insert the TOC. It will look something like this.

# Part III: Calc Spreadsheets

# Calc Basics

# Creating, Opening, and Saving Files

Using the core features of Calc is a lot like Excel, and pretty straightforward.

## Creating a New File

1   Open a new spreadsheet document by starting the program and choosing OpenOffice.org > Spreadsheet, or just choose File > New > Spreadsheet if the program is already running.

2   The new spreadsheet will appear.

---

**Note –** Within OpenOffice.org. you can choose File > New to create any kind of new document: Calc; Draw or Writer or the other options. Choose File > New > Spreadsheet; a new spreadsheet will appear; choose File > New > Text Document and a Writer doc will appear.

---

## Saving a Spreadsheet

1   Choose File > Save or click the Save icon on the main toolbar.

2   Navigate to the location where you want to save it, type the name, and click Save.

## Opening a Spreadsheet

1   Choose File > Open or click the Open icon on the main toolbar.

2   In the Open window, navigate to where the file is stored and click Open.

## Changing the Sheet Name

1   Open the spreadsheet.

2   Click on the tab at the bottom that you want to rename.

3   Right-click on it and choose Rename.

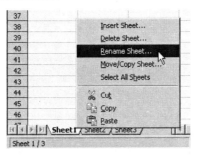

4   Name the sheet.

5   Click OK.

**6**   The new name will appear on the sheet.

## Opening a Text File as a Spreadsheet

It's easy to bring any text file of data into a Calc spreadsheet. You just need to make sure that each piece of data is separated by a comma, tab, etc.

**1**   In OpenOffice.org, choose File > Open.

**2**   Locate the text file. Don't click Open yet.

**3**   Click and hold down on the Files of Type list.

**4**   Scroll down through the list and select Text CSV.

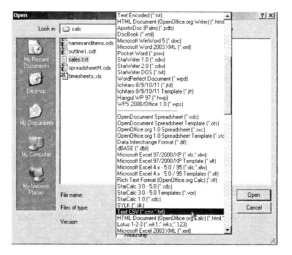

**5**   Click Open.

**6**   A conversion specifications window will appear. Select the correct field separator used to create the file, such as Tab or comma, and be sure the data in the display area looks correct.

**7**  Click OK.

**8**  The document will open correctly, this time in a spreadsheet.

# Entering and Deleting Data

Here are some core procedures for getting started adding data to your spreadsheet.

## Entering Data in a Spreadsheet

**1**  Click in the cell where you want content.

**2**  Type the information.

**3**  Press Enter. (You can also use the arrow keys to go to another cell.)

## Deleting the Contents of a Cell

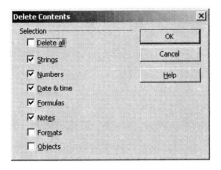

You can select the cell or cells and press Delete. You then get the window shown at right, where you can have some control over what gets deleted.

However, the quick way is to select the cell or cells and press Backspace. Then you get no window, and the contents just disappear.

# Templates

To create spreadsheet templates, or create spreadsheets based on templates, see *Saving Time With Templates and More* on page 37. You can use templates to change the file that appears when you create a new blank spreadsheet, and of course for standard template use.

# Managing Rows and Columns

This section covers how to resize, add, and remove columns, as well as how to see one chunk of rows or columns while you scroll to the other end of the sheet.

# Dragging a Cell, Row, or Column

It isn't quite the way you'd expect, so here are some tips.

## Dragging Rows or Columns

To drag a row or column to a different spot, click on the *heading* for the row for the row or column to select it, then click on one of the *selected cells* and drag the row or column.

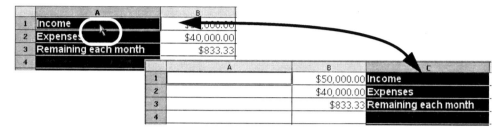

## Dragging Multiple Cells

To drag *two or more cells* to a different spot, just select them and drag them.

## Dragging One Cell

To drag *one cell* to a different spot, here's what you do. Cutting and pasting is easier.

1   Click on the cell and hold down the mouse

2   Drag the mouse down to select the cell below it, then back up.

3   Release the mouse.

4   Now drag the cell.

# Adding Row and Column Delete and Add Icons to the Toolbar

Icons are available for the functions you'll learn here; however, they're not usually on the toolbar by default. It's easy to add them.

1   Check to see if you have any of these icons on your toolbar. If you have all of them, skip this procedure. If you don't have them all, continue.

2   Click and hold down on the black arrow and choose Visible Buttons.

**3**    Scroll to the bottom of the list that appears. Find these icons and select one of them.

**4**    Choose Visible Buttons again and repeat the previous step to add all of the icons.

You might see all the icons on your toolbar now, or you might have to access one or more of them by clicking on the downward-facing black arrow.

## Deleting Rows and Columns

**1**    Select the row or column by clicking on the corresponding number or letter.

**2**    Click the Delete Row or Delete Column icon.

You can also right-click on the heading of a row or column and choose Delete.

# Inserting Rows and Columns

**1**   Click on the row below, or the column to the right, of where you want the rows or columns.

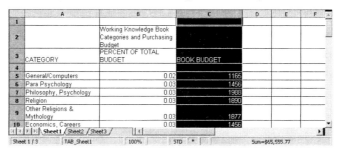

**2**   Click the Insert Row or Delete Column icon.

You can also right-click on the heading for a row or column and choose Insert or Delete.

# Resizing Rows and Columns

The example shows columns, but you can apply the same guidelines to rows.

## Dragging

Move the mouse pointer over the right-hand border of the column to resize, until the mouse looks like a two-ended arrow, as shown in the illustration at right.

Then drag the column border to the right, and release the mouse.

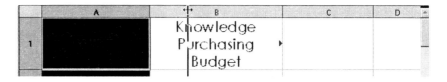

## Right-Clicking to Set Specific Height or Width

You can also right-click on the headings of one or more rows or columns, and choose the Height option. Set the height you want in the window that appears, and click OK.

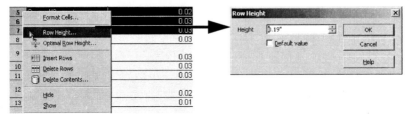

Usually, optimal width is best, so unless you absolutely need the row to be a certain height, skip setting a specific height. With optimal height, the row will resize to whatever height it needs to be, for the font size used.

## Right-Clicking to Set Optimal Height or Width

Select the headings for one or more rows or columns, and right-click. You'll see the Optimal Width or Optimal Height. You can specify additional spacing beyond the optimal height, but you don't usually need to type anything here. This will set the width or height to the best one for the content.

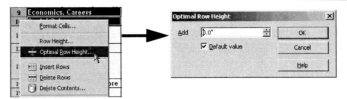

# Freezing and Scrolling Through Rows and Columns

The benefit and drawback of spreadsheets is that you can have many rows and columns. However, paper and monitors can only show a set number of those rows and columns at a time. If you want to see the headings in row 3 that identify the data, and the figures in row 27 at the same time, what do you do?

|   | A | B | C |
|---|---|---|---|
| 1 |   |   |   |
| 2 |   | Working Knowledge Book Categories and Purchasing Budget |   |
| 3 | CATEGORY | PERCENT OF TOTAL BUDGET | BOOK BUDGET |
| 27 | Landscape Architecture | 0.02 | 874 |
| 28 | Architecture | 0.02 | 1165 |
| 29 | Art and Art History, | 0.05 | 2912 |
| 30 | Drawing and Crafts | 0.04 | 2329 |
| 31 | Music | 0.04 | 3348 |
| 32 | Recreation, Sports | 0.03 | 1345 |
| 33 | Literature | 0.03 | 1210 |
| 34 | Mental Health | 0.01 | 901 |

Sheet1 / Sheet2 / Sheet3

Sheet 1 / 3 | TAB_Sheet1 | 100% | STD | * | | Sum=0

You essentially bring the two rows together, without having to look at the content between them. That's what *freezing* and *splitting* let you do. They're very similar, so just pick the one you like better.

## Freezing a Row

Let's say in your spreadsheet you've got three rows of headings, and the rest is data. So you want rows 1-3 to stay where they are, but you want to be able to scroll through everything else.

**1** Click in the row where you want scrolling to start, below the row you want to just stay put. In this case, you would click in row 4.

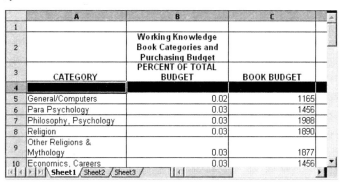

**2** Choose Window > Freeze.

**3** Scroll down; you'll see that everything starting with row 4 scrolls but rows 1-3 with the headings stay put.

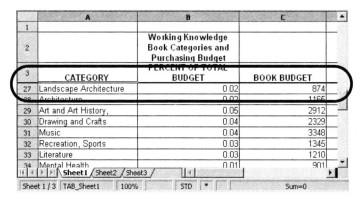

**4** Remove the freeze by choosing Window > Freeze again. The checkmark will be there but will be removed when you choose Freeze.

## Splitting the Window

This is similar to freezing. However, you can do it in two dimensions, and split the document into four quadrants. Then you can scroll in each of the four quadrants.

**1**    Click in the cell to the right of, and below, the cell where you want to split the spreadsheet.

**2**    Choose Window > Split.

**3**    The spreadsheet will look something like this, with scroll bars for every quadrant.

**4**    Choose Window > Split again to remove the split.

# Merging Cells

Let's say you're working on a spreadsheet that's very nicely formatted, except for the heading which would look at lot better centered over the content. You can merge several cells so that the text moves across all of them, as if they were one cell.

**1**    Select the cells you want to merge.

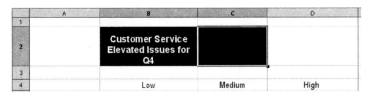

**2**    Click the Merge Cells icon on the toolbar. (Or choose Format > Merge Cells.)

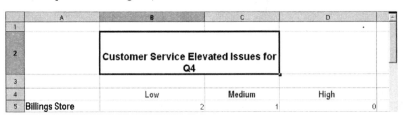

**3**    The two cells you selected will be merged. (Click the same icon again, or choose Format > Merge Cells, to split the cells again.)

# Text Formatting

Using the core features of Calc is a lot like Excel or any other spreadsheet you've used. In this section we'll go over the usual font select, bold and underline, as well as making text display currency symbols and other formatting. Formatting for borders is covered in *Cell Formatting* on page 269; formatting for numeric values is covered in *Number Formatting* on page 267.

## Standard Formatting for Text and Numbers

This works the same way it does in Writer.

♦ Basic formatting – Use the dropdown lists on the formatting toolbar for font, font size, etc. See *Making Text Look How You Want It: Basic Formatting* on page 71

♦ Advanced formatting – Use the Font and Font Effects tabs of the Cell formatting window for additional formatting; select text and choose Format > Character.

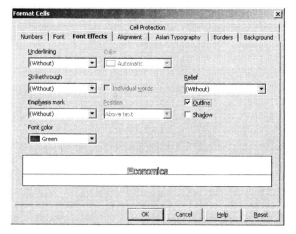

♦ Styles – You can even create styles in Calc. Styles work the same way as in Writer, except that you can only create two types of style, cell styles and page styles. Choose Format > Styles and Formatting to open the window. See *Saving Enormous Time and Effort With Styles* on page 147.

# Wrapping Text

When you enter text in a spreadsheet cell that's too wide, it looks like this.

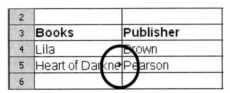

If there's text next to the cell where the text is too wide, it looks like this.

The first example is OK but will cause problems if you need to put text into the cell next to it. You're usually better off wrapping the text so that the text stays within its own cell.

**1**    Open the document and select the cells to wrap. You can just select the cells where the text is too wide, but it's most efficient to just select the whole spreadsheet.

Do this by pressing Ctrl + A or by clicking the small gray square in the upper left corner.

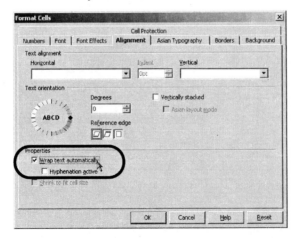

**2**    Choose Format > Cells.

**3**    When the Format Cells window appears, click the Alignment tab if it isn't on top.

**4**    Select the Wrap Text Automatically check box.

**5**   Click OK.

**6**   The text will wrap.

| 2 | | |
|---|---|---|
| 3 | **Books** | **Publisher** |
| 4 | Lila | Brown |
| 5 | Heart of Darkness | Pearson |
| 6 | | |

# Number Formatting

This section covers items like applying decimal places and date formatting automatically to a numeric value. This not only lets you apply the formatting easily to several selected cells at once, but lets you change the formatting easily, as well.

| Date | 12/08/06 |
|---|---|
| Amount | 1290 |
| Discount | 0.3 |

| Date | December 8, 2006 |
|---|---|
| Amount | $1,290.00 |
| Discount | 30.00% |

## Applying Numeric Formatting Using the Toolbar

Select the cells to format, then use the appropriate icon on the formatting toolbar. If you don't see one that you want to use, see *Adding Row and Column Delete and Add Icons to the Toolbar* on page 259 and add the icons you want.

Each icon applies the most commonly used formatting for the language you chose when you installed OpenOffice.org.

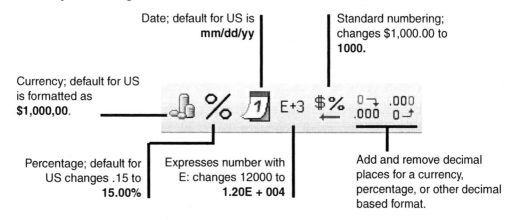

Date; default for US is **mm/dd/yy**

Standard numbering; changes $1,000.00 to **1000.**

Currency; default for US is formatted as **$1,000,00.**

Percentage; default for US changes .15 to **15.00%**

Expresses number with E: changes 12000 to **1.20E + 004**

Add and remove decimal places for a currency, percentage, or other decimal based format.

## Applying Formatting Using the Format Cells Window

When the icons on the toolbar can't do exactly what you want, you go a little deeper, into the number formatting section of the Format Cells window.

1   Select the cells to format.

2   Right-click on one of the selected cells and choose Format Cells.

3   In the Format Cells window that appears, select the Numbers tab if it isn't on top.

4   In the Category list, select the type of data you're dealing with, and in the Format list, select specifically what you want it to look like.

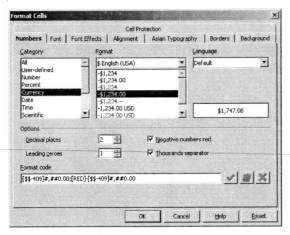

5   Specify the number of leading zeroes, if any, for the number. If the value for the leading zeroes doesn't stick, try formatting the number as Text or General if appropriate. This is the approach you'll need to use for postal codes.

6   Apply the Category of Text and the Format of @ if you just want the cell to accept normal text with no number formatting.

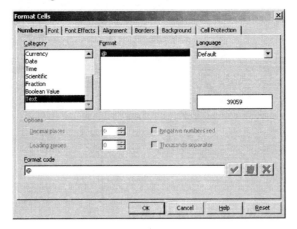

7   Click OK.

**Note –** If you want to create your own format from scratch, you can do so in the Format Code field. Press F1 to see the guide in the online help to what each code means.

**Note –** If you have trouble spellchecking, check the language in the Language dropdown list of the Numbers tab. For more information, see *Troubleshooting and Language* on page 97.

# Cell Formatting

The icons on the formatting object bar, and the cell formatting window (Format > Cells) are the power behind cell formatting. You'll also want to investigate styles (Format > Styles and Formatting) and Autoformats (Format > Autoformat) for time-saving ways to preserve and easily reapply complex formatting.

## Backgrounds and Borders

You can apply borders and background shading the same way you do in Writer for tables.

♦   Basic borders and backgrounds – Use the icons on the formatting toolbar to apply borders and backgrounds. Choose Format > Cells to get to the same border and background options as you had for tables. See *Formatting Tables* on page 182

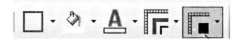

♦   Advanced borders and backgrounds – The advanced formatting options for tables are available by choosing Table > Table Properties. In Calc, the same options are available under Format > Cells.

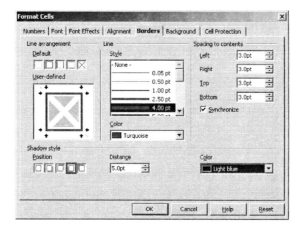

## Adding the Border Style and Border Color Icons

All the icons aren't on the toolbar by default. Here's how to add them.

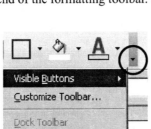

Line Color (of the border)

1    In a spreadsheet, locate the down-facing black arrow at the far right end of the formatting toolbar. Click and hold down on it, and choose Visible Buttons.

2    Scroll down through the list of icons. Find **Line Style** and if there isn't a checkmark next to it, select it.

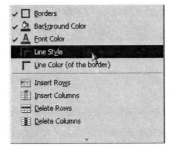

3    Click and hold down on the black arrow again, and choose Visible Buttons again. This time, scroll down again and find the **Line Color of the Border** option. If there isn't a check mark next to it, select it.

# Using AutoFormats and Cell Styles

You'll save huge amounts of time and effort using AutoFormats and styles.

◆    Autoformats – Autoformats are groups of formatting for background, borders, as well as
       numeric formatting like decimal places. They work the same way as in Writer. Choose
       Format > Autoformat to see the window. See *Creating and Applying AutoFormats: The
       Table Formatting Timesaver* on page 193.

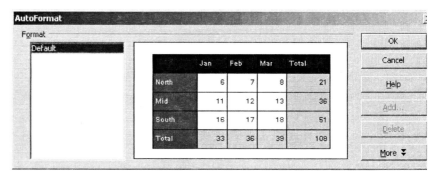

◆    Cell styles – Cell styles can include text attributes but also borders and backgrounds, and
       numeric formatting. See *Saving Enormous Time and Effort With Styles* on page 147.

# Cell and Sheet Protection

You can protect cells or an entire sheet from changes. The steps in this procedure are a bit odd
since cells are all protected by default, but both the sheet and the cell need to have protection
enabled for protection to work.

**1**    Select all the cells in the spreadsheet.

**2**    Choose Format > Cells.

**3**    In the Format Cells window, click the Cell Protection tab.

**4**     Unmark the Protected checkbox.

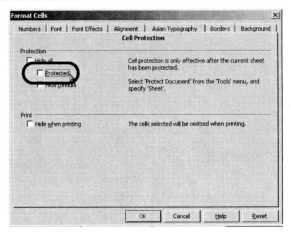

**5**     Click OK.

**6**     Select the cells that you want to protect from changes.

**7**     Choose Format > Cells and click the Cell Protection tab.

**8**     Mark the Protected checkbox.

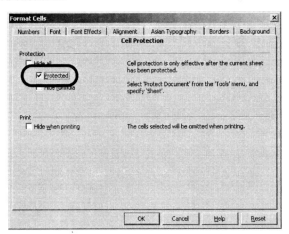

**9**     Click OK.

**10**  Choose Tools > Protect Document > Sheet.

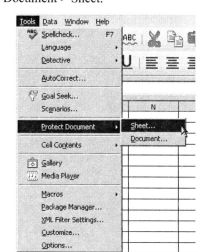

**11**  Enter a password.

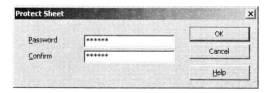

**12**  Now, when someone tries to change the contents of a protected cell, this message will appear.

**13**  To unprotect the cells, choose Tools > Protect Document > Sheet.

**14**  Enter the password and click OK.

# Data Entry Shortcuts

If you're an Excel user, you know a lot of shortcuts. Luckily, many of them work in Calc, and there are additional shortcuts, as well.

## Selecting Cell Data From a Dropdown List

**1**  Open a spreadsheet with a column of text values, like a few of book titles you need to reenter.

**2**   Click in the first cell under the column.

**3**   Right-click and choose Selection List (or press Ctrl D). You'll get a list of all the data in that authors column.

**4**   Select the one you want.

**5**   You'll see your selection in that cell.

# Entering a Value or Series Automatically

You don't always have an entirely different piece of data in every cell. Sometimes you just need the same number again and again, or you might need a series like 1, 2, 3 and so on. Use the Edit > Fill menu, or just drag.

## Using the Edit > Fill Menu to Repeat a Value

**1**   Open a spreadsheet.

**2**   Type a value that you want to repeat.

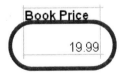

**3**   Select that value *and* all the other cells where you want that value to appear.

**4**   Choose Edit > Fill > Down.

**5**   The number 19.99 will be filled in all the cells you'd selected.

## Using Edit > Fill > Series to Repeat a Series

To enter a more complex series of numbers, use this approach.

### Standard Numeric Increment

**1**    Type a number, then select it and all the cells below that the numbers should fill.

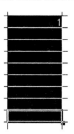

**2**    Choose Edit > Fill > Series and specify the direction, Linear, and the increment. Linear is a standard increment.

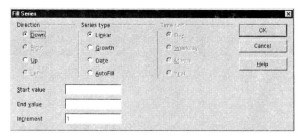

**3**    Click OK and you'll see the results. This is a linear increment of 3

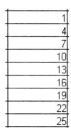

### Using the Growth Increment

If you want to increase at a faster rate, use the growth increment option. With this approach, each number is multiplied by, rather than added to, the increment number, to arrive at the next number.

**1**  Type a number, then select it and all the cells below that the numbers should fill.

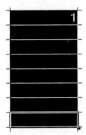

**2**  Choose Edit > Fill > Series and specify the correct direction, Growth, and the increment amount.

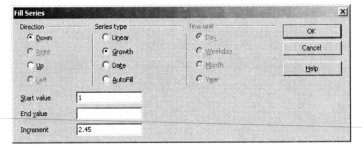

**3**  Click OK and you'll see the results.

| |
|---|
| 1 |
| 2.45 |
| 6 |
| 14.71 |
| 36.03 |
| 88.27 |
| 216.27 |
| 529.86 |

## Dragging to Increment by One

If you just want to increase a value by 1, in a series, do this.

**1**  Type the first number.

**2**  Drag down the lower right handle of the cell.

**3**    You'll see results like this. Note that the increase takes place in the 1's position immediately to the left of the decimal, not in the farthest right position.

|  |
|---:|
| $19.99 |
| $20.99 |
| $21.99 |
| $22.99 |
| $23.99 |
| $24.99 |
| $25.99 |
| $26.99 |

## Dragging to Repeat a Specific Series

Here's what to do to increase by a specific increment.

**1**    Open a spreadsheet.

**2**    Type the first two or three numbers of the series, as shown.

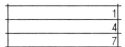

**3**    Select all the cells, drag down the handle in the bottom cell, and you'll see results like this.

|  |
|---:|
| 1 |
| 4 |
| 7 |
| 10 |
| 13 |
| 16 |
| 19 |
| 22 |
| 25 |

# Quickly Entering Months, Days, or Anything You Want With Sort Lists

Type the word **January** in a cell, and drag the handle down. You should get something like this.

This works because of the *Sort Lists* window. Anything in this window will automatically appear in the order shown when you type an item in the series and drag down the handle.

Sorting lists are great for sorting, of course (see *Sorting and Filtering Data* on page 331) and also just for shortcuts, a great way to quickly add a long list of items.

**1**   If you have the list in your spreadsheet already, select it. If it's in a text document, select it and copy it.

**2**   Choose Tools > Options > OpenOffice.org Calc > Sort Lists to see the lists.

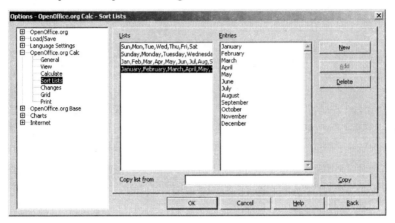

**3**   To add a new list, click New.

**4**   If you didn't copy or select items in the first step, just type the entries in the Entries list. Type the first entry, then press Enter to type the next.

If you copied text, just paste it. If you selected the items from the spreadsheet, click the Copy button at the bottom of the window.

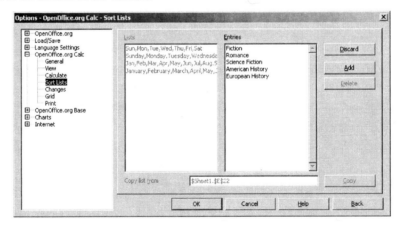

**5** Click Add; the list will appear.

**6** Click OK.

**7** In a spreadsheet, type the first item, then drag down and see the list appear.

## Entering a Series of Calculations Automatically

See *Repeating Calculations for a Row or Column* on page 292.

# Referencing Other Cells and Spreadsheets

It's fairly common to repeat content in a spreadsheet. A number that's displayed in one sheet might be reused in a calculation in another sheet, and so on. You want to refer to another cell, another cell in another sheet, or even a cell in an entirely different spreadsheet.

To do this, you can type a quick reference, or for longer references, you can just copy and paste, using the paste or the Paste Special feature.

## Basics for Referring to Another Cell

It would be a huge amount of work to retype calculations or content when you can just say "I want the contents of cell A43 over here." It's also more accurate to refer, rather than retyping, since you don't risk making typos when you skip retyping (it's a lower risk, at least).

## Simple Cell References

To refer to another cell, just type = and the cell number. Here's an example; I want to repeat the content from cell B6 in cell F2. So I click in cell F2 and type **=B6**. I can also click in F2, type = and then just click in cell B6.

## Absolute Versus Relative Cell References

To do an absolute cell reference rather than relative, use $ in front of each part of the reference; $B$3, for instance. For more on absolute and relative cell references, see *Absolute and Relative Cell References* on page 293.

# Referring to Cells From Other Sheets or Spreadsheets Using Paste Special

Let's say you're working away in the **budget.ods** spreadsheet and you realize you'd like to include a few cells with some data from a sheet in the **financials.ods** spreadsheet. You could copy and paste. This will just take the data from **financials.ods** and put it in **budget.ods**. However, then you're stuck with static data in your budget spreadsheet, and you know the accountants update financials.ods pretty much every day.

How do you keep the pasted data updated?

Use the Edit > Paste Special feature. This works for calculations too; you can copy data and calculations between sheets and the calculations will be updated.

1   Open the spreadsheet with the data you want (for instance, the financials.ods spreadsheet).

2   Select the cell or cells to copy, and copy them.

3   Go to the sheet you want to paste to (for instance, budget.ods), and click in the top left corner of where you want the cells to be pasted.

4   Choose Edit > Paste Special.

**5**   Select the Link option.

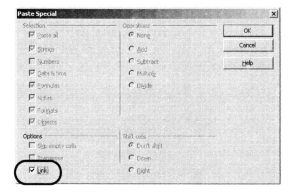

**6**   Click OK.

**7**   The cells will be pasted. When the originally copied cells are updated, the pasted cells will be updated, too.

# Inserting a Sheet From Another Spreadsheet

This is a nice feature you can use when you want to just bring in an entire sheet from another spreadsheet. You can choose, as you did in *Referring to Cells From Other Sheets or Spreadsheets Using Paste Special*, to link the data to the original source, too. However, the feature inserts the sheet as a separate sheet; you can't include it with other data on a sheet in your spreadsheet.

**1**   Go to the spreadsheet where you want to insert existing data.

**2**   Choose Insert > Sheet From File.

**3**   Select the spreadsheet with the data you want to insert.

**4**   In the Insert Sheet window, choose where you want the sheet to appear, the sheet to insert, and whether you want the sheet linked (so that the data will remain the same).

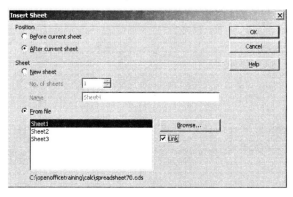

**5**   Click OK. The inserted sheet will appear as a new sheet.

# Adding a Linked HTML Table to a Spreadsheet

You can usually just copy and paste an HTML table from a web page to a spreadsheet. However, you can also insert the content. This will also let you link the content if you want.

This is documented in the online help as if it works with online URLs; however at the time of writing it only worked with saved files.

1   Click in the cell at the upper left corner of where you want the HTML table to appear.

2   Choose Insert > Link to External Data.

3   In the window that appears, make the appropriate selections.

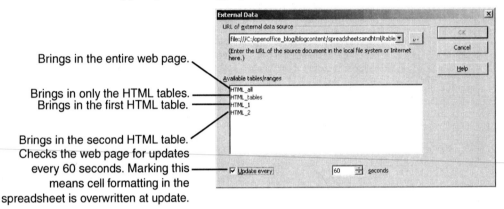

Brings in the entire web page.

Brings in only the HTML tables.
Brings in the first HTML table.

Brings in the second HTML table.
Checks the web page for updates
every 60 seconds. Marking this
means cell formatting in the
spreadsheet is overwritten at update.

4   Click OK. The content will appear.

# Summary of Cell Reference Syntax

This is the most direct way to refer to cells, but also more complex when you are referring to other spreadsheets. Here's a summary; use *Referring to Cells From Other Sheets or Spreadsheets Using Paste Special* on page 280 if you prefer.

Here's the syntax for cells in the same sheet in the same spreadsheet.

Syntax for a cell: *=ColumnRow*

Example for a cell: =E14 (or $E$14 for absolute reference)

Here's the syntax for cells in a different sheet in the same spreadsheet.

Syntax for a cell: *=$Sheetname.$Column$Row*

Example for a cell: =$Sheet2.$E$14

Here's the syntax for a cells in a different spreadsheet.

Syntax for a cell: {=DDE("soffice";"*pathtospreadsheet*";"*Sheetname.ColumnRow*")}

Example for a cell:

{=DDE("soffice";"C:\budgets\2006.ods";"EstimateSheet.B4")}

# Inserting and Printing Notes

To insert a note, click in the cell and choose Insert > Note: Type the note.

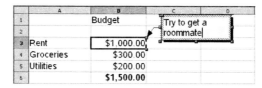

After you've inserted the note, a very small red dot in the upper right corner will indicate there's a note. To view the note, move your mouse over the cell.

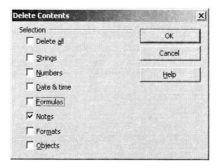

To delete a note, select the cell, press Delete, and in the window that appears, unmark everything except Notes.

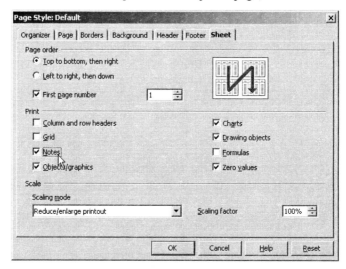

To print a note, choose Format > Page and click the Sheet tab. Be sure that Notes is marked. Then print as usual. The notes will be printed on a separate page, with the cell number listed.

# Creating Good Spreadsheets

Use the following tips to make spreadsheets that work well for you and for those you present them to.

## Organizing Spreadsheets

One of the most useful features for creating good spreadsheets isn't anywhere in the software—it's in your head. Constructing the spreadsheets well will make some features unnecessary, others more powerful, and life easier in general.

### Break Data Down Into Its Smallest Parts

Whenever possible, put the smallest piece of data possible into a cell. For instance, put First Name in one cell and the corresponding Last Name in the cell next to it.

| | A | B | C | D | E | F | G |
|---|---|---|---|---|---|---|---|
| 1 | Firstname | Lastname | Address1 | Address2 | City | State | Postalcode |
| 2 | Marion | Anderson | 404 Pearl | Suite 2 | Boulder | MT | 59901 |
| 3 | Paul | Verana | 88 Ludlow | | Kalispell | CO | 80026 |

This allows you to:

* Sort and filter by any piece of data
* Reverse the order the data is shown in
* Link from another cell or spreadsheet to the specific data you want.

### Put Everything You Use in a Cell

There are certainly exceptions to this, of course. But generally, put the parts of your calculations in cells and refer to them, rather than putting the numbers into the calculations directly.

Here's an example. The tax percentage is a separate cell, rather than a literal part of each calculation. If the tax percentage changes, it's easier to change in one place than three—or 300.

| | A | B | C | D |
|---|---|---|---|---|
| 1 | | **Income** | **Tax Percentage** | **Net Income** |
| 2 | 2001 | $45,889.00 | 35.00% | $29,827.85 |
| 3 | 2002 | $55,778.00 | | $36,255.70 |
| 4 | 2003 | $64,100.00 | | =B4 - (B4 * $C$2) |

## Reference, Don't Copy

If you need to use a piece of data that's already in the spreadsheet, simply refer to it. Don't retype or copy the data. Also considering referencing the data if it's in a different spreadsheet. See *Referencing Other Cells and Spreadsheets* on page 279.

| | A | B | C | D |
|---|---|---|---|---|
| 1 | | **Income** | **Tax Percentage** | **Net Income** |
| 2 | **2001** | $45,889.00 | 35.00% | $29,827.85 |
| 3 | **2002** | $55,778.00 | | $36,255.70 |
| 4 | **2003** | $64,100.00 | | $41,665.00 |
| 5 | | | | |
| 6 | | | | |
| 7 | | | Highest income: | =D4 |

## Don't Use a Spreadsheet as a Text Document

Spreadsheets are great for chunks of data and calculations. If you want to combine text with data, though, use a text document and reference the data in a separate spreadsheet. See *Skip the Tables—Use a Spreadsheet* on page 181.

This approach can be a lot of work to merge the cells and space the lines vertically, and can potentially cause problems with text flow.

| | A | B | C | D |
|---|---|---|---|---|
| 1 | | Income | Tax Percentage | Net Income |
| 2 | 2001 | $45,889.00 | 35.00% | $29,827.85 |
| 3 | 2002 | $55,778.00 | | $36,255.70 |
| 4 | 2003 | $64,100.00 | | $41,665.00 |
| 5 | | | | |
| 6 | | | Highest income: | $41,665.00 |
| 7 | | | | |
| 8 | | We believe that we can improve net income by 22% if we | | |
| 9 | | invest in some offshore accounts and divest ourselves of | | |
| 10 | | high tax investments We believe that we can improve net | | |
| 11 | | income by 22% if we invest in some offshore accounts | | |
| 12 | | and divest ourselves of high tax investments. We believe | | |
| 13 | | that we can improve net income by 22% if we e believe | | |
| 14 | | that we can improve net income by 22% if we | | |
| 15 | | | | |
| 16 | | Income | Tax Percentage | Net Income |
| 17 | 2004 | $88,000.00 | 42.00% | $57,200.00 |
| 18 | 2005 | $87,999.00 | | $57,199.35 |
| 19 | 2006 | $98,774.00 | | $64,203.10 |
| 20 | | | | |
| 21 | | | Highest income: | $64,203.10 |
| 22 | | | | |
| 23 | | We believe that we can improve net income by 22% if we | | |
| 24 | | invest in some offshore accounts and divest ourselves of | | |
| 25 | | high tax investments We believe that we can improve net | | |
| 26 | | income by 22% if we invest in some offshore accounts | | |
| 27 | | and divest ourselves of high tax investments. We believe | | |
| 28 | | that we can improve net income by 22% if we e believe | | |
| 29 | | that we can improve net income by 22% if we | | |
| 30 | | | | |

## Use Multiple Sheets Rather Than Multiple Documents

If you have a lot of related data, remember to use all the sheets, and create more if necessary. It's easier to keep track of one document than several. Additionally, if you reference data within the spreadsheet, you don't risk breaking the links as you do when linking between documents. To insert a new sheet, just choose Insert > Sheet.

| Daily Totals | Weekly Totals | Monthly Totals | Yearly Totals | **Summary Report** |

## Separate Calculations From Data

If you're working with complex spreadsheets with multiple sheets (big financial models, for instance), separate out the detailed calculations from the inputs and results. It is even possible to hide and lock access to the calculations sheets in cases where other users are going to use the document and you don't want them messing with the calculations. To control access, see *Cell and Sheet Protection* on page 271.

# Formatting Spreadsheet

Color, borders, and other visual cues are your friend. Spreadsheets can be very detailed and confusing, so emphasize the important information with formatting. See *Cell Formatting* on page 269.

# Presenting Spreadsheets

If you're building of presentation spreadsheets for multiple models that you'll present in a meeting, create a few summary sheets where you show the graphs, data, and other information for several different sets of variables. Show the input fields for the few key parameters that really drove the model. Then, you can plug in new numbers right in the meeting when other attendees want to see different values for the variables.

# Calculations and Functions

# Getting Started With Calculations

Calculations are reasonably simple; there are just a few basic rules. If you're familiar with Excel, you'll find most of Calc very easy to learn.

## Where to Type

You can click in the cell where you want the calculation results to show up, and just type there. What you're typing will show up in the formula toolbar and in the cell where you clicked.

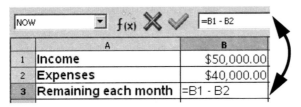

When you're done, press Enter, click the check mark, or use the arrow keys on the keyboard to go to another cell.

## Basic Syntax

To refer to the contents of a cell, just type its *cell reference*, which is the column and the row. If you want to put the 50,000 figure from this example in a calculation, just type **B1**. You can type the cell reference, or just click on the cell that you want to refer to and the cell reference will appear in your calculation.

|   | A | B |
|---|---|---|
| 1 | Income | $50,000.00 |
| 2 | Expenses | $40,000.00 |
| 3 | Remaining each month | |

To type a calculation, start with an equals sign, = , then type the calculation using cell references and standard math symbols. Use parentheses when necessary to make the calculation correct.

| | NOW ▼ f(x) ✗ ✓ | =(B1 - B2) / 12 |
|---|---|---|
|   | A | B |
| 1 | Income | $50,000.00 |
| 2 | Expenses | $40,000.00 |
| 3 | Remaining each month | =(B1 - B2) / 12 |

Start with = and type the formu using cell references and standa operators:

Addition +

Subtraction −

Multiplication *

Division /

## Changing a Calculation

If you want to change the calculation, click in the cell where it is. Then do whichever of the following seems the most appealing:

- Click in the formula toolbar and make the changes there.

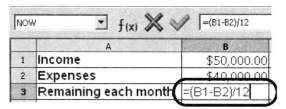

- *Or* double-click in that same cell and retype the formula there—it's pretty much the same, you're just typing in a different spot.

- *Or* double-click in that same cell and drag the color-coded boxes to different cells. This doesn't change the formula, just the cells in the formula.

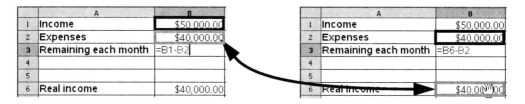

# Regular Calculations

Here are the basics for adding, subtracting, multiplying and dividing in standard calculations.

## Simple Calculations

To do math in OpenOffice.org, you just use + − / and * for plus, minus, divide, and multiply.

1    Click in the cell where you want the calculation results to appear.

2    Type the formula in the cell. This example would add the three reference cell contents together.

=(C38 + C39 + C40)

The parentheses and spaces are optional, but it makes the formula easier to read.

In another example if you had a more complex calculation, the parentheses would be more important.

=(B7 + B8 - B9) - ((12 * B3) + B4)

**3** Press Return when you're done. The total will appear.

| B45 | ▾ | $f_{(x)}$ | Σ | = | =(C38 + C39 + C40) |
| | | | | | |

| | A | B | C |
|---|---|---|---|
| 36 | Literature | 3.00% | $1,747 |
| 37 | Geography, Travel | 3.00% | $1,747 |
| 38 | World History | 5.00% | $2,912 |
| 39 | American History, World War II | 5.00% | $2,912 |
| 40 | State Histories, South American, Australian History | 4.00% | $2,329 |
| 41 | Biographies | 2.00% | $1,165 |
| 42 | Totals | 100.00% | |
| 43 | | | |
| 44 | | | |
| 45 | History Totals | $8,153 | |

# Quick Sum

There's a nice shortcut for adding a column or row of consecutive numbers.

**1** Open the spreadsheet.

**2** Go to the cell below, or to the right of, a column or row to add up.

| | | | |
|---|---|---|---|
| 38 | World History | 5.00% | $2,912 |
| 39 | American History, World War II | 5.00% | $2,912 |
| 40 | State Histories, South American, Australian History | 4.00% | $2,329 |
| 41 | Biographies | 2.00% | $1,165 |
| 42 | Totals | | |
| 43 | | | |
| 44 | | | |

---

**Note** – You don't select the columns or rows to add up; you click at the first empty cell *below* or *to the right* to it.

---

**3** Click the Sum icon in the formula bar.

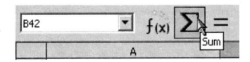

| B42 | ▾ | $f_{(x)}$ | Σ | = |
| | | | Sum | |
| | | A | | |

**4**    A proposed formula will appear at the top and you'll see a blue box around the cells that it thinks you want to sum (the blue box encircles all the adjoining numeric cells in the column).

| | A | B | C | D |
|---|---|---|---|---|
| AVERAGE ▾ *f(x)* ✖ ✔ =SUM(B4:B41) | | | | |
| 36 | Literature | 3.00% | $1,747 | |
| 37 | Geography, Travel | 3.00% | $1,747 | |
| 38 | World History | 5.00% | $2,912 | |
| 39 | American History, World War II | 5.00% | $2,912 | |
| 40 | State Histories, South American, Australian History | 4.00% | $2,329 | |
| 41 | Biographies | 2.00% | $1,165 | |
| 42 | Totals | =SUM(B4:B41) | | |
| 43 | | | | |

**5**    It's usually what you want, so press Enter. The total will appear.

**6**    Press Return or an arrow key to get out of the cell. **Don't click in another cell.**

The quick sum feature will add up consecutive numbers. Here are two examples of what it will put into the formula automatically. The autosum will go up to the first missing row, but it will start at the first number it finds.

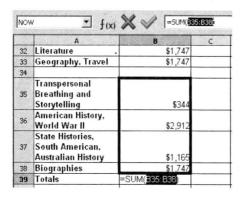

| | A | B | C |
|---|---|---|---|
| NOW ▾ *f(x)* ✖ ✔ =SUM(B35:B38) | | | |
| 32 | Literature | $1,747 | |
| 33 | Geography, Travel | $1,747 | |
| 34 | | | |
| 35 | Transpersonal Breathing and Storytelling | $344 | |
| 36 | American History, World War II | $2,912 | |
| 37 | State Histories, South American, Australian History | $1,165 | |
| 38 | Biographies | $1,747 | |
| 39 | Totals | =SUM(B35:B38) | |

| | A | B | C |
|---|---|---|---|
| SUM ▾ *f(x)* ✖ ✔ =SUM(B34:B38) | | | |
| 28 | Art and Art History, | $2,912 | |
| 29 | Drawing and Crafts | $2,329 | |
| 30 | Music | $2,329 | |
| 31 | Recreation, Sports | $1,747 | |
| 32 | | | |
| 33 | | | |
| 34 | Geography, Travel | $1,747 | |
| 35 | Transpersonal Breathing and Storytelling | $344 | |
| 36 | American History, World War II | $2,912 | |
| 37 | | | |
| 38 | | | |
| 39 | Totals | =SUM(B34:B38) | |

# Cell References

Now that we've covered the basics, we'll go on to a couple more advanced cell reference tasks and how the relate to calculations.

## Repeating Calculations for a Row or Column

Let's say you've got this spreadsheet. You need to multiply everything in the Wholesale Price column by 1.8 and put the result in the Retail Price column.

| | Title | Wholesale Price | Retail Price |
|---|---|---|---|
| 5 | | | |
| 6 | For Love of Flight | $10.0 | =D6 * 1.8 |
| 7 | Up in the Air | $10.0 | |
| 8 | OpenOffice and Me: The Untold Story | $14.0 | |
| 9 | Lila, the Lilies, and Lyle | $19.0 | |
| 10 | Mark Johnson Owes Me Money | $19.0 | |
| 11 | Java Jive: The Scandal Behind the Programming Language | $6.0 | |
| 12 | Head First Perl | $22.0 | |
| 13 | The Secret Life of Variables | $6.0 | |
| 14 | Head First Java | $10.00 | |

You could retype or copy and paste to get that formula into all the other cells in the Retail Price column. However, the quickest way to get exactly what you want is to just drag the formula down. You're looking for the tiny square handle in the lower right corner of the calculation cell.

| Wholesale Price | Retail Price |
|---|---|
| $10.00 | $18.00 |
| $10.00 | |

The drag the handle down as far as you want it.

| Wholesale Price | Retail Price |
|---|---|
| $10.00 | $18.00 |
| $10.00 | |
| $14.00 | |
| $19.00 | |
| $19.00 | |

Here's what the results look like, with the correct calculation in each cell.

| | Title | Wholesale Price | Retail Price |
|---|---|---|---|
| 5 | | | |
| 6 | For Love of Flight | $10.00 | $18.00 |
| 7 | Up in the Air | $10.00 | $18.00 |
| 8 | OpenOffice and Me: The Untold Story | $14.00 | $25.20 |
| 9 | Lila, the Lilies, and Lyle | $19.00 | $34.20 |
| 10 | Mark Johnson Owes Me Money | $19.00 | $34.20 |
| 11 | Java Jive: The Scandal Behind the Programming Language | $6.00 | $10.80 |
| 12 | Head First Perl | $22.00 | $39.60 |
| 13 | The Secret Life of Variables | $6.00 | $10.80 |
| 14 | Head First Java | $10.00 | =D14 * 1.8 |

# Absolute and Relative Cell References

When you click in cell B2 and type the reference **=A1**, you're not really referring to A1. You're referring to "the cell one to the left of this cell." You'll see this if you set this up, and then copy and paste that formula into different cells.

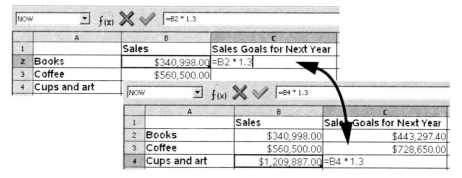

Cell references are like this, *relative* by default. This is usually what you want.

However, what if you don't want that cell reference to move—what if you always want a particular cell referred to? In this example, the amounts are multiplied by one number at the right.

If you copy and paste the formulas down in this example, then you multiply by zero in the second and third cells.

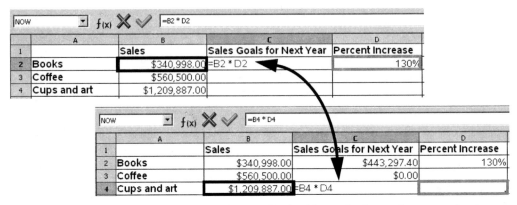

What you would do in this situation is to refer to cell D2 with an *absolute reference* so that it always stays the same.

**Note –** You can read more about referring to cells in different sheets and spreadsheets in *Referencing Other Cells and Spreadsheets* on page 279.

To do this, just type **$D$2**, with a **$** in front of the column and the row. (To make only the row or only column absolute, just put the **$** in front of one of them.)

| NOW | | | =B4 * $D$2 | |
|-----|---|---|---|---|
| | A | B | C | D |
| 1 | | Sales | Sales Goals for Next Year | Percent Increase |
| 2 | Books | $340,998.00 | $443,297.40 | 130% |
| 3 | Coffee | $560,500.00 | $728,650.00 | |
| 4 | Cups and art | $1,209,88... | =B4 * $D$2 | |

*Relative reference* to            *Absolute reference* to
the cells in column B.              the cell D2.

# Functions

Functions are preset calculations like Average, Internal Rate of Return, when Easter falls for a given year, etc. Calc has a huge number, which I'm not going to cover in detail. The online help has good definitions and examples of each, and the Function Wizard walks you through how to use each one.

## Using the Help

The simplest approach is to use the help (press F1), look up your function, and find the syntax.

One way to find all the functions and the help for them is to press F1, type **Function Wizard** in the Find screen, then click the List of **Categories and Functions** link. You'll find the Categories and Functions window, where you can click on a category and get to syntax and examples for all the functions in that category.

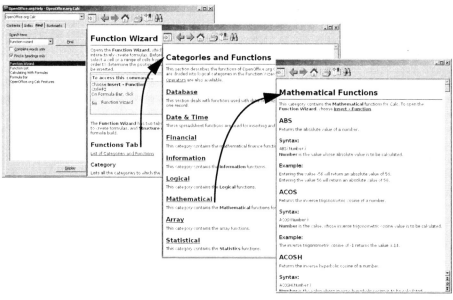

## Typing a Function Manually

Once you've found the syntax and an example, just type the function. Start with = then use the function name, then typically use parentheses and cell references as necessary.

The syntax for the average of the cells in B12, B42, and B90, for instance, is:

**=AVERAGE(B12;B42;B90)**

The syntax for the average of the cells in the *range* B12 through B90, however, is:

**=AVERAGE(B12:B90)**

You generally separate ranges of cells with a colon, and individual cells with semicolons.

If you'd like more help to get started, use the function wizard.

# Using the Function Wizard

**1** Click where you want the calculation to show up.

**2** Click the Function Wizard icon on the toolbar.

**3** The Function Wizard window appears.

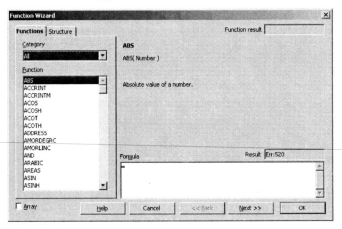

**4** Find the category your function is in, then select the function, or just scroll through the whole list alphabetically.

**5** Select the function. Read the information about the function. If you're ready you can just type everything here in the Formula field and the preview result will be displayed in the Result field.

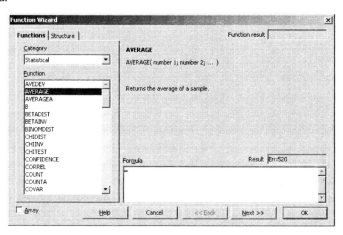

**6** To get more help, double-click the function name to make the fields appear, and a little extra help in the function entry field below

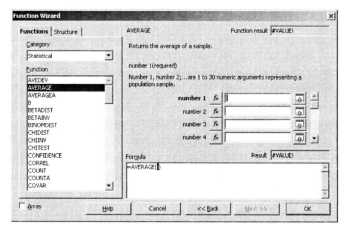

**7** You have a few options at this point for entering the cells in the function.

◆ You can just type in each **number** field in the wizard, typing the appropriate cell reference in each of the fields. Scroll down to see more.

◆ Or you can just click in the cell in the spreadsheet, instead of typing.

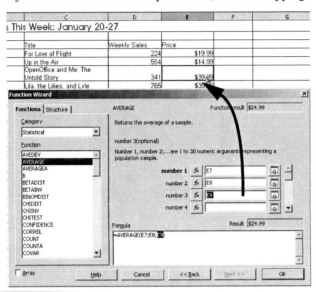

◆ If you can apply the function to a range, you can just click in the top cell in the wizard, labeled **number 1**, and drag your mouse in the range in the spreadsheet itself.

Drag around the cells in the range; the
wizard window is minimized

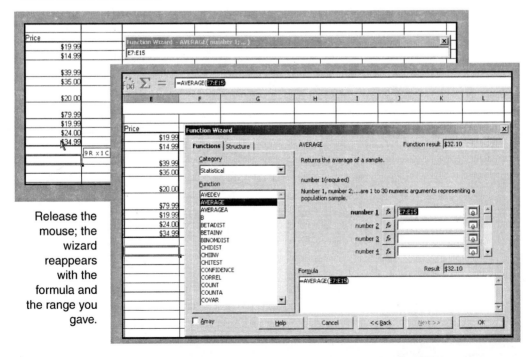

Release the
mouse; the
wizard
reappears
with the
formula and
the range you
gave.

**8**   When you've filled in your formula, just click OK. The function result will appear in the spreadsheet. Double-click the cell if you want to verify that the formula and range are correct, visually.

| Weekly Sales | Price |
|---|---|
| 224 | $19.99 |
| 554 | $14.99 |
| 341 | $39.99 |
| 765 | $35.00 |
| 665 | $20.00 |
| 211 | $79.99 |
| 122 | $19.99 |
| 344 | $24.00 |
| 445 | $34.99 |

| Average price | $32.10 |
|---|---|

➡

| Average price | =AVERAGE(E7:E 15) |
|---|---|

# More Information About Calc Functions

There are hundreds of valuable functions in the Calc program. For an excellent guide to using these, see the web site **http://www.openofficetips.com**.

# Using Subtotals

Let's say you've got a list of groups of items, like book sales sorted by author, and you want to get subtotals for the books sold for each author. You could insert rows and do some additions but it's quicker to use the Subtotals feature.

**1**   Select the data **and the headings** for the data you want subtotals for.

**2**   Choose Data > Subtotals. The Subtotals window will appear.

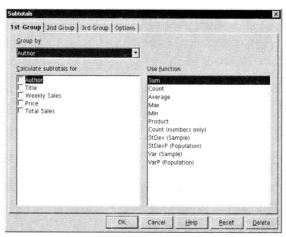

**3**    Select the items you want subtotals for.

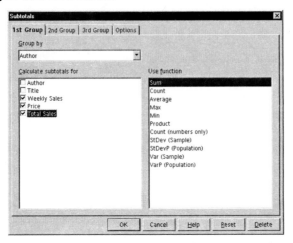

**4**    Click the Options tab and *unmark* the Pre-Sort Area According to Groups option. Unmarking this option means the data stays as it is and doesn't get rearranged.

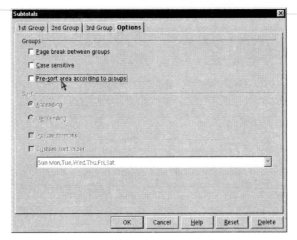

**5**   Click OK. You'll see the subtotals as shown, as well as the totals at the bottom.

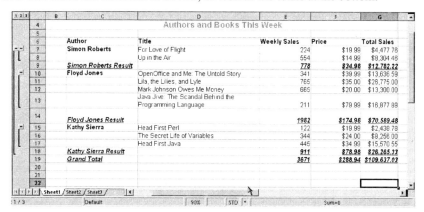

When you created subtotals, you got *groups* by default. Groups are marked by the + and – signs at the left side of the work area. Click the + and – signs at the left, as well as the 1, 2, and 3 at the top left. You can see the data and subtotals or only subtotals for each group.

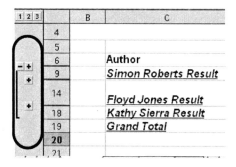

# Page Setup, Headers and Footers, and Printing

# Page Size, Margins, Headers and Footers

The main attributes you'll need to set for spreadsheets are the orientation (landscape or portrait), and putting titles and page numbers in headers and footers.

## Page Size, Margins, and Orientation

This works similarly to setting up pages in Writer, but with a few differences.

1    Open the spreadsheet and choose Format > Page.

2    The Page Style window will appear. Click on the Page tab if it's not already showing.

3    Here, you can specify page size, orientation, margins, and positioning of the cells within the paper.

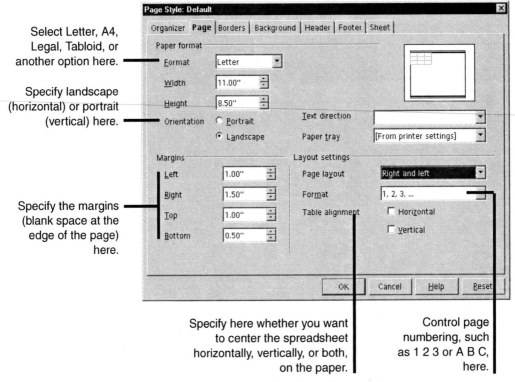

Select Letter, A4, Legal, Tabloid, or another option here.

Specify landscape (horizontal) or portrait (vertical) here.

Specify the margins (blank space at the edge of the page) here.

Specify here whether you want to center the spreadsheet horizontally, vertically, or both, on the paper.

Control page numbering, such as 1 2 3 or A B C, here.

4    Check the preview area in the upper left to see the effect of your choices.

5    Click OK.

## Adding Information to a Spreadsheet Header or Footer

1    Open the spreadsheet.

2    Choose Format > Page.

3    In the Page Style window, click the Header tab or the Footer tab.

4    Click the Edit button at the bottom.

**5**   The editing window will appear, showing what's currently in the header or footer.

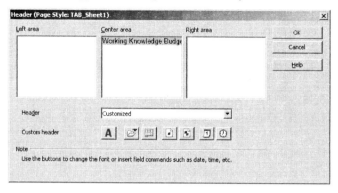

**6**   One of the quick ways to control what goes in the header or footer is to use the Header or Footer dropdown list. Click the list to see the options and select one.

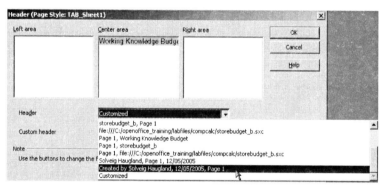

**7**   To add information to a specific area, click in the left, center, or right area, then click on an item in the dropdown list, or on one of the Custom Header icons.

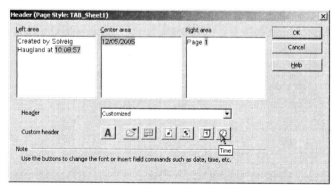

**8**   Click OK.

**9**   Click OK again in the page style window.

**10**  Choose File > Page Preview to see the effect of the settings.

## Page Styles

You can easily preserve the page formatting and headers and footers by saving them as page styles. Creating page styles works the same way as in Writer. See *Saving Enormous Time and Effort With Styles* on page 147.

# Printing to PDF

PDF "freezes" your document so that no one can change. And everyone can read the PDF format using the Adobe Reader program on virtually every computer in the world. This means you can create only OpenOffice.org documents and send a PDF version of them to people who don't have OpenOffice.org.

PDF is available for all components of OpenOffice.org, so I've put it in the first part of this book, with the other time-saving techniques. See *PDF, Publishing, and the Web* on page 51.

# Printing Spreadsheets

Here's how to print spreadsheets. If you need to do additional changes to get it to print exactly the way you want it, you can take advantage of the setup options in *Power Spreadsheet Printing Setup* on page 311.

## Printing the Whole Spreadsheet to the Default Printer

Click the Print icon at the top of the window. This will print one copy of the whole document straight to whatever printer is your default printer.

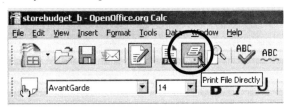

## Printing Basics

**1**    Choose File > Print.

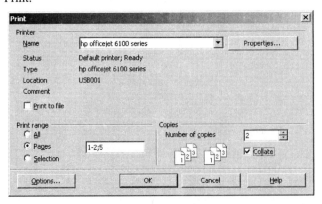

**2** Select the printer to print to.

**3** Enter the number of pages to print, and the number of copies.

**4** Click Options to set the options shown. You can also choose Tools > Options > OpenOffice.org Calc > Print to set these options for every document.

**5** Click OK.

# Using Page Preview to See How Documents Will Look Printed

Page Preview shows you how your document will look, including page breaks.

**1** Choose File > Page Preview.

**2** Click the page left and page right icons to scroll through the pages.

**3** You can see one page at a time.

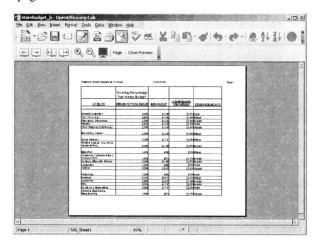

# Printing a Specific Range of Pages

When you choose File > Print, you can specify the range of pages in the print window. If you want to print pages 1-7, for instance, just type **1-7**. If you want to print 1-7 and 10-12, though, you need to put a *semicolon* between the nonconsecutive pages:
**1-7;10-12**.

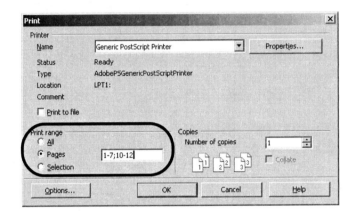

# Printing a Specific Sheet or Sheets

1    Press Ctrl and at the same time click on the tab for one of the sheets you want to print.

2    Click on the tab for another sheet. Release the Ctrl key.

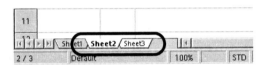

3    Choose File > Print.

4    In the print window, click Options.

5    In the Options window, choose to print only the current sheet.

6    Click OK.

7    Click OK in the print window to print the selected sheets.

# Printing Heading Rows or Columns on Multiple Pages

Typically, it's nice to have headings like these print on every page to help identify the data. If you don't do anything, though, they'll only print on the first page. Here's how to print additional rows, columns, or both on each page.

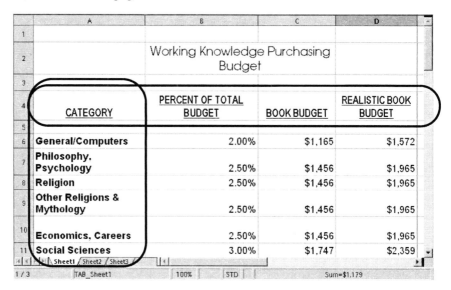

**1**    Choose Format > Print Ranges > Edit.

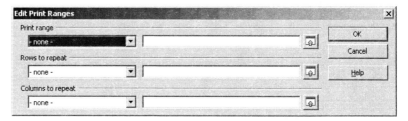

**2**    Click in the Rows to Repeat field.

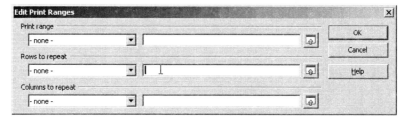

**3**    Click in the first cell of the row(s) to repeat.

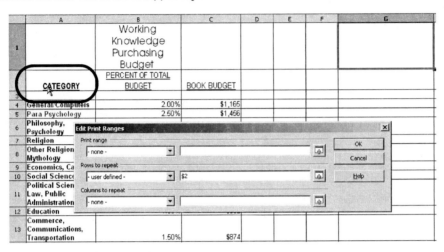

**4**    Click in the Columns to Repeat field.

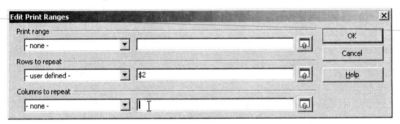

**5**    Click in the first cell of the column(s) to repeat.

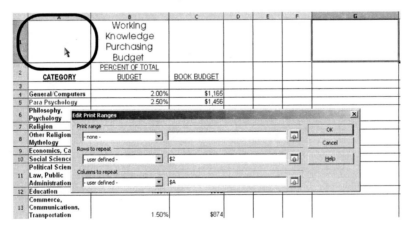

**6**   The window should look like this.

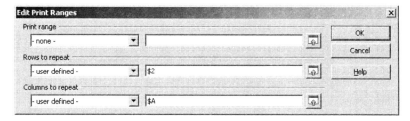

**7**   Click OK.

**8**   Choose File > Page Preview, and go to the second page. You'll see that the specified row and column are repeated.

## Printing Specific Cells

**1**   Select the cells to print.

**2**   Choose Format > Print Range > Define.

**3**   Select additional cells if you want to add print ranges and choose Format > Print Range > Define again.

**4**   The print range is set. Choose File > Print Preview to verify what will be printed. Note that print ranges on different pages will not be condensed and printed on the same page.

**5**   To remove it, choose Format > Print Range > Remove.

## Keeping Specific Cells From Printing

In a spreadsheet, select a cell and choose Format > Cells. Click the Cell Protection tab and select the Hide When Printing option. Click OK.

# Power Spreadsheet Printing Setup

Here's where you can exert extra control over exactly how many sheets of paper your spreadsheets print on, and more.

**1**   Choose Format > Page and click the Sheet tab.

**2**   Changing entries here will allow you to change printing direction; for instance, to print across all columns first, then to go back down to the left and start again.

**3**  You can change the number of pages the spreadsheet will be printed on, to squish it onto a few pages or make sure it's printed on enough to make it visible. Reduce the scaling from 100% to 90%, for instance, to get more on a sheet of paper.

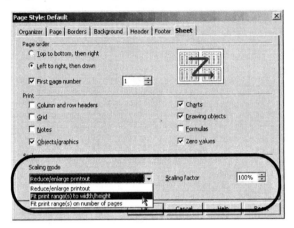

**4**  Click OK.

# Emailing Your Spreadsheet in One Step

This is related to printing, though of course not quite the same thing. You can email your spreadsheet to someone else in one step. See *Emailing Your Document in One Step* on page 229.

# Creating Charts in Writer and Calc

# How Charts Work

Here's a little overview of what charts are like.

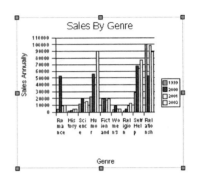

## Creating Charts Is Simple

Just select your data, choose Insert > Chart or Insert > Object > Chart, and follow the wizard. However, the reason it's simple is that you don't have much control over it. To control the chart, you modify it.

## To Modify a Chart, Click a Lot

If you're ever found, or read about, a secret bookcase behind a fireplace, you're going to have no problem with charts.

Opening the secret bookcase usually requires something like twisting the left candlestick twice, then pulling out the copy of War and Peace. Modifying a chart means clicking, then double-clicking to be able to modify certain aspects of the chart. To modify other aspects, you click again, and so on.

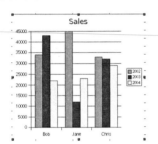 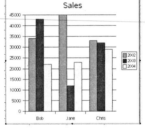 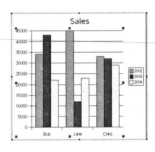

| Click the chart once | Double-click the chart | Click on a part to modify |
| --- | --- | --- |

# Chart Modification Tools

Once you've selected the thing to modify in the right way, there are are four places you can look for modification icons or tools.

**1. Format menu**      **2. Formatting toolbar**      **3. Right-click**

**4:** Just double-click on part of the chart.

## Charts Are Very Similar in Writer and Calc

You can create charts based on data in spreadsheets, and tables in Writer. It works the same way in each, except that in Writer you select the data and choose Insert > Object > Chart, and in Calc you choose Insert > Chart.

Also, in Writer charts you can't change the data range easily. Calc charts, however, behave very nicely, updating when necessary and allowing you to right-click on the chart and change the range of data covered by the chart.

## Always Have Data Headings, and Select Them When Creating the Chart

When you're charting, select the headings for the rows and columns. They like to be included, and the charting feature needs them to make all the axis titles and the legend.

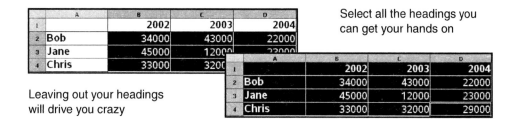

Select all the headings you can get your hands on

Leaving out your headings will drive you crazy

---

**Note** – At the time of writing, there was a new beta version of the upcoming replacement to this chart software. Go to the www.openoffice.org web site to download it.

---

# Creating a Chart

Creating a chart is pretty straightforward. The key things are to select your data along with the data headings, and in the wizard, mark all the options you could want.

**1**  Select the table, or the cells, that you want to chart. Be sure to select the headings as well as the data.

**1**  In Writer, choose Insert > Object > Chart. In Calc, choose Insert > Chart.

**2**  The first window in the chart Wizard will appear. The area you selected was automatically defaulted in as the data that you selected. Be sure that both First Row as Caption and First Column as Caption are marked.

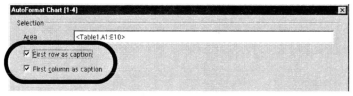

**3**  Click Next.

**4**  In the next window, select the Show Text in Preview option so you can see which data is on which axis.

**5**  Select the chart type you want.

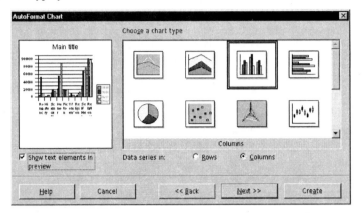

**6**  Click Next.

**7**  Select a variant on the chart, and add gridlines if you want.

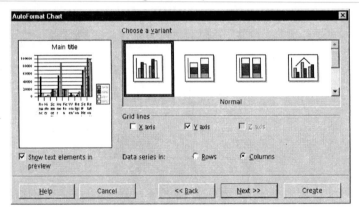

**8**  Click Next.

**9**   In this window, select the Title, X Axis, and Y Axis options, and name them.

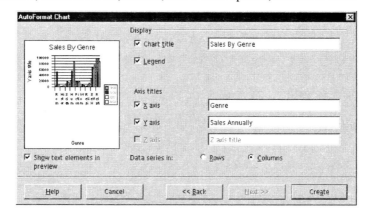

**10**   Click Create. The chart will appear in your document. Resize it if necessary by dragging the handles.

# Modifying a Chart

Creating a chart is very straightforward. Once you've got it created, though, you'll usually want to change it. Partly because that's just how life is, but partly because you just don't have a huge amount of control over the chart when you create it in the first place. The real design control comes when you modify it.

Let's say you want to control statistical aspects of your chart data, for instance, and you want just one of the bars of the bar chart to be bright red. That kind of thing needs to be done as a modification, after the chart is created.

## Chart Modification Principles

This is an overview but it's very important. If you don't read any of the other intro sections, please read this.

## Selecting the Part of the Chart You Want to Modify

It's all about clicking the right number of times on the right things. You usually have to click, then double-click, to do anything useful, and you can keep going if you want.

Here are the basics. Select it (**click once**) to be able to wrap text and modify the data range, **double-click** it to do basic stuff like changing the background color and axes, and **click again** on the central data part to modify the bar colors and other attributes. If you want to keep modifying the data part, **click on it again** to modify statistical attributes of the whole data range, then **click again** on a particular bar or portion of the chart to modify just that part—for instance, make to make a particular salesperson's sales bar bright red.

Here's the detail.

**1. Click on the chart once to select it.** The chart will look like this, with green handles. When you right-click on the chart you get the options in the context menu. Clicking on the Data Range modification option, for instance, gives you the window shown. (You get the Modify Data Range option in Calc, but not in Writer.)

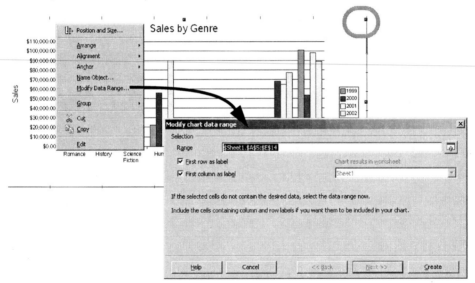

**2. Then double-click the chart.** At this point you start to be able to do useful modifications to the chart format. There's a gray border and the handles are black. When you choose the Axes > All Axes option, for instance, you get the Axes window.

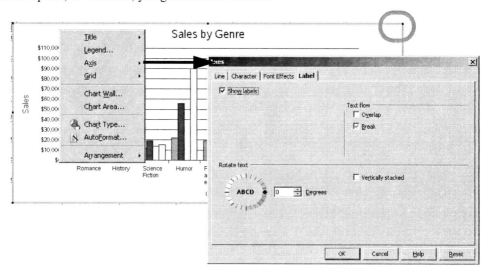

**3. To keep on modifying the data, click again once on the data part.** Green handles show up around the data area inside the main chart area. When you right-click on the data area and choose Object Properties, you get the shown Chart Wall option.

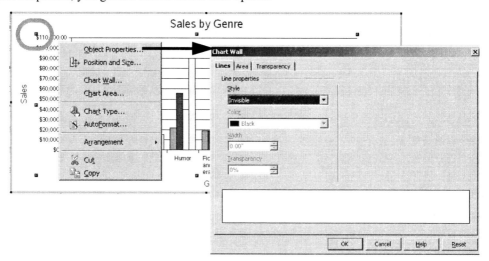

**4. To keep on modifying the data, click *again* once on the data part.** I'm showing a smaller part at this point to emphasize that it's the *data* portion of the chart that's involved. Blue handles appear on the selected area.

When you right-click on the data area and choose Object Properties, you get the shown Data Series window, with more options than previously. To change statistical aspects of the data, use the Statistics tab.

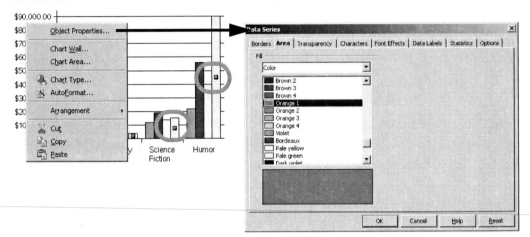

**5. And if you want to modify aspects of just one part of the chart, like one bar, click yet *again*, on that part.** You get green handles on the one part of the chart that you selected. When you right-click on the data area and choose Object Properties, you get the shown Data Series window, with more options than previously.

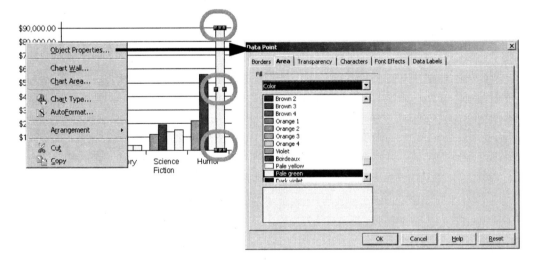

## Tools for Modifying Charts

Once you've clicked to get to the type of modification you want, here are your options for making that modification.

- ◆ **Toolbar:** When you double-click, the chart Formatting toolbar appears. Move your mouse over each one to see what it's for; a tooltip will appear.

- ◆ **Format menu:** Click on the Format menu to see another set of formatting options.

- ◆ **Right-clicking:** Right-click on the part of the chart you want to modify and you'll see options.

- ◆ **Double-clicking:** Double-click on the part of the chart you want to modify and you'll get a window related to that part.

# Chart Modification Procedures

Here are some steps for modifying specific aspects of the chart.

## Changing the Chart Type

Select the chart, then double-click it to get a gray border and black handles. Choose Format > Chart Type and select a different type and subtype. Click OK.

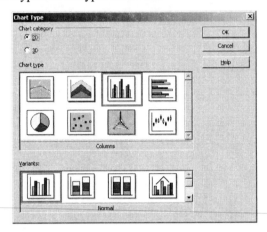

## Changing Data From Rows to Columns

Select the chart, then double-click it to get a gray border and black handles. The Formatting toolbar will appear (if it doesn't, choose View > Toolbars > Formatting). Click either the Data in Rows or Data in Columns icon.

## Modifying Chart Background and Other Basics

Select the chart, then double-click it to get a gray border and black handles. Right-click on the chart and choose the option you want.

◆ When you choose **Chart Area**, you get this window. The changes look like this.

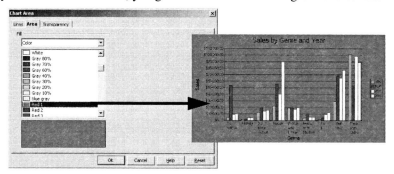

◆ When you choose **Chart Wall**, you get the same type of window, but the changes look like this.

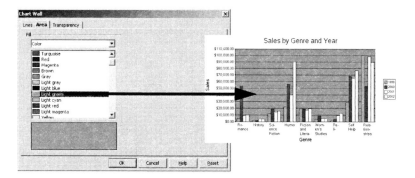

## Changing Chart Colors

You can change them one by one in *Modifying Specific Bars or Points* on page 327. The best approach, however, is to change the default values.

**1**   Choose Tools > Options > Charts > Default Colors.

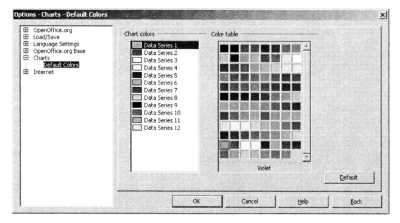

**2**    Select different colors for each series. The series just means the first chunk of data. If you have three pieces of data in your chart, like sales for Bob, Joan, and Sam, only the first three color series will be used.

**3**    Click OK. Existing charts won't be affected but new ones will be.

# Modifying Chart Text

Here's how to modify the text in the chart: titles, axes, and the legend.

## Showing or Hiding Any Text Element

Select the chart, then double-click it to get a gray border and black handles. The Formatting toolbar will appear. Click the appropriate icon of the first four: Title On/Off, Legend On/Off, Axes/Titles On/Off, or Show/Hide Axis Descriptions.

## Modifying the Chart Titles

Select the chart, then double-click it to get a gray border and black handles.

*    Changing the text – Double-click on the text you want to modify and type the new text in the text box that appears.

*    Changing the formatting – To modify the title formatting, select the chart, then double-click it to get a gray border and black handles. Choose Format > Title and choose which title to modify. In the window that appears, set the options, then click OK.

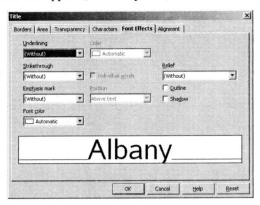

## Modifying the Text in the Chart Data Area

Here's how to modify the text in the chart, such as the names of the years or the formatting of the currency. Select the chart, then double-click to get a gray border and black handles.

♦   Changing the text – To change the text within the chart itself, change the text in the cell headings that the chart is based on. The chart will update automatically.

♦   Changing the formatting – To modify the axis title formatting, select the chart, then double-click it to get a gray border and black handles. Choose Format > Axis and choose to change the X or Y axis, or All Axes.

In the window that appears, set the options you want to change.

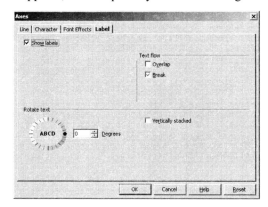

## Modifying the Legend

Select the chart, then double-click it to get a gray border and black handles.

♦   Changing the text – To change the legend text, change the text in the cells that the chart is based on. The chart will update automatically.

♦   Changing the formatting – To modify the legend formatting, select the chart, then double-click it to get a gray border and black handles. Choose Format > Legend or right-click on the legend and choose Legend.

In the window that appears, set the options you want to change.

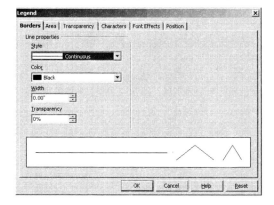

# Modifying Data

Here's how to modify how the data is represented in the chart.

## Modifying the Data in the Chart

Change the values in the cells that the chart is based on. The chart will update.

## Modifying the Chart Data Range in Calc

Click on the chart once to get the green handles. Right-click and choose Modify Data Range. In the window that appears, enter a different range and click Create.

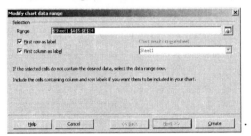

You can also simply select the new range of cells and drag it onto the chart.

## Modifying Statistics

Select the chart, then double-click it to get a gray border and black handles. Click on the data area again to get green handles around the data, then click a fourth time on the data area to get blue handles within the data.

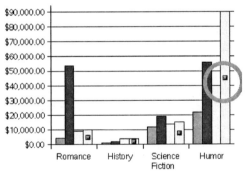

Right-click on part of the data area and choose Object Properties. Click on the Statistics tab, make your choices, and click OK.

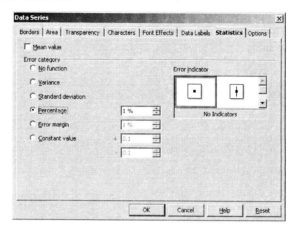

## Modifying Specific Bars or Points

**1**   Select the chart.

**2**   Double-click it to get a gray border and black handles.

**3**   Click on the data area again to get green handles around the data, then click a fourth time on the data area to get blue handles within the data.

**4**   Click a fifth time on the specific line, bar, or pie section to modify.

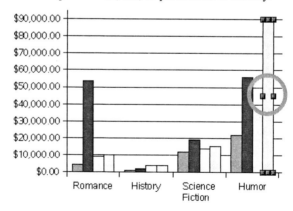

**5**   Right-click on part of the data area and choose Object Properties.

**6**   Make your choices, and click OK.

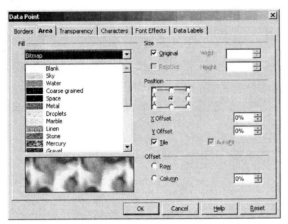

You'll see the changes applied only to the item you selected.

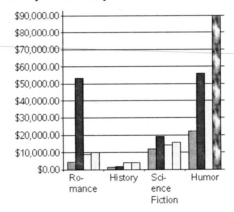

## Rotating Axis Text

**1**   Click the chart, then double-click it.

**2**   Choose Format > Axes and select the X Axis, Y Axis, or All Axes.

**3**   In the window that appears, click the Label tab.

**4**   In the Rotate Text field, type 45 or the rotation that you want. Mark Overlap and unmark the Break option.

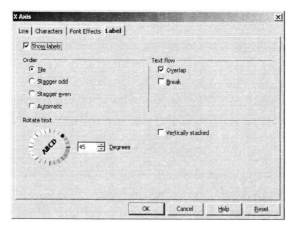

**5**   If you want to reduce the font size, click the Characters tab. Specify smaller font.

**6**   Click OK.

**7**   The text will be rotated.

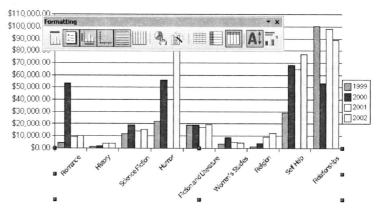

## Rotating the Y Axis Title to be Horizontal

**1**   Click the chart, then double-click it.

**2**   Choose Format > Axis > Y Axis, or right-click on the label for the Y axis and choose Title > Y Axis Title.

**3**   In the window that appears, click the Alignment tab.

**4** In the Text Direction field, change the number to 0

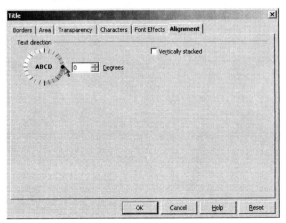

**5** Click OK.

**6** The Y axis title will be horizontal and easier to read.

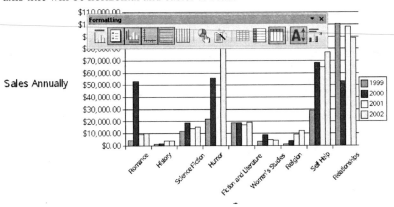

# Sorting and Filtering Data

# Sorting

You can sort data in your spreadsheets pretty much anyway you want: by one or more columns, ascending or descending, or even by specific sort orders you set up yourself.

## Quick Sort

**1**  Select all the data you want to sort. This will sort data only by the first column, but you need to select all the columns to be sure the data stays together correctly.

| B | C |
|---|---|
| Wagg | Kris |
| Haugen | Sylvia |
| Fishburn | Larry |
| Bates | Bert |

**2**  Click the A-Z or Z-A quicksort icon.

**3**  The data will be sorted.

| B | C |
|---|---|
| Bates | Bert |
| Fishburn | Larry |
| Haugen | Sylvia |
| Wagg | Kris |

# Sorting Using the Sort Window

Here's the best way to sort basic data. Let's say you've got a big list of names and you'd just like to see them in alphabetical order so it's easier to use.

**1** Select all the data you want to sort, ***including the headings***. This will make it easier to specify which columns to sort by. Select just the data to sort, not the whole sheet.

**2** Choose Data > Sort.

**3** In the Sort window, select the column to sort by, and whether you want to sort in Ascending (A to Z or 1 to 10) or Descending order.

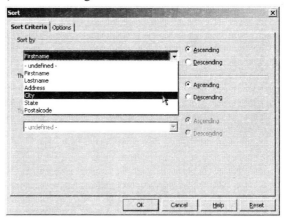

**4** Click the Options tab and mark the **Range Contains Column Labels** option.

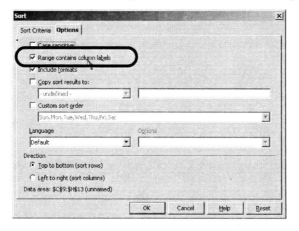

**5** Click OK.

## Sorting Left to Right

Sometimes the categories you want to sort by are on the vertical axis, in rows, as in this example. The sorting process is similar to the standard top-to-bottom approach; you just need to specify that you're sorting left to right instead of top to bottom.

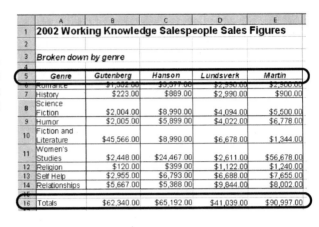

| | A | B | C | D | E |
|---|---|---|---|---|---|
| 1 | 2002 Working Knowledge Salespeople Sales Figures | | | | |
| 2 | | | | | |
| 3 | Broken down by genre | | | | |
| 4 | | | | | |
| 5 | Genre | Gutenberg | Hanson | Lundsverk | Martin |
| 6 | Romance | $1,302.00 | $3,577.00 | $2,990.00 | $2,300.00 |
| 7 | History | $223.00 | $889.00 | $2,990.00 | $900.00 |
| 8 | Science Fiction | $2,004.00 | $8,990.00 | $4,094.00 | $5,500.00 |
| 9 | Humor | $2,005.00 | $5,899.00 | $4,022.00 | $6,778.00 |
| 10 | Fiction and Literature | $45,566.00 | $8,990.00 | $6,678.00 | $1,344.00 |
| 11 | Women's Studies | $2,448.00 | $24,467.00 | $2,611.00 | $56,678.00 |
| 12 | Religion | $120.00 | $399.00 | $1,122.00 | $1,240.00 |
| 13 | Self Help | $2,955.00 | $6,793.00 | $6,688.00 | $7,655.00 |
| 14 | Relationships | $5,667.00 | $5,388.00 | $9,844.00 | $8,002.00 |
| 15 | | | | | |
| 16 | Totals | $62,340.00 | $65,192.00 | $41,039.00 | $90,997.00 |

1   Select the data you want to sort, including the headings.

2   Choose Data > Sort.

3   In the Sort window, click the Options tab.

4   Select the options shown: select Left to Right (Sort Columns) to specify left-to-right sorting, and also mark the Range Contains Row Headers option to indicate that the first column of data is headers, not data to be sorted.

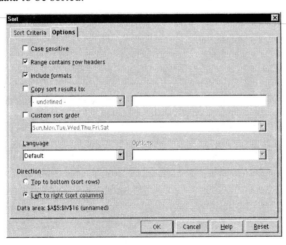

5   Click the Sort Criteria tab.

**6**   Select the normal sort options; the row to sort by and Ascending or Descending.

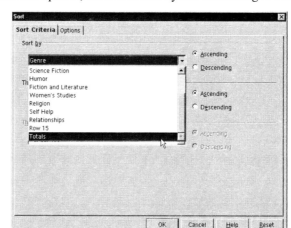

**7**   Click OK.

**8**   The data will be sorted from least to greatest (ascending) total sales.

| | A | B | C | D | E |
|---|---|---|---|---|---|
| 1 | 2002 Working Knowledge Salespeople Sales Figures | | | | |
| 2 | | | | | |
| 3 | Broken down by genre | | | | |
| 5 | Genre | Lundsverk | Gutenberg | Hanson | Martin |
| 6 | Romance | $2,990.00 | $1,352.00 | $3,377.00 | $2,900.00 |
| 7 | History | $2,990.00 | $223.00 | $889.00 | $900.00 |
| 8 | Science Fiction | $4,094.00 | $2,004.00 | $8,990.00 | $5,500.00 |
| 9 | Humor | $4,022.00 | $2,005.00 | $5,899.00 | $6,778.00 |
| 10 | Fiction and Literature | $6,678.00 | $45,566.00 | $8,990.00 | $1,344.00 |
| 11 | Women's Studies | $2,611.00 | $2,448.00 | $24,467.00 | $56,678.00 |
| 12 | Religion | $1,122.00 | $120.00 | $399.00 | $1,240.00 |
| 13 | Self Help | $6,688.00 | $2,955.00 | $6,793.00 | $7,655.00 |
| 14 | Relationships | $9,844.00 | $5,667.00 | $5,388.00 | $8,002.00 |
| 16 | Totals | $41,039.00 | $62,340.00 | $65,192.00 | $90,997.00 |

# Sorting Using Two or More Columns as Criteria

Sometimes you need to sort by two or more columns to get the data in the order you need. If you have, for instance, 5000 names of the people in your company, with three locations, you probably want to sort the employees first by location. However, then you have at least 1000 people at each location, in no particular order. To make the data easier to read, sort first by the location, and then by last name.

**1**   Select the data including headings.

**2**   Choose Data > Sort.

**3**    In the Sort Criteria tab, select to sort by up to three columns.

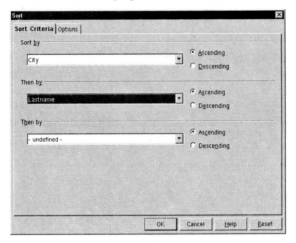

**4**    Click the Options tab and make sure the Range Contains Column Labels is marked.

**5**    Click OK. The data will appear sorted as you specified.

## Sorting Using Months and Weeks

You can sort alphabetically or by numbers but you can also sort based on other things that have a particular order like the days of the week or months.

**1**    Select the data including headings.

**2**    Choose Data > Sort.

**3**    Click the Options tab; you'll see the option to sort by other information.

**4**    Select the Custom Sort Order to use.

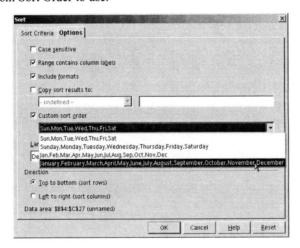

**5**    Select the Range Contains Column Labels option.

**6**    Click the Sort Criteria tab and choose to sort by the column containing data corresponding to the sort you chose in the other tab.

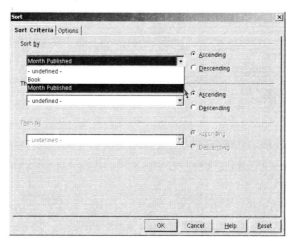

**7**    Click OK.

## Creating Your Own Sort Order

You can automatically sort by month or day of the week because OpenOffice.org comes with these custom sort orders already set up. You can set up similar sort orders that contain whatever you want. To create your own sort order, see *Quickly Entering Months, Days, or Anything You Want With Sort Lists* on page 277.

# Filtering

There are a couple ways to do filter out data so that you see only what you want: a quick simple autofilter that's often good enough as is, and the filter you can define the way you want.

## Using the AutoFilter

Here's what the autofilter looks like.

Let's say that you've got an enormous list of people in a spreadsheet, and you just want to see the ones from a particular town. That's a good example of when to use the autofilter. Autofilter lets you pick one value for a column, like "Boulder" for the City column, and view the rows in that spreadsheet with "Boulder" in the City column.

**1**   Choose Data > AutoFilter.

**2**   Dropdown arrows will appear at the top of each column. This means you can restrict what you see in the spreadsheet to rows with a particular value.

|   | A | B | C | D | E | F |
|---|---|---|---|---|---|---|
| 1 | Firstname | Lastname | Address | City | State | Postcode |
| 2 | Jane | Roberts | 101 1st Str | Fargo | ND | 56567 |
| 3 | Mark | Crowe | 90122 105th Avenue | Kalispell | MT | 59901 |
| 4 | Stan | Marston | 1058 W Ninth | Billings | MT | 57788 |
| 5 | Kathy | Hanson | 910 Harrison Dr | Portland | OR | 90033 |
| 6 | Bryan | Togerson | 78 West County Line Rd | Boulder | CO | 80302 |
| 7 | Simon | Johnson | 12 Main St | Fargo | ND | 56567 |
| 8 | Don | Barton | 445 Ludlow | Kalispell | MT | 59901 |
| 9 | Jeff | Bates | 366 W 7th | Billings | MT | 57788 |
| 10 | Jenna | Curlioner | 88 E 105th | Portland | OR | 90033 |
|  |  |  | 944 Madison |  |  |  |

**3**   Click and hold down the arrow and select a value.

**4**   The spreadsheet will filter out everyone except the rows with that value.

|   | A | B | C | D | E | F |
|---|---|---|---|---|---|---|
| 1 | Firstname | Lastname | Address | City | State | Postcode |
| 3 | Mark | Crowe | 90122 105th Avenue | Kalispell | MT | 59901 |
| 8 | Don | Barton | 445 Ludlow | Kalispell | MT | 59901 |
| 19 | Beth | Jerlin | 455 Reserve Drive | Kalispell | MT | 59901 |
| 27 | Michelle | Fortnum | 39 Working Way | Kalispell | MT | 59901 |
| 29 | Tracy | Falude | 1 Working Way | Kalispell | MT | 59901 |

**5**   To go back to showing all, click and hold down on the column's arrow (blue now) and choose All.

**6**   When you're done, choose Data > Filter > AutoFilter again to turn off the filter.

**Note –** If you leave an autofilter selection like just Kalispell within the State column, then make another selection in another column like Last Name or State, you'll see only records for items that meet **all** the criteria. This means you'll see far fewer records than you want, typically.

## Creating a Standard Filter

The autofilter works great for some situations, but sometimes you want something a little more complicated. With the autofilter you can just select one value for a column (or the top 10). What if you wanted to just show records for a value that is above a particular level; say, all the invoices for $100 or more? Or you need to view all the records for invoices you've submitted to Frye's, Best Buy, or Circuit City. You can't do that with the autofilter, so it's time to create your own filter.

Let's say you're still working with the same spreadsheet as before. You need to narrow down your spreadsheet to people who are from Boulder *or* from Kalispell, *and* who have been with the organization at least five years.

**1**   Select all the cells containing data, including the headings.

**2**   Choose Data > Filter > Standard Filter.

**3**   The Standard Filter window will appear.

**4**   Fill in the first row with your first criteria, listing the column, the operator (equal to, greater than, etc.), and the amount to compare values to.

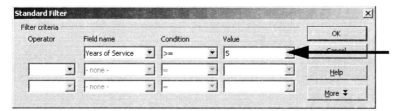

This condition says "Show me all the records for people who have five or mo years of service

**5**   Enter additional filters, if necessary. Select And or Or, depending on whether they are combined or independent.

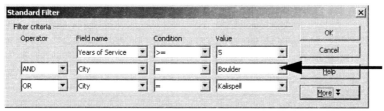

These condition now say "Show me all the peop who've been here five years or more, **and** who are from **either** Kalispell or Boulder."

**6**   Click OK. The data meeting the criteria will appear in your spreadsheet.

**7**   To remove the filter, choose Data > Filter > Remove Filter.

# Part IV: Impress Presentations

# Creating and Running Presentations

# Creating Presentations and Templates

Creating presentations is just like creating other files; you just get to choose the template in a window that pops up.

## Creating a Presentation

**1**    Start the program and choose OpenOffice.org Impress, or with OpenOffice.org already running, choose File > New > Presentation.

**2**    The Impress Wizard will appear.

**3**    What you do depends on whether you want it blank or based on a template.

♦    If you want it blank, just leave the selection as is.

♦    If you want to create it based on a template, select the From Template option. Select a category from the list, and then select the template.

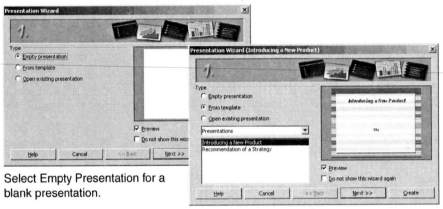

Select Empty Presentation for a blank presentation.

Or select From Template, select the correct category, then select a template.

**4**    You can continue through the wizard by clicking Next and applying transition options. However, it's simplest to apply those features later, so just click Create.

**5** The presentation will appear. How it looks depends on whether it's blank or based on a template, and on what template you chose.

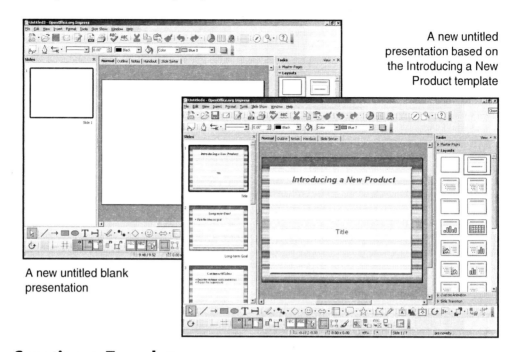

A new untitled presentation based on the Introducing a New Product template

A new untitled blank presentation

## Creating a Template

You'll save a lot of time and effort using templates; see *Creating a New Template* on page 41 for more information.  .

# Managing Slides

To do anything with slides, select the thumbnail for the slide on the left area of the work area. You can usually right-click to get several options.

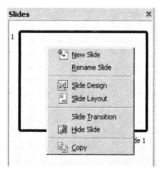

## Deleting a Slide

Select the slide thumbnail and press the Delete key on your keyboard.

## Creating a New Slide

You'll need more than one slide, of course, in your presentations. Find the Slides thumbnail section on the left side of the work area. Right-click below the existing slide and choose New Slide.

## Rearranging Slides

Drag the thumbnail for the slide down or up to where you want it.

## Renaming Slides

Right-click on the slide, choose Rename Slide, and type the name. Click OK.

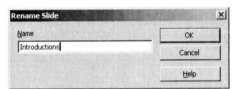

## Redocking the Slide Thumbnail Pane

The navigation pane at the left lets you view the thumbnails for each slide. You can view or hide it by choosing View > Slide Pane.

You can dock or undock the pane by dragging it to the middle of the work area.

I don't think undocking it, i.e. making it float rather than sitting at the left side, is very useful. If the pane accidentally comes undocked, here's how to redock it. This will depend on your version and operating system.

◆ Just drag the Slides Pane back to the left edge of the OpenOffice.org work area

◆ Hold down Ctrl and drag it back

◆ Hold down Ctrl, then double-click the gray area next to the word **Slides** in the slides pane. Not the top title bar Slides but the second time Slides appears

# Changing the Slide Layout

Slides can have different layouts, depending on what you want to put in them. You can have headings (or not), area for bullets (or not), graphics (or not), etc.

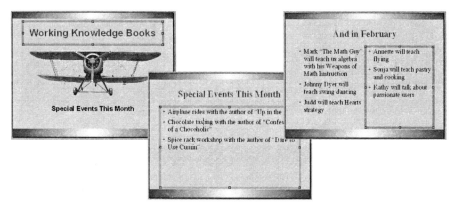

The slide layout is controlled by what you choose in the Layouts area of the window. You have a lot of choices, but the top few are the most useful.

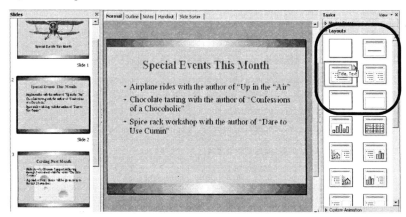

To specify a layout, select the thumbnail for a slide on the left side of the work area, click the Layouts heading on the right-hand side, and click the layout you want.

To apply a layout to all slides in your presentation, select all the slide thumbnails in the left side of the work area. Then right-click on the layout and choose Apply to Selected Slides.

# Templates

To create presentation templates, or create presentations based on templates, see *Saving Time With Templates and More* on page 37.

# Formatting Text and Bulleted Lists

This covers formatting, regardless of whether you're in normal editing form or the master page. See *Creating and Modifying Master Pages (Backgrounds)* on page 353.

## Standard Formatting for Text and Numbers

This works pretty much the way it does in Writer.

* Basic formatting – Use the lists on the formatting toolbar for font, colors, etc. See *Making Text Look How You Want It: Basic Formatting* on page 71

* Advanced formatting – Use the Character formatting window and other advanced windows for additional features; select text and choose Format > Character to open the window.

For paragraphs, select text and choose Format > Paragraph. See *Formatting Using the Paragraph and Character Windows* on page 78.

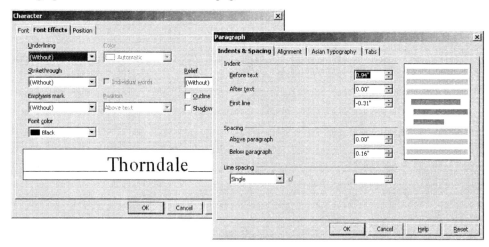

◆ Bullets and numbering – You don't have an advanced bulleting toolbar; the icons for indenting and promoting on the standard toolbar are fine.

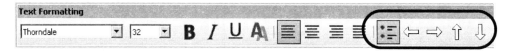

To do advanced formatting like choosing different bullets, choose Format > Bullets and Numbering. See *Creating and Formatting Lists* on page 119.

# Creating a Custom Presentation

Sometimes you need to give a presentation on the same topic to several different groups of people, but they don't need to get exactly the same information. You could create several different files, but it's more efficient to create custom versions of the same presentation file.

**1** Create all your slides, even the ones you only want to show to one of the audiences you're presenting to.

**2** Choose Slide Show > Custom Slide Show.

**3**    Click New. The Define Custom Slide Show window will appear.

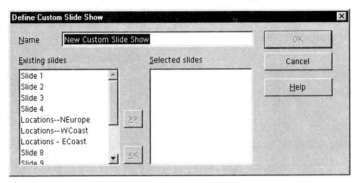

**4**    In the Name field, type the name for the first custom presentation.

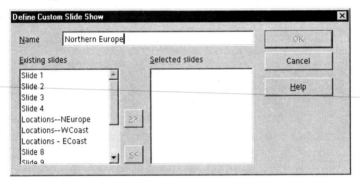

**5**    Select the slides in the left column that you want in the custom presentation, and click the arrow icon to insert them.

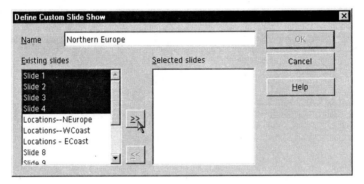

**6**    Click OK. The custom presentation is listed in the Custom Slide Shows window.

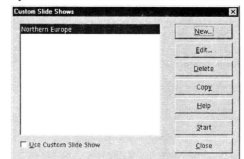

**7**    Click New again to create another version of the presentation, and add slides the same way. Click OK when you're done.

**8**    Choose Slide Show > Custom Slide Show again to display the Custom Slide Shows window. Select the custom presentation to show, select Use Custom Slide Show checkbox, and click Start.

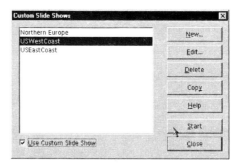

# Running a Presentation

Just open a presentation, then press F5. You can also choose Slide Show > Slide Show. Press your right and left arrows on your keyboard to move forward and backward in the presentation, or just click or press the space bar to move forward through the presentation.

Press Esc to stop running it at any time.

When you get to the last slide, you'll see a window like this. When you click, the presentation will stop running.

**Click to exit presentation...**

# Guide to Creating Good Presentations

Use these tips to create presentations that work for your audience as well as for you.

## Formatting Presentations

If your presentation looks good, and is easy to format and re-format, you're halfway to a great document.

## Keep the Bullets Short and the Font Legible

Remember the "1/25th rule", which states that the smallest font shall be no smaller than 1/25th the height of the screen. Far too many presentations are unreadable.

Impress doesn't have the Powerpoint feature that lets you automatically compress a bunch of text onto a slide by reducing the font. I think that's a good thing, since your text really shouldn't be in a smaller font than the default sizes in the Impress templates.

One way you can keep the font legible is to reduce the amount of text in each bullet. You're not presenting all the information in the slide—the bullets are points you will talk to. The content is in you, not the bullets, so feel free to type topics, not sentences.

## Use Master Pages for Formatting

One of the best things you can do for yourself is to set up presentations with the content and the formatting as separate as possible. Do this by using master pages as much as possible. When you need to change the formatting, you can simply change the master page, rather than the manual formatting in each slide. See *Creating and Modifying Master Pages (Backgrounds)* on page 353.

## Be Prepared

Your audience might be very interested in one of your topics, or not at all interested in some slides that you thought you would spend time on. Be sure to provide additional slides, just in case you finish quickly, or in case your audience wants more information on a particular topic.

## The Audience Wants Information, Not Fade From Left

Effects are fun. But unless they add value to the presentation, you don't need them. Which is not to say that your presentation shouldn't be entertaining: just use effective effects. Create great content, with lots of illustrations rather than a series of plain bullet points, engaging metaphors, and try not to burrow too far down into technical detail if it's not important to give people what they came for.

For an excellent guide to creating presentations that aren't all bullets and slide transitions, see Kathy Sierra's blog entry here:

http://headrush.typepad.com/creating_passionate_users/2005/06/kill_your_prese.html

## Use Custom Presentations for Multiple Audiences

Let's say you need to give three different presentations on the quarterly results to three different audiences, with some slides that are the same and some different. Do *custom presentations* with multiple versions of some slides, rather than entirely different documents, so that you can reuse the shared slides, and keep everything together. This will save you a lot of work, and preserve accuracy in your presentation. See *Creating a Custom Presentation* on page 349.

# 22

# Creating and Modifying Master Pages (Backgrounds)

# How Master Pages Work

Master pages affect nearly everything about your presentation except the content. The master page is like a template of styles for the slide it's applied to. It's a great, timesaving way to apply formatting to your presentation. You can have a different master page for every slide in your presentation, though you typically don't want to.

## Master Pages Mean You Don't Have to Format Each Slide

Here's a slide I created. Everything in it is part of the master page, except the content. All comes from the master page; I didn't do any formatting on this slide.

Background formatting: Two rectangles with a red gradient, and a gray page background color

Text formatting: Avant Garde title and Arial Narrow text, red diamond-shaped bullets

**Slide**                                                    **Corresponding master page**

Using master pages, without manual formatting, also means it's easier to change the whole presentation just by applying a new master page.

## Master Pages Are Different Than Slide Layouts

Here's a comparison of master pages versus slide layouts.

Master page                    Slide layout

- Master pages affect formatting and backgrounds
- Slide layouts affect the structure of the slide and what text and object components are in it. See *Changing the Slide Layout* on page 347.

## You Can Use Existing Master Pages, Create Your Own, or Import New Ones

Any presentation you create has a few master pages included by default. If those don't do it for you, you can create your own, or import master pages from an existing presentation or presentation template.

## Everything With Master Pages Is Easier When They're in Templates

Keeping your master pages around, and importing master pages, is simplest when you create a template of all the presentations you work with.

It's easy to do. Just open the presentation, choose File > Templates > Save, select a category, name the presentation, and click OK.

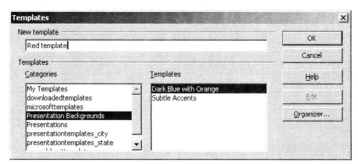

# Applying an Existing Master Page to a Slide

When you create a new presentation, there are a few built-in master pages ready for you to use. Here's how to apply one of those—or any other presentation you create or load.

### Applying a Master Page to the Whole Presentation

**1**   Click the Master Pages item at the far right.

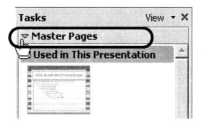

**2**   Click on a master page in the Available for Use section. The master page will be applied to **all the slides** in the presentation.

You can also right-click on the master page and choose Apply to All Slides.)

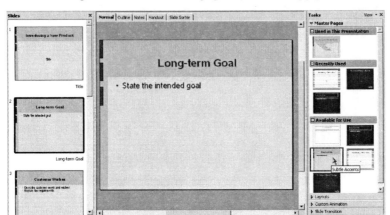

## Applying a Master Page to One or More Slides

In the left-hand pane, select the thumbnails of the slides you want to apply the master page to, then just make the appropriate selection in the right-hand pane.

**1**   To select two or more slides, click on the thumbnail for the first one, hold down Ctrl, click on the next one, and so on.

Long-term Goal

**2**   Click on the Master Pages item on the right side, and find the master page to apply.

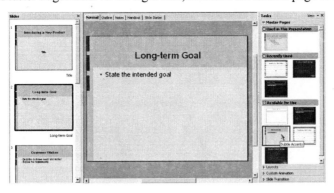

**3**    Right-click on the master page and choose Apply to Selected Slides.

**4**    The master page will be applied to the selected slide or slides.

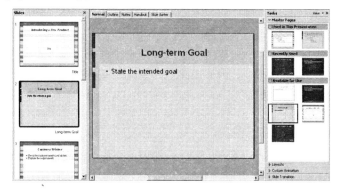

# Creating and Modifying Master Pages

You have the most control over formatting when you modify or create master pages.

## Important Note on Creating Master Pages

Once you create a master page, you need to do one of the following so you won't lose it:

◆    Keep it applied to at least one slide in the presentation. If you apply a different master page to the whole presentation, *your own master page will disappear.*

◆    Make the presentation into a template; the master pages of all your templates are available for use in a new presentation. See *Creating a New Template* on page 41.

## Modifying a Master Page

1    Select a slide that has the master page you want to modify. If there isn't a slide with that master page applied, select a slide in the left pane, then right-click on a master page in the right pane and choose Apply to Selected Slides.

2    Choose View > Master > Slide Master. The master view will be displayed.

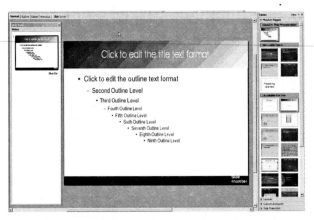

3    Reformat the master page any way you want.

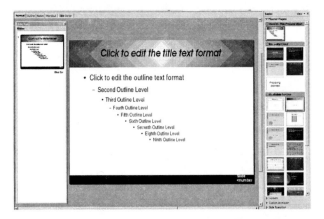

- Choose Format > Page and click on the Background tab to apply a color, gradient, or bitmap to the background.

- Insert a graphic to use as the background. Choose Insert > Picture > From File and select a file. Then right-click on the graphic and choose Arrange > Send to Back. Resize and reposition the graphic as necessary. To make the graphic lighter or grayscale, see *Applying Grayscale, Black/White, or Watermark Effects* on page 430.

- Format the color and font for all the text boxes in the slide. Use the dropdown lists at the top of the work area, or choose Format > Character.

- Format the bullets by choosing Format > Bullets and Numbering. To apply the same bullet to all levels, just use the Graphics or Bullets tab. Click the Customize tab to apply the bullets you want to each level.

- Use any of the drawing tools (View > Toolbars > Drawing) to draw items you want in every slide, such as a narrow bar at the left, or top and bottom.

- Double-click any of the footer placeholders and substitute other content. Choose Insert > Fields > Page Number or Insert > Fields > Date, or see *Adding Footer Information to a Presentation in Standard, Notes, or Handouts View* on page 364. See also *Adding Footer Information to a Presentation in Standard, Notes, or Handouts View* on page 364.

**4**   Choose View > Normal. The slide where the master page was applied, and any new slides you apply it to, will have the new formatting.

# Creating a Master Page

Master pages are somewhat twitchy when you start creating them. Here are a couple tips.

- Only create one new master page per presentation file. To make a second master page, just create another new blank presentation, follow these steps again, including making it into a template. Any master page in a presentation you make into a template is available anytime you create or format a presentation, so you don't need to have all master pages in the same template. If you do want to load multiple master pages into the same presentation, see *Importing and Applying a Master Page From Another Presentation* on page 361.

♦ Sometimes the formatting dropdown lists will become dimmed and unavailable when you're formatting a master page. As an alternative, just use the windows available under the Format menu: Format > Character, Format > Bullets and Numbering, etc.

Follow these steps to create a new master page.

**1**   Create a new presentation.

**2**   Choose View > Master > Slide Master.

**3**   Right-click in the left-hand slide pane and choose New Master.

**4**   Format the new master page any way you want. add objects, format text and bullets, and change any other aspects of the master page.

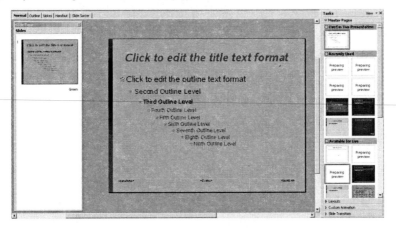

♦ Choose Format > Page and click on the Background tab to apply a color, gradient, or bitmap to the background.

♦ Insert a graphic to use as the background. Choose Insert > Picture > From File and select a file. Then right-click on the graphic and choose Arrange > Send to Back. Resize and reposition the graphic as necessary. To make the graphic lighter or grayscale, see *Applying Grayscale, Black/White, or Watermark Effects* on page 430.

♦ Format the color and font for all the text boxes in the slide. Use the dropdown lists at the top of the work area, or choose Format > Character.

♦ Format the bullets by choosing Format > Bullets and Numbering. To apply the same bullet to all levels, just use the Graphics or Bullets tab. Click the Customize tab to apply the bullets you want to each level.

♦ Use any of the drawing tools (View > Toolbars > Drawing) to draw items you want in every slide, such as a narrow bar at the left, or top and bottom.

♦ Double-click any of the footer placeholders and substitute other content. Choose Insert > Fields > Page Number or Insert > Fields > Date, or see *Adding Footer Information to a Presentation in Standard, Notes, or Handouts View* on page 364. See also *Adding Footer Information to a Presentation in Standard, Notes, or Handouts View* on page 364.

**5**   Choose File > Templates > Save.

**6**   In the window that appears, select a category, type a name for the master page, and click OK.

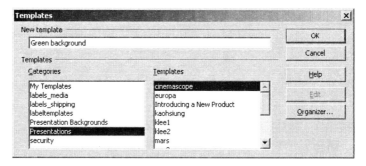

**7**   Choose View > Normal to go back to standard mode.

**8**   Your master page will be available in the presentation where you created it, as well as in all new presentations. The page might not be displayed immediately, but it will be available immediately in the presentation creation wizard in the category you selected, and in the Available for Use section of any presentation, soon (either immediately or after a restart).

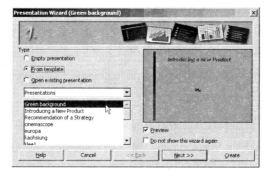

**9**   To create another master page, repeat these steps.

# Importing and Applying a Master Page From Another Presentation

Let's say you've been told to use the master page from another presentation on the presentation you've already started. Here's how.

**1**   Open the source presentation containing the master page you want to use, and make it into a template. See *Creating a New Template* on page 41.

**2**   Open the presentation that you want to import that master page *into*.

**3**   Choose Format > Slide Design.

**4**    The Slide Design window will appear

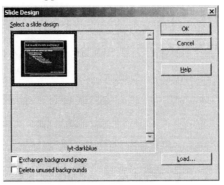

**5**    Click Load. The Load Slide Design window will appear.

**6**    In the My Templates category, select the name you gave to the source presentation when you made it into a template in the first step. Select the Preview checkbox to see the template.

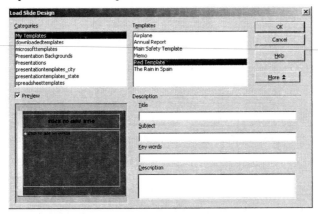

**7**    Click OK. The source presentation's background appears in the Slide Design window. Leave the checkboxes *unmarked* if you want to *add* the new background but not remove others.

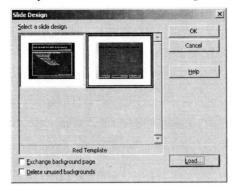

**8**    Click OK.

**9** Your document should look like this, with the imported master page applied to the selected slide.

**10** Click the Master Pages item at the right side of the work area, if master pages aren't displayed. You'll see the imported master page listed.

**11** If you wanted to apply the new master page to all other pages, you could right-click on the master page and choose Apply to All Slides.

# Adding Footer Information to a Presentation in Standard, Notes, or Handouts View

You can add information like dates, page numbers, plain text, and so on, to presentations in multiple ways.

## Using Text Boxes and Fields

You can go to the  Notes View or Handouts View, and simply use the text box tool to add whatever content you want. Choose View > Master > Slide Master for normal view; choose View > Master > Notes Master or for the handouts view; or simply put the text straight into the normal view. For more information about using text boxes and inserting fields, see *Adding Page Numbers and Text to Handouts* on page 370.

## Using the Header and Footer Window

You can apply many pieces of information all at once using this window. This approach uses the pre-existing footer boxes already available in Handouts and Normal view.

**1**     Choose Insert > Page Number or Insert > Date.

**2**     The Header and Footer window will appear. Select the options you want.

Select Date and Time, then type the date to insert, or choose to insert the current date that will update.

Select Footer and type content to add any text to the footer.

Select Slide Number to add the slide number to each slide.

Select this option to skip the content on the first slide.

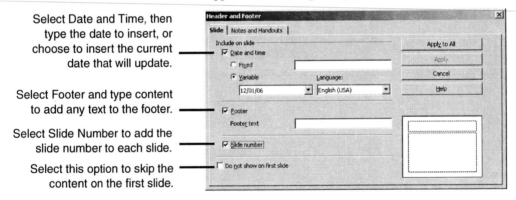

**3**     Click the Notes and Handouts tab and set the appropriate options.

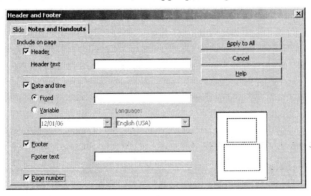

**4**   Click Apply, to apply to the current slide, or Apply to All to apply to the whole presentation.

**5**   The presentation will look like this. Edit the position and formatting by choosing View > Master > Slide Master or View > Master > Notes Master.

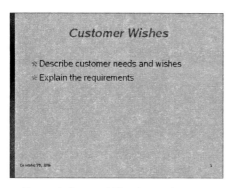

Normal view and Handouts view

Notes view

# 23

# Using Handouts, Outline, and the Slide Sorter

## About the Impress Views

The normal drawing view for presentations is fine enough. But if you want to look at several slides at once; if you want to focus on the text, or perhaps make notes on each slide, you need another way to look at your content.

Luckily, there are other views so that you can easily do all those things. Here are the different views you can use. I'll talk throughout the chapter about how each is particularly useful.

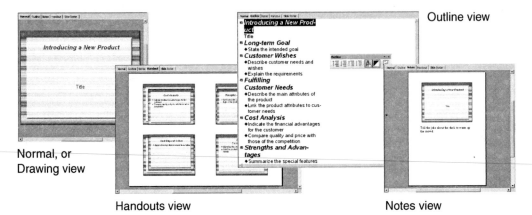

Outline view

Normal, or Drawing view

Handouts view

Notes view

# Creating and Printing Handouts

Handouts are nice for, well, handing out. They let you give out a guide to your presentation, without wasting paper by printing a slide on each page, and with a place for notes.

---

**Note** – Creating a presentation with lines for note taking is a bit of a pain, since this isn't provided with OpenOffice.org. However, there's a template in the Book Resources section on my blog, and you can easily copy and paste the lines from that template.

---

## Creating Handouts

**1**    Open the presentation and click the Handouts tab.

**2**   You'll see the Handouts layout.

**3**   To switch from landscape to portrait orientation, choose Format > Page and click the correct option. Then click OK.

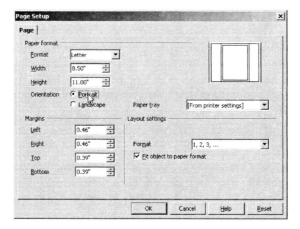

**4**   If you want to change the number of slides in the handouts, select a different layout.

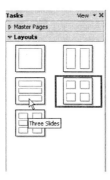

**5**  If the layout looks a little odd with slides overlapping, you can click on a different number of handouts, like 1 or 2, then click back on the number of handouts you want per page.

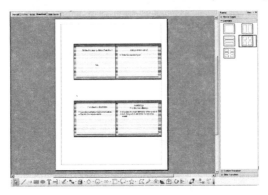

**6**  You can't resize the slides but you can reposition them. Drag the slides to the new location.

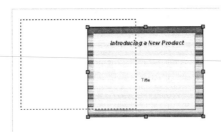

**7**  That's all you need to do. To print, see *Printing Handouts* on page 375. To add lines next to each, see *Creating Handouts With Lines for Notes* on page 371.

## Adding Page Numbers and Text to Handouts

To add a page number or other text to appear on every page, just use the text box and insert a page number or other fields. See also *Adding Footer Information to a Presentation in Standard, Notes, or Handouts View* on page 364.

**1**  Make sure you're in Handouts view.

**2**  Be sure you can see the Drawing toolbar; if you don't see it, choose View > Toolbars > Drawing.

**3**  Click the Text icon.

**4** Draw a text box at the bottom of the work area. If you want type the word **Page**.

**5** To insert the page number, click in the box and choose Insert > Fields > Page Number.

**6** Select the contents of the text box and format them with the dropdown lists in the Text Formatting toolbar. If you don't see it, choose View > Toolbars > Text Formatting.

**7** Move the text box so that it's inside the page margins. If you need to make the margins bigger or smaller, choose Format > Page and click the Page tab.

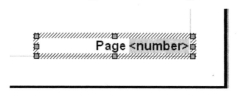

**8** Add any additional content you want to repeat on each page.

- ◆ To add other content such as the author, title, date, etc., just repeat these steps and insert the Author, Title, or Date field by choosing Insert > Fields.

- ◆ To add other text, just use the text box icon and type the content you want.
  To add a graphic such as a logo on each page, choose Insert > Picture > From File.

- ◆ To add a drawing object like a rectangle or oval, draw the item using the appropriate shape on the toolbar.

## Creating Handouts With Lines for Notes

In other office suites you can typically choose a layout with three slides down the left side and lines for writing notes by them, like this. In OpenOffice.org, you need to create the lines yourself, or copy them from another presentation or template.

**1** Open the presentation and click the Handouts tab0.

**2**   The presentation's Handouts view will appear.

**3**   It'll be better for note-takers if the handouts are in vertical (portrait) format. Choose Format >
Page, select Portrait, and click OK.

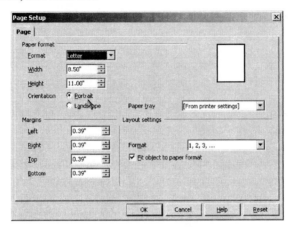

**4**   In the layout setup window, select the three-to-a-page layout. You can select another layout
but three is usually all that will fit if you want lines to fit on the page, as well.

**5**   The slides now should look something like this.

**6**    Drag the slides so that they're in one row down the left side, evenly spaced.

**7**    At this point, create the lines according to the method of your choice:

- *Inserting a Graphic of the Lines*
- *Copying From a Template*
- *Creating Your Own Lines*

## Inserting a Graphic of the Lines

Here's the easiest possible approach. Go to the download site for this book, on my blog at http:// openoffice.blogs.com, find the **Book Resources** link, and in the Templates section download the lines graphic. Click the Handouts tab to find the Handouts view.

Next, choose Insert > Picture > From File and find lines.jpg. Then just position the graphic. Resize the proportions as necessary by dragging the handles up or over.

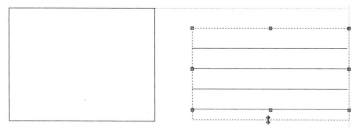

## Copying From a Template

Go to the download site for this book, on my blog at http://openoffice.blogs.com, look for the **Book Resources** link, and download the Impress handouts lines template from the web site.

Open it, and click the Handouts tab to find the Handout view. Copy the lines from the presentation.

Then just go to your own presentation, and paste the lines into the presentation.

## Creating Your Own Lines

**1**  Click on the line icon in the toolbar at the bottom of the work area.

**2**  Draw a line near the top of the slide, to the right.

**3**  Now, you just need to create additional lines, more evenly spaced. You can do this a couple different ways; I recommend using the Duplicate feature.

Select the line and choose Edit > Duplicate. In the Duplicate window, specify the lines to duplicated. Try 3 or 4 lines, .50 of an inch for the Y axis (since you want each line to appear vertically), and Black for the colors. Click OK.

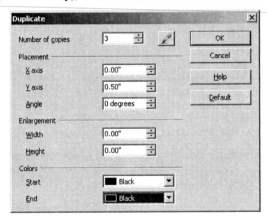

**4**  The lines will appear.

**5**   Repeat the previous steps to create lines for the other two slides.

**6**   Save changes.

---

**Note** – In other presentations, you might find the slides in the three-up layout are on the small side and not big enough to match the lines. In this case, you can do one of two things, since you can't change the size of the slides manually. Delete the extra line for each slide, or delete the lines, change the slide format back to two-up, change it three-up again, drag the slides to the left side of the page again, and paste the lines again.

---

## Printing Handouts

**1**   Choose File > Print.

**2**   In the Print window, click the Options button.

**3**   Select the Handouts checkbox only.

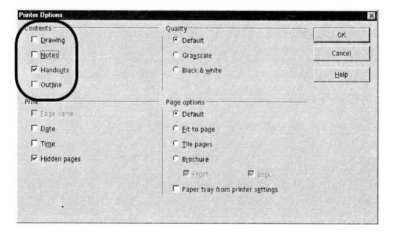

**4**   Click OK.

**5**   Select the correct printer.

**6**   Click Print.

# Using Notes View

Notes view is for speakers and lets you put in notes on things you should say when showing a particular slide.

**1**   Click the Notes tab at the top of the work area.

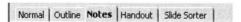

**2**  Type the notes you want in the text area at the bottom of each slide.

**3**  Select the text and format it, if you want, using the Text Formatting toolbar. If you don't see it, choose View > Toolbars > Text Formatting.

To print notes, see *Printing the Handouts, Outline, or Notes View* on page 394.

To add page numbers and other footer or header content, go into the master view by choosing View > Master > Notes Master. Then see *Adding Page Numbers and Text to Handouts* on page 370 and apply the same principles using text boxes and other elements.

To add page numbers and other content using the Header and Footer window, see *Adding Footer Information to a Presentation in Standard, Notes, or Handouts View* on page 364.

# Using Outline View

Once you have a presentation created, or if you're taking over someone else's project, you'll need to take a look at the presentation from a broader point of view. The Outline view helps a lot with this; I really like it.

## Using Outline View for Text Editing

**1**  Switch to the Outline View by clicking on the Outline tab.

**2**   The presentation will appear in outline view.

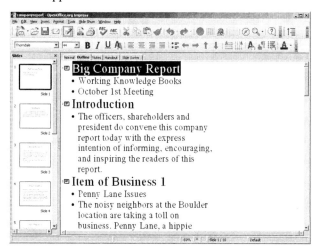

**3**   The Outline toolbar might be a little scrunched, so find it in the upper area of the work area.

Click and hold down on the dotted line at its left and drag it into the work area.

**4**   To take a look at only headings (titles of each heading) click the First Level icon.

The subpoints will all disappear and the titles only will be displayed.

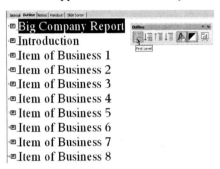

5   To change how big the display is, double-click the view percentage field at the bottom of the work area.

In the Zoom window, type 33% and click OK.

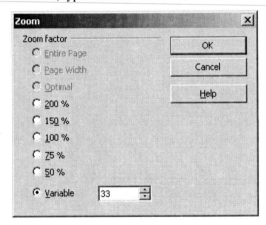

# Creating and Combining Slides Using Outline View

You can use the Promote and Demote icons to make any line of text a heading, a first-level bullet, a second-level bullet, and so on.

1   Switch to the Outline View by clicking on the Outline tab.

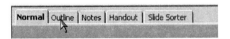

**2**   Click the Demote or Promote icon in the toolbar at the top as necessary. In this illustration, the items on the left were promoted or demoted to make a new slide, and to turn a couple of slides into bulleted items.

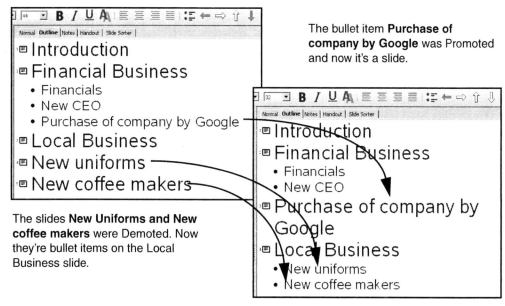

The bullet item **Purchase of company by Google** was Promoted and now it's a slide.

The slides **New Uniforms and New coffee makers** were Demoted. Now they're bullet items on the Local Business slide.

To print outline view, see *Printing the Handouts, Outline, or Notes View* on page 394.

# Using the Slide Sorter View

The Slide Sorter view lets you view all the slides in the presentation more easily.

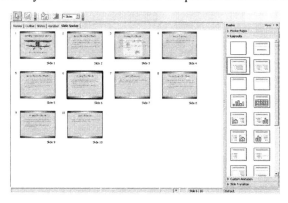

## Hiding Slides

It's convenient to be able to hide a slide that you don't want everyone to see. You can also hide the slide without deleting it, which saves time in case you need to get the slide back later.

**1**   Click the Slide Sorter tab at the top of the work area.

**2**   Right-click on the slide and choose Hide Slide. The hidden slide will look like the slide on the right.

## Applying Slide Transitions

You can apply a slide transition to one or more of the slides using Slide Sorter view.

**1**   Click the Slide Sorter tab at the top of the work area.

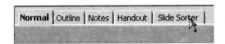

**2**   Select the slides, right-click and choose Slide Transition. Then follow the instructions in *Applying Slide Transitions* on page 389.

## Specifying the Number of Slides Displayed

**1**   Click the Slide Sorter tab at the top of the work area.

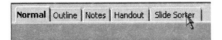

**2**   Find the small box at the top and click the arrow to change the number of slides shown in a row.

## Rearranging Slides

**1**   Click the Slide Sorter tab at the top of the work area.

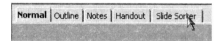

**2**   Click on the slide you want to move and drag it to where you want it. A thick bar shows where the slide will be moved to when you release the mouse.

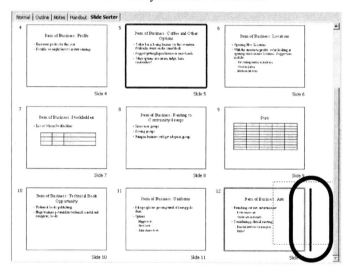

**3**   Release the mouse.

# 24

# Object Animation, Slide Transitions, and Interaction

# Applying Custom Animation to Objects and Text

You have a variety of options for applying objects to effects. Here's how to get started with a basic object.

## Applying an Effect to an Object

1    Click on the object you want to apply the effect to.

2    Click on the arrow by the **Custom Animation** label at the right side.

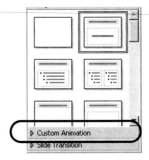

3    You'll see the animation tab with all the options.

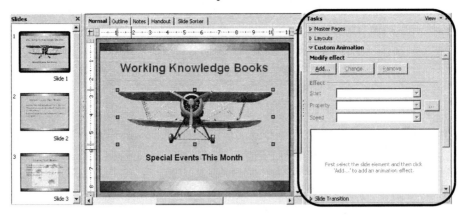

**4**    Click Add. The Custom Animation window will appear.

**5**    Select the effect you want.

**6**    The Automatic Preview option is marked by default so you'll see the effect run.

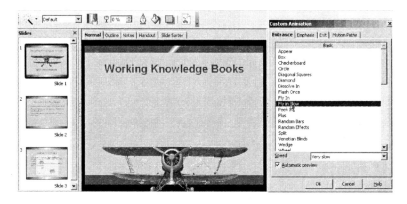

**7**    Select a different speed, if you need to.

**8**    Click OK.

**9** The Custom Animation definition area will look like this. If the effect is still not what you want, you can right-click on the effect and choose Effect Options to modify it; click the browse icon (circled) to modify it; or change the selections in the dropdown lists shown.

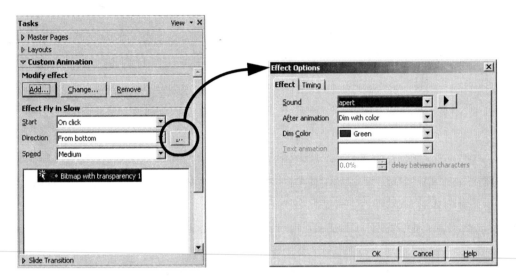

**Note** – When you run the presentation, you need to click or press the arrow key once to make the *slide* appear, then click to run the *effect*.

## Applying an Effect to Bulleted Items

You can apply effects to text as well as object. One note: the default effect is to run the effect on all the bulleted items on a slide at once, rather than one by one. You usually need to change that yourself.

**1** Click somewhere in one of the bulleted items.

**2** Click on the arrow by the **Custom Animation** label at the right side of the work area, if the effects aren't already displayed.

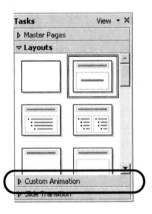

**3**    In the custom animation area, click Add.

**4**    In the effects list, scroll to something you like and select it.

**5**    You'll see the effect run.

**6**    Click OK.

**7**    To apply additional changes, select the effect in the custom animation area and click the effect options browse icon. (You can also right-click on the effect and choose Effect Options.)

**8**    In the Effect Options window, click on the Text Animation tab. From the Group Text list, select By First Level Paragraphs. This is the option that makes each paragraph (each bulleted item) appear separately.

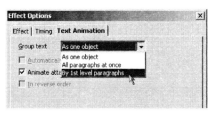

**9**    Click OK.

# Applying a Sound to an Item With an Effect

**1**   Click on an object.

**2**   Click on the Custom Animation item.

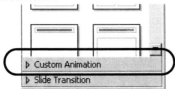

**3**   Apply the effect you want. (Click Add and select an effect, then click OK.)

**4**   The effect will be displayed in the list. Click the small icon with three dots.

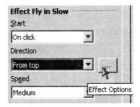

**5**   The Effect Options window will appear.

**6**   Click in the Sound list and select a sound.

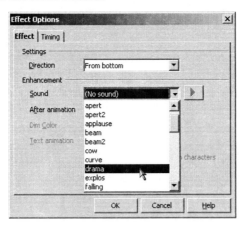

**7**   Click OK.

# Applying Slide Transitions

Slide transitions run an effect when you first display the slide.

**1**    Select the thumbnail for the slide, in the left pane.

**2**    Click the Slide Transitions item on the right side of the work area.

**3**    Select an effect from the list.

To apply an effect to all slides, click the Apply to All Slides icon.

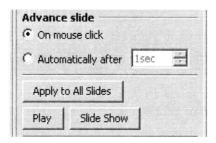

**4**    Automatic Preview is marked so you'll see the effect run.

**5**    Select a different speed for the effect from the speed list, if necessary.

# Playing Movies and Sounds

Running a movie or sound file along with a presentation isn't, quite yet, all it could be in OpenOffice.org. Your operating system will control the movies you can play, and those are limited on Linux. Movies play reasonably well on Windows; here's how you do it.

**1**    Go to the slide and choose Insert > Movie and Sound.

**2**    In the dialog box that appears, find the movie file.

**3**    The movie will appear in a black box in the screen. The movie shows up pretty small; you might be tempted to resize it but, at least in my experience, this makes the whole program crash. Leave the movie size as is.

**4**    When you run the presentation, the movie or sound will start as soon as you go to the slide. Here's what they look like; the sound placeholder is a black box, and the default size for the movie is as shown. Note that, as with objects and graphics in general, there is no wrapping so you might want to use a two-column or no-text layout for movies and sounds.

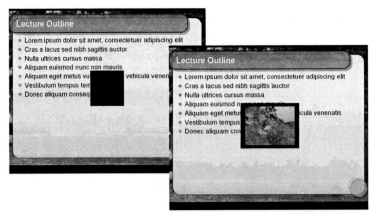

# Additional Effects: Interaction

Interaction is kind of like applying different kinds of hyperlinks to objects in your presentation. It's different than the standard object effects, which are pretty much just for show. Interaction lets you do things like go to a specific page, play a sound, open a file, or run a program, when you click on a particular object. They're fairly useful; I use Interaction for the quiz program I run as part of my training classes so that I can click on an object and go to the answer for a particular question.

**1**  Open your presentation and go to the slide where you want the interaction.

**2**  Create or insert an object of some sort to apply the interaction to. If you want to simply have a button that you click to run the effect, then draw a rectangle or similar object in the slide.

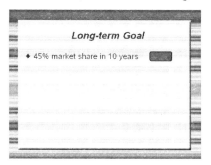

**3**  Right-click on the object and choose Interaction.

**4**    In the window that appears, click on the dropdown list and select the type of action.

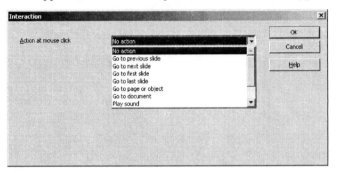

**5**    Depending on what you select, different options will appear. Here's what going to a particular
        slide, and going to a text document, look like. The Target area in the lower right window
        should allow you to go to a specific heading or other element within the document, but that
        isn't currently working. However, it works well enough to simply open any document when
        you click on the object.

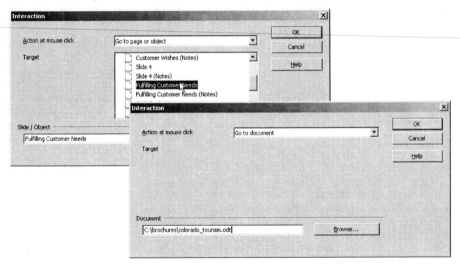

**6**    Click OK to apply the interaction.

When you move your mouse over the object, you'll be able to see what the interaction is. Note that
this runs regardless of whether you're in play mode or not, so don't click on it unless you want to
run the effect.

To remove the interaction, draw a box around the object to select it. Then right-click, choose
Interaction, and in the Interaction window select No Action. Click OK.

# Printing
# Presentations

# Printing Presentations

Printing is reasonably simple; you can also export to PDF and other formats. See *Exporting Presentations* on page 395.

## Printing Presentations

**1**   Choose File > Print.

**2**   Select the correct printer.

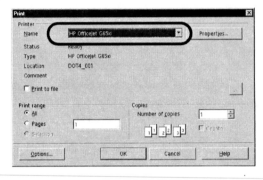

**3**   Click Print.

## Printing the Handouts, Outline, or Notes View

When you print, you normally get one slide on each piece of paper—the Drawing, or Normal, view. You can also print your handouts (handouts view), the text only (outline view), or presenter notes (notes view). These are the views.

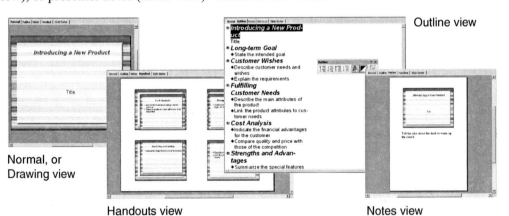

Normal, or
Drawing view

Outline view

Handouts view

Notes view

**1**  Choose File > Print. Click the Options button to see the Print Options window.

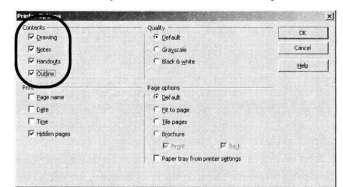

**2**  Select the versions of the presentation you want to print. You don't have to choose just one; you can print all versions at the same time.

**3**  Click OK and print as usual.

# Exporting Presentations

There isn't a standalone presentation player for Impress, but you can export the presentation to HTML or Flash, and then show the presentation in a browser or Flash. Here's how to export a presentation to either of those formats.

## Exporting a Presentation to PDF

Printing to PDF, Adobe's portable document format, is one of the very nice additions in OpenOffice.org. PDF "freezes" your document so that no one can change it, and everyone can read the PDF format using the Adobe Reader program on virtually every computer.

This means you can create only OpenOffice.org documents, and send a PDF version of them to people who don't have OpenOffice.org.

In addition, PDF is a very common way to put documents on the Web, and all links in an OpenOfice.org document are carried over to the PDF version.

All this means that PDF has nearly infinite uses for tasks such as:

◆  Working with Microsoft Office users

◆  Web publishing

◆  Printing brochures, technical manuals, and other documents

PDF is available for all components of OpenOffice.org, so I've put it in the first part of this book, with the other cross-program cool time-saving techniques. See *PDF, Publishing, and the Web* on page 51. Note that you can only export the normal view of the presentation to PDF, not the handouts view or other views.

# Exporting a Presentation to HTML

**1** Choose File > Export.

**2** In the Export window, create a new directory for the export and select the HTML export file type.

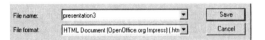

**3** Click Save.

**4** In the first Export window, keep New Design selected and click Next.

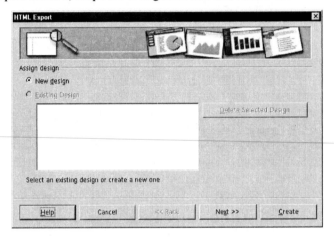

**5** In the next window, leave Standard HTML format selected and click Next.

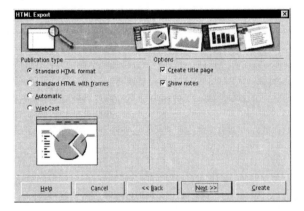

**6** In the next window, set the quality of the JPG graphics, and set the monitor resolution.

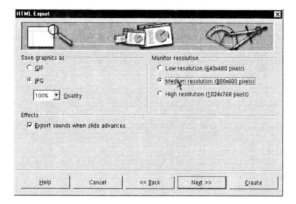

**7** Click Next.

**8** In the next window, enter your name and a home page if you like.

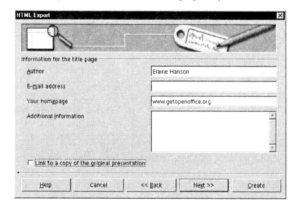

**9** Click Next.

**10** In the next window, select one of the button formats.

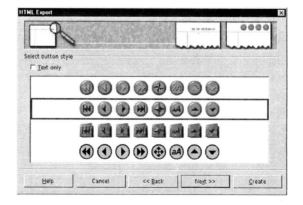

**11** Click Create.

**12**   You'll be prompted to name this design. Type the name and click Save.

**13**   Go to the directory where you exported the presentation.

**14**   Find the HTML file with the same name as the presentation. Open it in a browser.

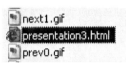

**15**   The presentation's TOC file will be displayed.

**16**   Click one of the links. The left slide below shows what a converted HTML page looks like; the right slide is from the original presentation.

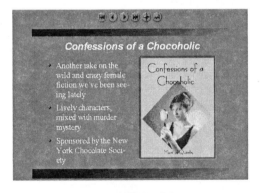

Converted HTML slide

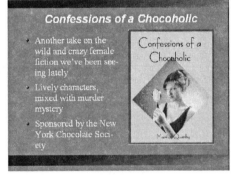

Original slide

## Creating a WebCast From Your Presentation

Follow the instructions in *Exporting a Presentation to HTML* on page 396. Instead of HTML in step 5, choose WebCast.

## Exporting a Presentation to Flash

**1** Choose File > Export.

**2** Select MacroMedia Flash as the file type, in the dropdown list, and type the name for the exported presentation.

**3** Click Save.

**4** OpenOffice.org will process for a while; when it's done, you'll see the file in the location where you specified.

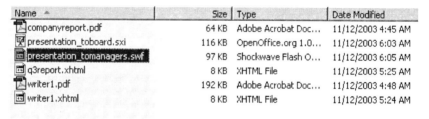

# Emailing Your Presentation in One Step

This is related to printing, though of course not quite the same thing. You can email your presentation to someone else in one step. See *Emailing Your Document in One Step* on page 229.

# Part V: Drawings

# Using Text, Objects, and 3D

# Drawing Tools in Impress and Draw

Draw is one of the least-used, least-known, best programs I know of. I talk it up every chance I get. I think it's a wonderful combination of great features and ease of use. I hope you'll take a look at it and see the power.

---

**Note** – If you need to create graphics that appear in Writer documents, do them here first. Use Draw to create your graphic designs, and then either export that drawing to a GIF or JPG and insert the picture in the document where you want the illustration, or simply import the drawing itself into the document. See *Exporting a Drawing to a JPG or Other Graphic Format* on page 432.

---

# Creating a New Drawing

Drawings are pretty much like Impress except that they don't run like presentations—they simply have the drawing, text, and multi-slide capability of Impress.

## Creating a New Drawing

1    Start OpenOffice.org and choose OpenOffice.org Drawing or, if the program is already running, choose File > New > Drawing.

2    The new empty drawing will appear.

## Saving a Drawing

1    Save the document by choosing File > Save or File > Save As.

2    Go to the correct directory and name the file.

3    Click Save.

## Changing the Page Setup

1    Choose Format > Page.

2    Click the Page tab if it's not on top.

**3** From the Format list, select the page size if you need to change it, or specify a different Width and Height. Change the orientation and margins as necessary. The preview area shows the effect of your changes.

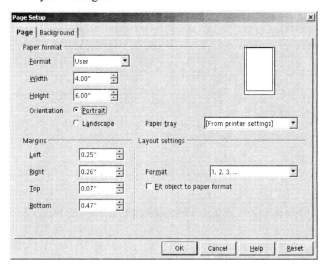

**4** Click OK.

**5** You might get a message like this one; click Yes.

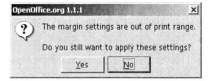

# Creating a New Slide in an Existing Drawing

You don't need a new file for each drawing. You can create a new slide in the same drawing.

**1** In the Pages area at the left, right-click below the last slide thumbnail and choose New Page. *(The words* slide *and* page *are used interchangeably in the software.)*

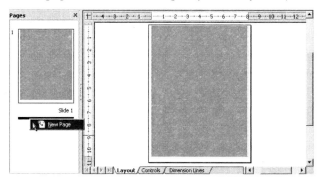

**2**  A new slide will appear. Click on the thumbnail to draw in the slide.

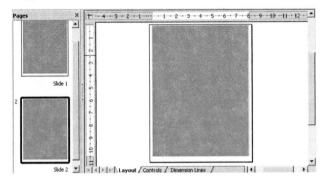

# Basic Drawing

Here's how to get started with drawing ovals, lines, and other shapes.

## Drawing Shapes

**1**  Find the Drawing toolbar. (To see it, choose View > Toolbars > Drawing.)

**2**  Find the tool you want to use and click on it.

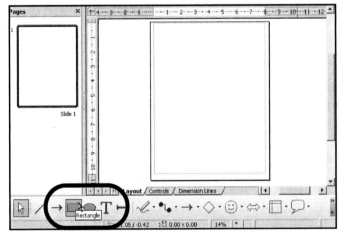

**3**   Click and hold down in the drawing area. Move the mouse over and down to create the shape you want, then release. The shape will appear.

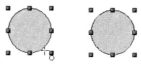

> **Note –** To maintain proportions of a shape, or to draw a perfect circle or square, hold down the Shift key while you draw.

**4**   To see more interesting shapes, click on the black triangles for the other icons on the formatting toolbar. Drag the small bar at the top of the palette to the right or left, to keep the palette displayed.

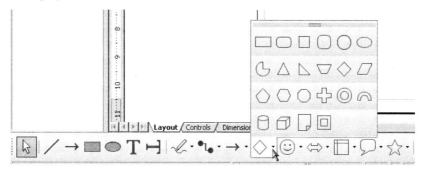

# Resizing an Object

You can resize by dragging or by using the Position and Size window.

### Resizing by Dragging

**1**   Select the object and move your mouse over one corner until the mouse becomes a two-ended arrow.

**2**   Hold down the Shift key if you want to maintain the proportions.

**3**   Drag your mouse toward the center of the object to make it smaller, or away from the center to make it bigger.

**4**   Release the mouse and the Shift key.

### Resizing Using the Position and Size Window

Let's say you need to create a rectangle that's exactly 4.67 inches wide by 3.80 inches high. You could draw that, roughly, keeping an eye on the rulers. But it's much easier to use the Position and Size window.

1    Select the object. Right-click on it and choose Position and Size.

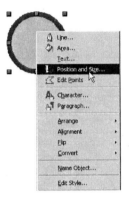

2    Click the Position and Size tab.

3    Select the Keep Ratio option if you want to keep the object's proportions as they are. Then in the Width and Height fields, specify the dimensions you want.

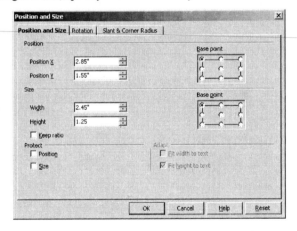

4    Click OK.

# Rotating an Object

You can rotate using the object handles, and the Position and Size window.

## Rotating an Object Using the Object Handles

**1**   Click the object once to make the square green handles appear.

**2**   Click again to make the round red handles appear.

**3**   Move your mouse over one of the corner handles; when the mouse looks like the illustration, drag the handle to rotate the object.

**4**   The object will rotate.

## Rotating an Object Using the Position and Size Window

**1**   Select the object. Right-click on it and choose Position and Size.

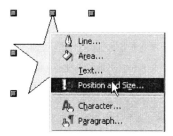

**2**   In the Position and Size window, click the Rotation tab.

**3**   Set the rotation degrees in the Angle field, or click an option in the lower right Default Settings
box.

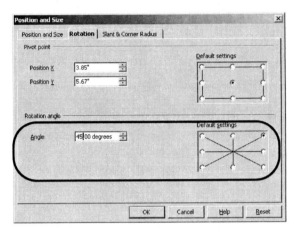

**4**   Click OK.

# Applying and Removing Borders and Fills

If you want something different than the default color in a shape, you have a bunch of other
choices. You can apply a variety of fills to shapes: not just color but gradients, bitmaps, and
crosshatches.

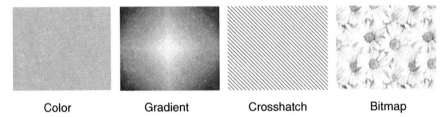

Color            Gradient            Crosshatch            Bitmap

## Applying Borders Using the Toolbar

**1**   Select the object.

**2**   To change the border style, select a style from the indicated list.

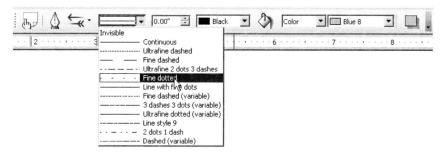

**3**   To change the border width, use the Line Width field.

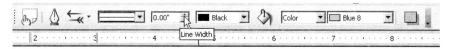

**4**   To change the border color, select a color from the color list shown.

**5**   The object's border will change.

## Applying Fills Using the Toolbar

**1**   Select the object.

**2**   Click and hold down on the indicated list. This is where you select the *type* of fill you want: color, gradient, hatching, or bitmap.

**3** Select the actual fill you want from the list next to it.

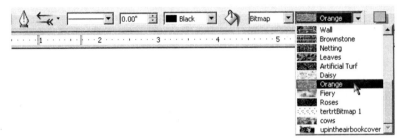

**4** The object's fill will change.

## Removing Fills and Borders Using the Toolbar

To remove a border, from the border style list select Invisible.

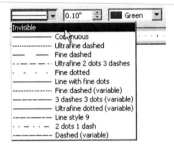

To have no fill in an object, from the fill list select Invisible.

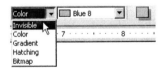

### Using the Area Window to Specify the Object Fill

If, instead, you want a little more control, then select the object and choose Format > Area. Click the Area tab. Select the fill type you want, and set the associated options. See the online help for more information about each type

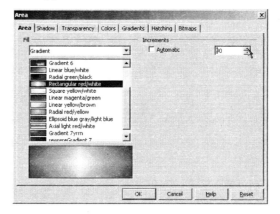

# Text Boxes and Fontwork

Text boxes are reasonably simple: just draw the text, then type inside them. Fontwork is an advanced tool for creating formatted text.

## Drawing and Typing in a Text Box

**1**  Find the Text tool icon on the toolbar, or choose View > Toolbars > Drawing.

**2**  Click on the Text tool and draw a text box.

**3**  Type content.

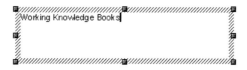

# Formatting Text Boxes

Formatting works the same way as in Writer, essentially. See *Making Text Look How You Want It: Basic Formatting* on page 71 and *Formatting Using the Paragraph and Character Windows* on page 78 for more information.

## Formatting Text Using the Dropdown Lists

1   Select the text to format it; double-click if necessary to get into text editing mode.

2   Click on the font list at the top of the work area and select the font you want.

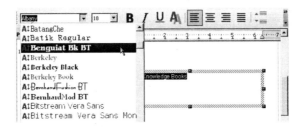

3   Select the font size you want from the font size list at the top of the work area.

## Formatting Text Using the Character and Paragraph Formatting Windows

1   Select the text to format it; double-click if necessary to get into text editing mode.

2   Choose Format > Character or Format > Paragraph.

3   Apply the formatting options you want.

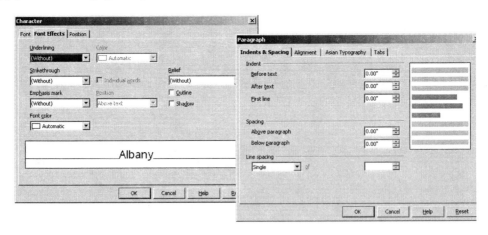

4   Click OK.

## Formatting Text Using the Text Formatting Window

1   Select the text to format it; double-click if necessary to get into text editing mode.

2   Choose Format > Text.

**3**    Apply the formatting options you want. The Fit Width to Text, Fit Height to Text, and Fit to Frame options are the most useful. To position the text within the text frame, use the Text Anchor area.

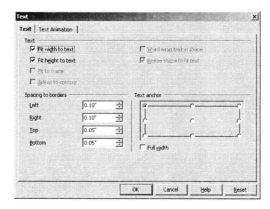

**4**    Click OK.

# Curving Text Using FontWork

This works in Writer, as well as in Impress and Draw.

**1**    Be sure you see the Drawing toolbar at the bottom of the work area. If you don't, choose View > Toolbars > Drawing.

**2**    Click the Fontwork icon.

**3**    The Fontwork window will appear. Select the pattern you like.

**4**    Click OK.

**5**   A curved piece of text will appear in your document, with the Fontwork toolbar.

**6**   Double-click in the middle of the text. The actual editable text will appear. Type the text that you actually want.

**7**   The text will change to what you typed.

**8**   You can apply different formatting with the dropdown lists at the top of the window.

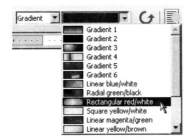

**9**   You can click on the text to see the Fontwork toolbar. Use the icons to modify it if you want; for instance, you can click and hold down on the Fontwork Shape icon to select a different shape.

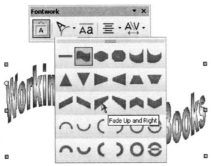

# Using 3D Shapes and Text

The 3D features are a nice extra in OpenOffice.org. While not strictly useful in most circumstances, they're an excellent way to make your drawings look interesting.

You can use the prefab 3D tools, or convert any object to 3D.

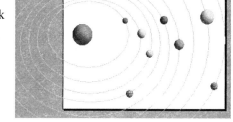

## Viewing the 3D Toolbar

The 3D shapes aren't always on your toolbar by default. Here's how to make sure you have this icon.

If you have this icon at the bottom of your toolbar on the Drawing toolbar, you can skip this step.

**1**   Be sure you can see the Drawing toolbar; if you can't, choose View > Toolbars > Drawing.

**2**   Find the black downward-facing triangle on the Drawing toolbar.

**3**   Click and hold down on the triangle, and choose Visible Buttons > 3D Objects.

**4**   The icon will appear in your toolbar.

**5**   Click and hold down on the 3D Objects icon; you'll see the palette.

# Drawing 3D Shapes

1  Make sure you can see the drawing toolbar.

2  Click and hold down on the 3D Objects icon.

3  Click the icon you want to use in the 3D Objects palette.

4  Click in the drawing area and draw the shape.

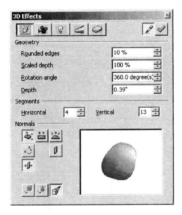

5  With the sphere still selected, you can apply colors, borders, and other formatting. You can combine 3D objects to create drawings, or just use them as is.

# Applying 3D Effects

1  Right-click on a 3D object and choose 3D Effects.

2  The 3D Effects window will appear. You have several different tabs, so apply the effects you want.

**3**   Click the green check mark to apply the effect and see the change in appearance.

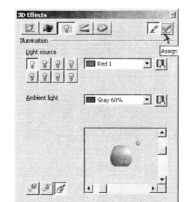

**4**   Close the window.

# Converting Text to 3D

You can convert text to 3D, with some pretty nice results.

**1**   Use the Text tool on the toolbar to draw a text box and type some content.

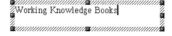

**2**   Expand the text box if necessary to keep the text all on the same line.

**3**   Move your mouse over the invisible text box border so that the mouse pointer is a crosshairs as shown.

**4**   Right click on the text box border and choose Convert > To 3D. (*Not* to 3D Rotation Object.)

**5**  The converted text will appear. Change the fill using the dropdown list at the top, and apply any other fill or line options you want.

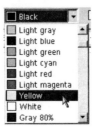

**6**  You can resize and rotate the text.

♦  Drag the middle bottom green box on the text box to make the text higher.

♦  Click the text, then click again to change the green handles to *red*. Grab a handle and move it around; you'll see the text rotate.

# Creating Intersecting 3D Objects

This is fun. You can use the Enter Group feature to get 3D objects to intersect and coexist, as shown in this bowl drawing. (3D shapes do require a lot of memory.)

**1**  Draw two 3D objects.

**2**  Select one and cut it (Ctrl X).

**3**  Select the other, then press F3 (to Enter Group).

**4**  Paste the first object.

**5**  Move the first object over the second object; they'll intersect.

**6**  Double-click elsewhere in the diagram to exit the group, or just right-click and choose Exit Group.

# Copying, Pasting, and Arranging

This section covers a couple specific aspects of copying and pasting in Draw and Impress, and performing some useful tasks: aligning, distributing, and putting objects in the back and front.

## Selecting Text and Objects

It's important to be able to select the exact items you want. Here's how.

### Selecting Objects

When you select an object to copy or position, you want it to have blue or green square handles, not round red handles. (The object has square blue handles when you select one, and square green handles when you've selected two or more.) Click on the object once to get square blue handles.

If the object has round red handles, click somewhere else, then click on the object again. Red handles are for rotation, which is fun but usually not what you want.

### Selecting Multiple Objects

Select the first object, hold down Shift and click the next object, and so on.

You can also draw a box around the objects with the standard pointer tool. Just draw, the dotted box will appear, and when you release, all the items will be selected.

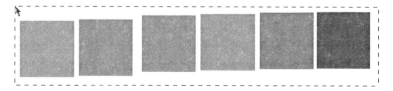

### Selecting Text Boxes

To modify the text in a text box, just click on the text, then double-click on the text to get into the right modification mode. Now you can use the text modification tools like the font dropdown list, to make the change.

At other times, though, you want to affect the whole text box. You want the *text box* to come to the front of the drawing, you want a border around the *box*, or you want to copy the *whole box*. In this case, you click just once on the text to get into the right modification mode. Now you can use the other modification tools.

## Copying and Pasting

**Note** – See *Selecting, Copying and Other Tips* on page 64 for how to do text copying and pasting.

**1**   Click on an object and be sure the handles are square.

**2**   Press Ctrl + C or choose Edit > Copy.

**3**   To paste, press Ctrl + V or choose Edit > Paste.

**4**   The pasted object will appear on top of the object you copied. **It looks nothing happened.** However, if you drag the object away you'll see that there are two.

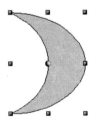

When you paste, you just see one selected item.

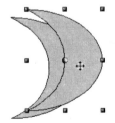

Drag the selected item and you'll see the first one below it.

## Duplicating Objects Multiple Times

If you need to make, say, 20 copies of an object, you might want to use the Duplicate feature.

**1**    Select the object.

**2**    Choose Edit > Duplicate.

**3**    Specify how many copies you want to make, and how far horizontally (the X axis) and vertically (the Y axis) each additional copy should be. You can set other options but these are the essentials.

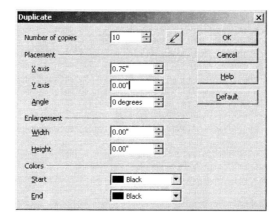

**4**    Click OK. The copies will appear.

## Duplicating, Rotating, and Enlarging Objects

**1**    Select the object.

**2**    Choose Edit > Duplicate.

**3**    Specify the number of copies and set the options for the X and Y axis.

**4**    Specify angle of rotation for each copy, and the amount each copy should be enlarged compared to the previous one.

**5**  Specify the color of the beginning object and the last object.

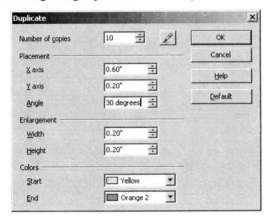

**6**  Click OK. You'll see the duplicated objects.

# Aligning Objects

Let's say you're doing a graphic design with a lot of different elements that need to all be in a straight line. You could do this manually, or with the grid, but alignment is simplest.

Objects that were drawn
manually and are uneven.

Objects aligned at the top.

**1**  Select the objects to align.

**2**  Right-click on one of the selected objects and choose Alignment > and an option. You can choose at left, right, or center for horizontal, and at top, bottom, and center for vertical.

Here's what the various alignments look like.

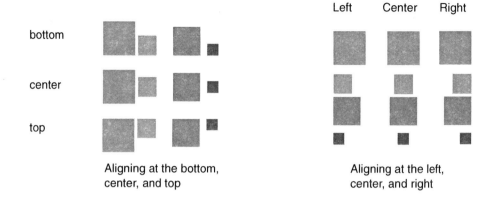

Aligning at the bottom,
center, and top

Aligning at the left,
center, and right

## Distributing Objects

Aligning is great but it doesn't cover everything you need. If you want objects to be evenly spaced, you need even *distribution*.

Unevenly distributed objects

Evenly distributed objects

**1**   Select the objects to distribute.

**2**   Either right-click on the selected objects and choose Distribution, or choose Modify > Distribution.

**3**   In the Distribution window, choose Horizontal or Vertical distribution.

**4**   The specific distributions are all pretty similar, so you can usually choose Center.

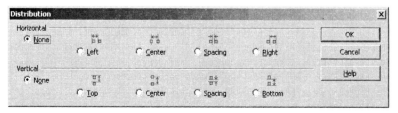

**5**    Click OK.

# Sending Objects to the Back and Front

When you're putting together a diagram with several objects, you want to make sure that some are in front of others. For instance, if you've got people with thought bubbles, the text needs to be on top, then the thought bubbles, then the picture.

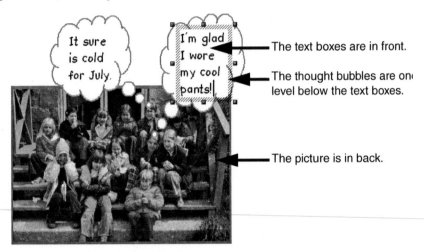

The text boxes are in front.

The thought bubbles are one level below the text boxes.

The picture is in back.

To put something in back, front, or just raise or lower it a level, you can:

♦    Click on the object, right-click on it, and choose Arrange and an option, such as Bring to Front.

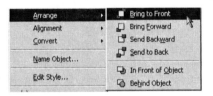

♦    Click on the object and choose Modify > Arrange > and an option.

# Grouping Objects

When you need to keep some objects together, it's a good idea to group them. Grouping is also useful if you want to take several objects, and align them with a group of other objects.

**1**    Select the objects.

**2**    Right-click on them and choose Group. You could also choose Modify > Group.

Once you've grouped the items, right-click on the items and choose Ungroup to ungroup the items. You can also choose Enter Group if you want to change an item in the group, but leave the items grouped.

# Using the Grid

A grid is a set of horizontal and vertical axes in the drawing area, represented by a series of horizontal and vertical dots. It's a nice way to make sure your drawings are even and symmetrical. You can use the grid as just a visual guide, or you can set up Draw and Impress so that objects you move or create *snap* to the grid. Snapping means that all objects automatically align with the axes of the grid, both in their position and their dimensions.

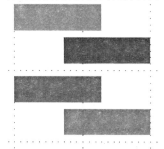

If your grid is a series of horizontal and vertical lines a half inch apart, for instance, and you've turned on the "snap to grid" feature, you can't move an object to be .56 inches from the left margin. And you can't draw an object that's .72 inches by .96 inches.

# Grid Basics

Here's how to get going with basics like turning the grid on.

## Viewing the Grid Toolbar Icons

To turn on the grid and do other grid tasks, choose View > Toolbars > Options.

## Displaying the Grid

Click the Display Grid icon; click it again to turn it off.

## Snapping to the Grid

Click the Snap to Grid icon; click it again to stop snapping. The grid doesn't have to be displayed in order to be snapped to.

# Making the Grid Lines Darker

When you turn on the grid, it looks like the picture on the left. This isn't much use if you want to use it as a visual guide. Here's how to make it darker (the version on the right).

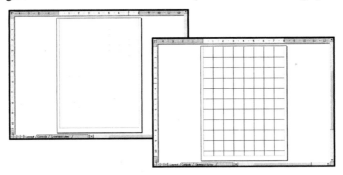

**1** Choose Tools > Options > OpenOffice.org > Appearance.

**2**    Scroll down to the section showing the Drawing/Presentation grid, choose Black.

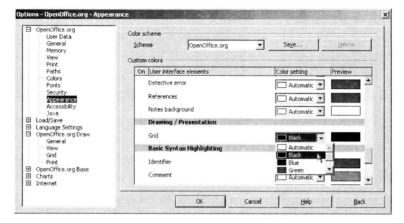

**3**    You can also give the grid more visual points. In the left pane of the same main window, scroll down to OpenOffice.org Draw (or OpenOffice.org Impress) and select Grid.

**Note** – You only do this if you're using the grid visually because now when you move objects they'll snap to the nearest grid point, and they're 1/50th of an inch apart. Having the dots that close together doesn't help you when you're snapping.

**4**    Specify something like an inch between axes and 50 points between the axes, or a half inch and 25 points.

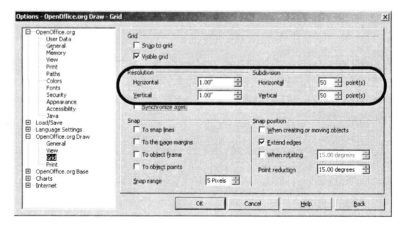

**5**    Click OK.

# Editing Graphics

Draw is a drawing program, vector-based, so it's primarily about making shapes, not editing individual pixels. It isn't Photoshop or Gimp. However, you do have several useful photo editing tools at your disposal.

## Opening a Graphic

Just choose File > Open and find the graphic file, as you would normally, or choose Insert > Picture > From File.

## Applying Grayscale, Black/White, or Watermark Effects

Click on the graphic; the picture toolbar will appear. If it doesn't, choose View > Toolbars > Picture.

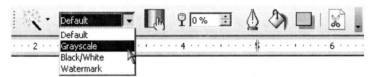

Use the indicated dropdown list to apply the effect you want.

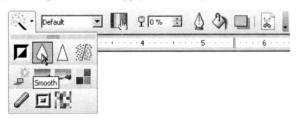

## Applying Filters

Click on the graphic; the picture toolbar will appear. If it doesn't, choose View > Toolbars > Picture. Use the indicated dropdown list to apply the effect you want.

The following examples show some of the effects.

Original

Posterized

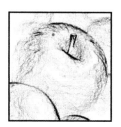

Charcoal sketch

# Changing Brightness, Contrast, and Other Attributes

**1**   Click on the graphic; the picture toolbar will appear. If it doesn't, choose View > Toolbars > Picture.

**2**   Click the Colors icon.

**3**   Use the indicated controls to change red, green, or blue values; and increase brightness, contrast, or gamma.

# Cropping

Click on the graphic; the picture toolbar will appear. If it doesn't, choose View > Toolbars > Picture. Click on the Crop icon.

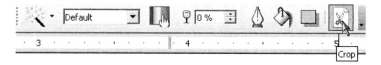

In the window that appears, specify the distance on each side to crop, then click OK.

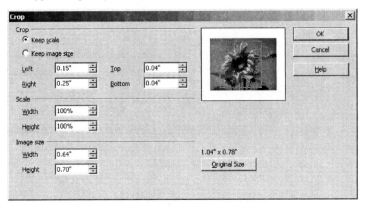

# Exporting a Drawing to a JPG or Other Graphic Format

Once you've created your drawing, with all the other features covered in this section, how do you get them into another document? The simplest approach is to make a graphic file out of your drawing, just a JPG or GIF, and insert that file in your Writer document, spreadsheet, web page, or other document.

**1**    Open your drawing if it's not already open.

**2**    Select all the items in the drawing.

**3**    Choose File > Export.

**4**    In the export window, specify a file name and location to export the file to. Click the file type list and select the format such as JPG.

**5**    Click Save.

**6**    You might be prompted for additional options. Leave them as is, or check the online help for more options, then click OK.

# Lines, Curves, Connector Lines, and Arrows

# Drawing and Modifying Lines

This section covers how to draw the different types of lines available in OpenOffice.org.

## Drawing a Straight Line

**1** Locate the Drawing toolbar, and the Line icon. Choose View > Toolbars > Drawing if you don't see this toolbar.

**2** Click on the Line icon.

**3** Click and hold down the mouse in the work area, then draw the mouse to draw the line. Release when you're done.

---

**Note –** Hold down the Shift key as you draw to make the line absolutely straight.

---

## Drawing Irregular Lines

Sometimes you might want to create a very specific line or unfilled shape, like a hexagonal stop sign or a flight of stairs. In this case, you need to use the Curve toolset.

**1** Turning on the grid so that your mouse snaps to the grid will make drawing the line easier. Choose View > Grid > Snap to Grid.

**2** Locate the Curve icon on the Drawing toolbar. Click and hold down on the black triangle by it to display the palette.

**3** Drag the title bar of the palette to separate it and make it stay displayed while you're drawing.

**4**  Click in the icon that corresponds to what you want to draw.

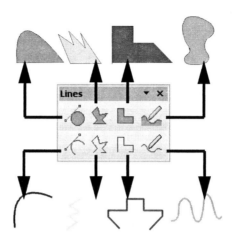

**5**  Draw a shape. Click and hold down to draw a line in one direction, then click to change directions. When you're done, double-click.

# Modifying a Line

You can change the style, width, and color, as well as the symbols on each end, for any line.

## Modifying Lines Using the Toolbar

Select the line, then use the arrow end, line style, line width, and color dropdown lists.

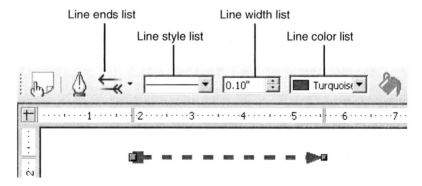

## Modifying Lines Using the Formatting Window

Select the line, then choose Format > Line and make your selections. Click OK.

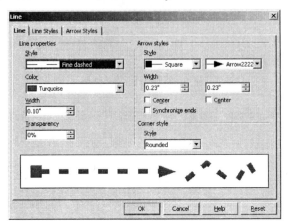

**Note –** You can create your own line styles and arrow styles by clicking on the corresponding tab in the Line window. They will show up in the main Line tab, as well as in the dropdown lists on the toolbar.

# Drawing Dimension Lines

Dimension lines are a handy tool that lets you automatically display the length of an object.

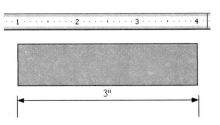

## Setting up the Scale

When you display the dimension of an item, it's often in plans for creating an object. You're drawing to *scale*; that is, you're not drawing the plans for the book case or house the actual size of the object you're going to build.

You can display the actual dimension by specifying the scale you're using. If your diagrams for what you're going to do to the back yard are on a scale of 1 to 80, then you can set that up. The dimensions displayed on the dimension line will be the actual dimensions of your yard.

1 Choose Tools > Options > OpenOffice.org Draw > General. In the Scale list, select your scale from the list, or type the scale you're using.

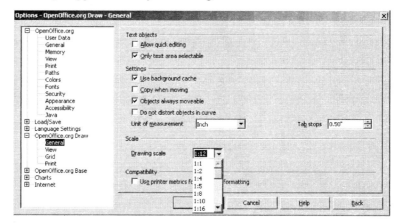

2 Click OK.

# Drawing the Dimension Line

1 Create the drawing as you want it, then locate the Lines and Arrows icon on the Drawing toolbar.

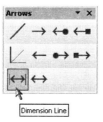

2 Click on the Dimension Line icon.

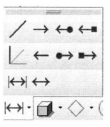

3 Hold down the Shift key to draw a straight line, and draw the line immediately next to the items to measure.

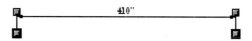

**4** Double-click the measurement that appears and change the font size, color, and font using the dropdown lists in the toolbar.

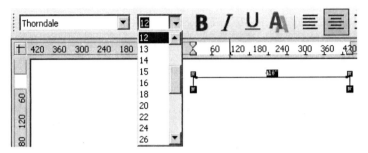

**5** If you'd like to change aspects of the measurement, select the dimension line, right-click it, and choose Dimensions.

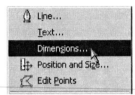

**6** Make your selections, then click OK.

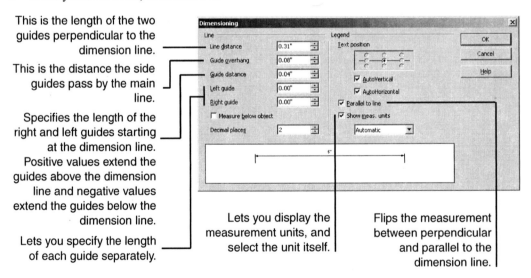

This is the length of the two guides perpendicular to the dimension line.

This is the distance the side guides pass by the main line.

Specifies the length of the right and left guides starting at the dimension line. Positive values extend the guides above the dimension line and negative values extend the guides below the dimension line.

Lets you specify the length of each guide separately.

Lets you display the measurement units, and select the unit itself.

Flips the measurement between perpendicular and parallel to the dimension line.

**7**    Draw any additional lines and format them as necessary. It's generally easiest to draw one line, format it the way you want, then copy and paste it, and drag it to the measurement and position you want.

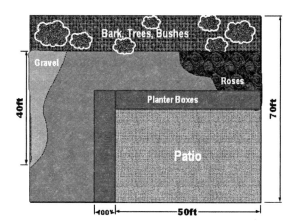

# Using Connector Lines for Diagrams

Connector lines automatically attach themselves to the objects they're connected to, and wherever you move the objects, the lines follow. This is very convenient for diagrams. They're a lot like the connector lines you get in Visio.

## Connecting Objects Using Connector Lines

**1**    Draw the objects you want to connect.

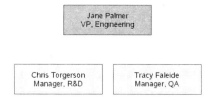

**2**    Click and hold down the mouse on the Connectors icon on the toolbar.

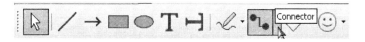

**3**   Click on the connector icon you want. You can change the line type later.

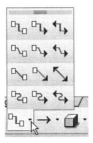

**4**   Without clicking, move your mouse over one object until a connector point lights up.

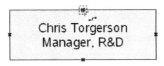

**5**   Click and hold down the mouse, and draw a line to another object; the "handles" on the second object will light up. Release the mouse.

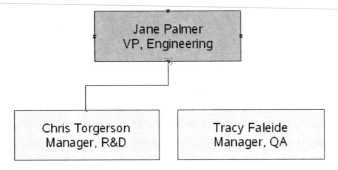

**6**   The line will look something like this.

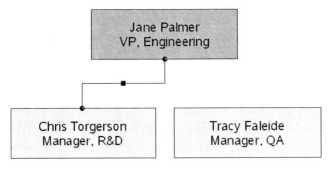

**7**    When you move the objects, the lines will follow.

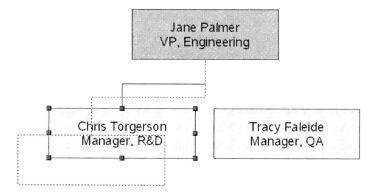

## Adjusting Connector Lines

You can change a connector line from curved to straight, as well as other attributes.

**1**    Select a line to modify. Right-click on it and choose Connector.

**2**    The Connector window will appear. Select the options to change the line.

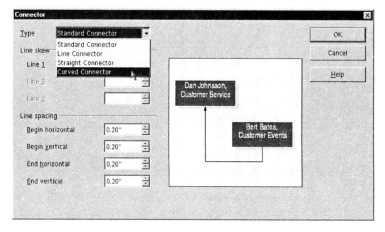

**3**    Click OK.

# Creating Colors, Gradients, and Other Fills

# Creating Area Fills

OpenOffice.org comes with premade colors, gradients, bitmaps, and crosshatches that show up in the fill dropdown lists. You can create your own, as well, which makes being creative with OpenOffice.org a lot more fun. Anything you create shows up in the fill dropdown lists on the object formatting bar, and in the Area window. Here are some colors I made for my own use.

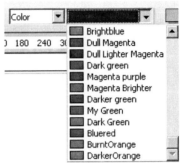

# Creating a Color

Let's say you want a little more subtlety and control over the color, or you just don't like the existing colors. You can create any color you want in OpenOffice.org, and they will show up throughout the program in Writer, Calc, and Impress, as well as in Draw.

---

**Note –** You can also do this by opening a drawing or presentation and choosing Format Area, then clicking the Colors tab. However, those colors are available only in Draw.

---

1    Choose Tools > Options > OpenOffice.org >Colors.

2    Type the color name in the Name field.

3    Click Edit. The Color window will appear.

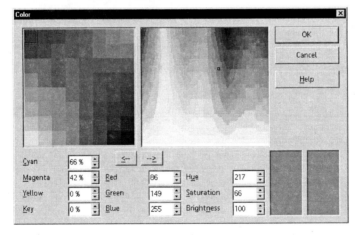

**4**   In the window that appears, double-click in a square on the left that contains the color palette you want.

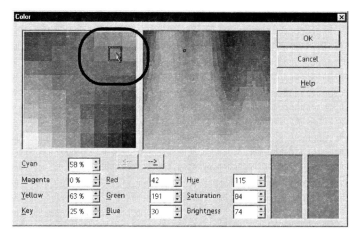

Then click in the area at right until you have a dark green you like. You can also type the RGB or CMYK values, and Hue, Saturation, and Brightness values.

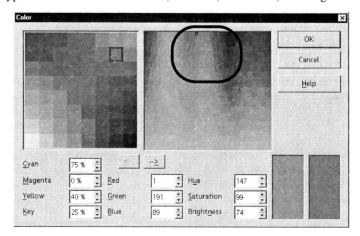

**5**   Click OK. You'll be sent back to the original color window.

**6**   In the original color window, click Modify. The name you typed in the Color list will now
show the color you created.

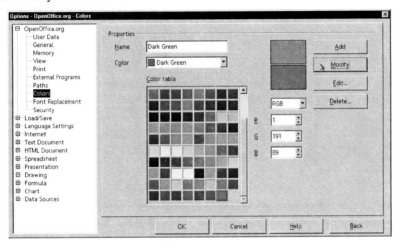

**7**   Click OK.

# Creating a Gradient

**1**   Choose Format > Area.

**2**   In the Area window, click the Gradient tab.

**3**   In the Type field, select the type of gradient. In the Angle field, select the degrees.

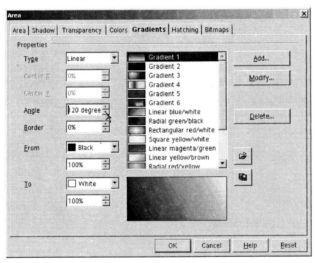

**4**   In the From and To fields, select the colors you want. In the percentage field below each
color, select the percentage for each color.

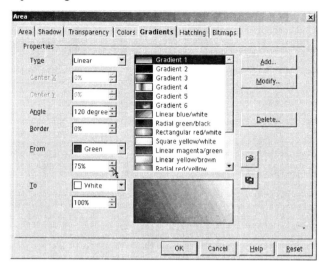

**5**   Click Add. A window will prompt you to name the gradient.

**6**   Click OK.

**7**   Click OK again in the Area window.

**8**   The gradient now shows up in the gradient lists.

# Creating a Bitmap

**1**   Choose Format > Area.

**2**   In the Area window, click the Bitmap tab.

**3**   Click the Import button.

**4**   In the window that appears, find a graphic you want to use and select Open.

**5**   A window will prompt you to name the bitmap. Name it and click OK.

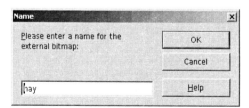

**6**   The bitmap will appear at the bottom of the window. Click OK.

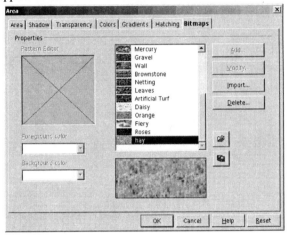

# Creating a Hatching

**1**   Choose Format > Area.

**2**   In the Area window, click the Hatching tab.

**3**   Select the spacing, angle, number of lines, and color you want.

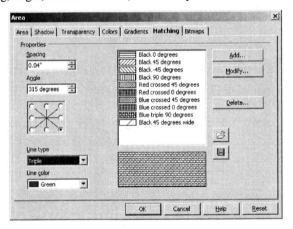

**4**   Click Add and name the hatching.

**5**   Click OK.

**6**   Click OK in the Area window.

# Part VI: Mail Merge and Databases

# Understanding Databases and Mail Merges

# What Databases Are For

Not everyone needs a database. Sometimes a big text file, or a spreadsheet, is big enough to track your friends' addresses, your DVDs, or other information.

You need a database if you have one or more of the following (this isn't a complete list, but it's a good start).

- A huge amount of data
- A need to view or print a subset of the data, like your friends from Minnesota or the DVDs that you've loaned out
- A need to view or print the data in multiple ways like in a report and in labels
- A need to arrange the data in multiple ways easily, like sorting it by zip code and by last name

If you need to do things in this list, you probably need a database.

# What Databases Are Made Of

The database can be made of nearly anything:

- One or more text files
- A spreadsheet
- An address book
- The OpenOffice.org Base database file
- A database file in Access, Oracle, mySQL, or another format

# What Mail Merges Are and How They Work

One of the main reasons you'll create a database is to do mail merges. Here's an overview of what they are and how they work.

## What's a Mail Merge?

A mail merge is a system for letting you make one document and generate a personalize copy to everyone in a database. For instance, you can write your holiday letter and send a copy to everyone in your address book.

Or you can send a copy of a letter requesting payment to everyone in your invoices database who hasn't paid you yet.

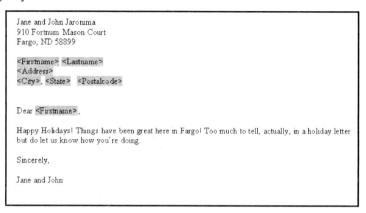

Another example is that to make mailing labels, one for each of your customers.

John Johnson
90 Pearl
Boulder, CO 80708

Miranda Hobbeson
12 Ludlow
Kalispell, MT 59900

Sonja Bereson
6 Main
Billings, AK 99821

Mail merge is a great way to do a lot of work without a lot of effort.

# The Parts of a Mail Merge

Here's how it works.

- Mail merge data – You have some **data file**: your list of customers, your address book, your huge database, whatever. It can be a plain text file, a spreadsheet, Microsoft Access, the OpenOffice.org Base database, or nearly anything else. The file can therefore have pretty much any extension: **.txt** for text files, **.ods** for spreadsheets, etc.

- Mail merge configuration – You need to let OpenOffice.org know that you want it to be one of your databases for making mail merges. So you create a little **configuration file**, with the extension .odb, that holds the information about where the data is, that this is a special mail merge file, and so on. To create the database, see *Creating Databases and Queries* on page 455.

- Mail merge document – And of course you need a **document**, where the data from your data file shows up. You take this document, point it at the mail merge configuration file, decide which fields, or types of data, you want in the mail merge document: everybody's first name, their address, their outstanding balance, their birthday, or whatever other data you have decided to put in that data file. Then you print, and you get a copy of that document for every person (or *row*) in that data file. To create the document, see *Creating and Printing Mail Merge Documents* on page 483.

Here's a visual take on how it all works.

### Mail merge data in a file or any data source

| Firstname | Lastname | Address | City | State | Postalcode |
|-----------|----------|---------|------|-------|-----------|
| John | Johnson | 90 Pearl | Boulder | CO | 80708 |
| Miranda | Hobbeson | 12 Ludlow | Kalispell | MT | 59900 |
| Sonja | Bereson | 6 Main | Billings | AK | 99821 |

### OpenOffice.org mail merge configuration file

Data is in a **spreadsheet** at C:\data\addresses.ods...and so on...
There's **one table** of data...
My name is **addressdatabase.odb**...
The fields are Firstname, Lastname, Address, City, State, Postalcode

### One OpenOffice.org mail merge document prints one copy for each row in the data file

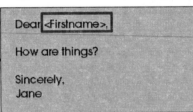

Dear <Firstname>,

How are things?

Sincerely,
Jane

# Creating Databases and Queries

# Creating a Database From a File

**Note** – If you've got data in another database that you can't access using OpenOffice.org, export to
.CSV text files. Then use those text files to create a database using the instructions here. You could
also bring the CSV files into spreadsheets using the instructions in *Opening a Text File as a
Spreadsheet* on page 257, then use the spreadsheets as the data for the database. Or for yet
another option, once you have the text files in a spreadsheet, import the data directly into a true
Base database; see *Importing Content From Another Database or Spreadsheet* on page 465.

One of the easiest things to do is enter your data in a spreadsheet, then connect to that when you
create the database. You can also use a bunch of text files, or even your address book, as the data
for the database.

In a spreadsheet, each sheet in the spreadsheet you point to becomes a table. Tables are what
actually hold the data. With text files, each file in the directory you point to becomes a separate
table.

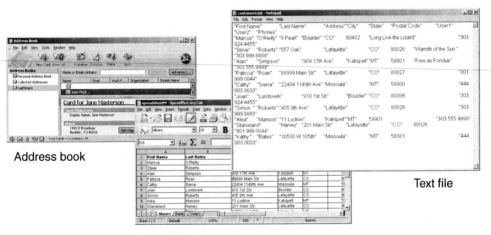

Address book

Spreadsheet

Text file

1    Choose File > New > Database.

2    In the Database Wizard window, select Connect to an Existing Database.

**3**  From the list, you can select Text, Spreadsheet, or the type of Address Book you're using; make the selection you want (except for LDAP address book). Or select another type of database if you're using something more complex.

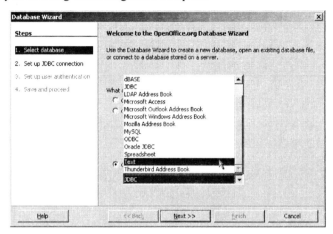

**4**  Click Next.

**5**  Make the appropriate selections based on what you chose. Here are some tips.

♦  Address book – The wizard will automatically find the address book so you don't need to point to the address book file.

♦  Spreadsheet – Specify the location of the spreadsheet. Then click Next.

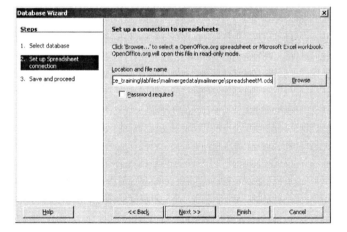

◆    Text file – Specify the location of the directory where your text files are. Each text file will become a separate table in your database. Then from the Field Separator list, select the correct separator and click Next.

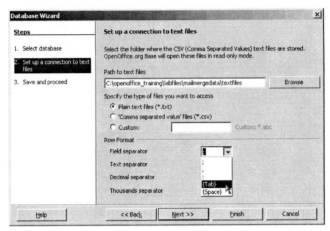

**6**    In the last window, choose to register the database. You don't have to open the database for editing unless you want to.

**7**    Click Finish.

**8**    When prompted, save the database. This is the **.odb** database file, separate from the data file itself. The name you choose here will show up in lists when you create mail merges.

# Connecting to an Existing Database

Follow the instructions in *Creating a Database From a File* on page 456. However, in the first window, select the type of database you're using, such as Access, instead of a flat file.

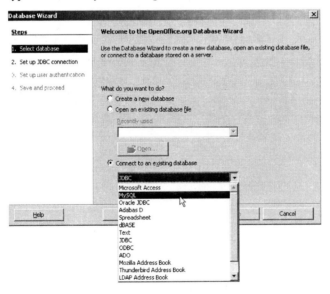

Then, depending on the selections you made, enter the necessary information. See the online help *Database Wizard* topic for more information about what to enter for each item.

Finish saving the database as described in *Creating a Database From a File* on page 456.

# Creating a Base Database

OpenOffice.org has a database tool built into it, called Base, so that you can create your own database from scratch. It's more work than connecting to existing data like a spreadsheet.

When you create a database based on spreadsheet or other file, you have a database, which is the basic .odb file, and the *tables*, which contain the actual data. In the case of a spreadsheet example, a mycustomers.odb file is the database, which *points to* sheets in the spreadsheet like minnesotacustomers, northdakotacustomers, etc. Each sheet is a table.

In a Base database, you still have a database and tables. The tables contain the actual data. However, you enter the data into the tables, rather than having the database point to some other file where the data already is.

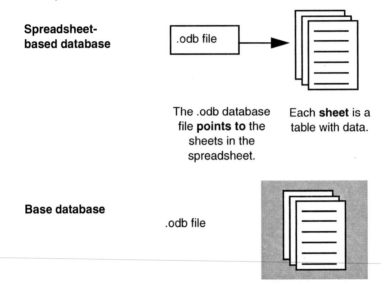

**Spreadsheet-based database**

.odb file

The .odb database file **points to** the sheets in the spreadsheet.

Each **sheet** is a table with data.

**Base database**

.odb file

The .odb database file **contains** the separate tables. Each **table** and its data is stored in the .odb file.

I'm not going to go into all the aspects of creating databases, since books far longer than this have been written on this topic. I'll just outline here how to use the tool; consult your favorite database guide for how to create a good one.

**1**    Choose File > New > Database.

**2**    Choose to create a new one.

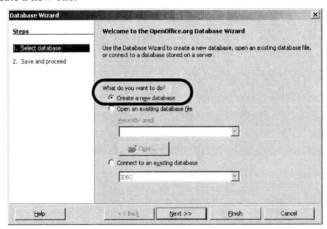

**3**    Click Next.

**4**    Choose to register the database, open it for editing, and create tables using the wizard.

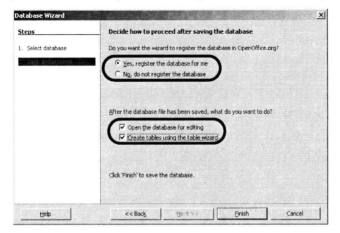

**5**    Click Finish and save the database.

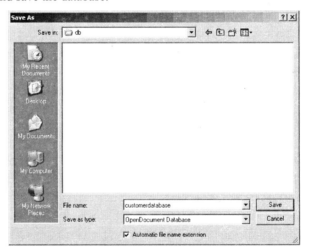

**6**    The table creation wizard will appear. Select the type of fields you want.

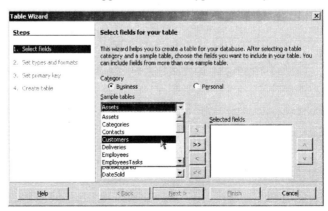

**7**    Add the fields you want, using the >> or > buttons to add all or one of the fields at once. Then use the up/down buttons at the right to arrange the fields in the order you want them in. Be sure you do this, since this is the order you'll need to enter data in, it's the default order for data entry, forms, and you'll be really annoyed with the table if the fields aren't in the order you want them.

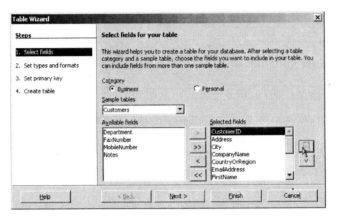

**8**    Click Next. In the Field Types window you can generally leave things as is. However, note that the CustomerID doesn't allow letters by default. If you want your customer IDs to be something like AKL-4-899, change the type to CHAR.

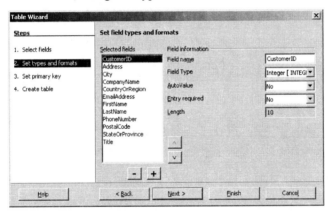

**9**   Click Next. In the Set Primary Key window, the easiest thing to do is to automatically add a
primary key field that's autonumbered. A primary key ensures each record is unique.

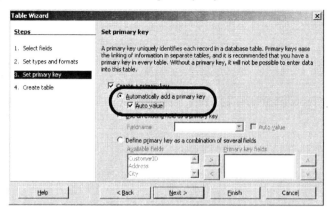

**10**   Click Next. Name the table, or leave it as is. Select the Enter Data Immediately option if you
want to open the table for manual data entry.

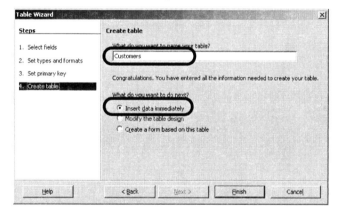

**11**   Click Finish. The table will open, showing the field names and a blank row.

---

**Note –** The database and table still aren't saved. When you close the database editing window,
click Save if a message prompts you to save.

---

# Entering Data in a Base Database Manually

**1**   Choose File > Open and open the database file.

**2**   In the left area of the database window, click the Tables icon.

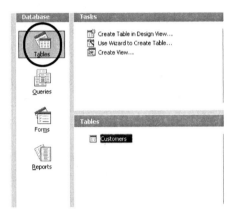

**3**   Double-click the name of the table you want to enter data in.

**4**   Simply type in the data you want. When you press Tab, you'll go to the next record in the table and the previous record will be saved.

**5**   When you're done, click the Save icon if it's not dimmed. Close the table.

**6**    You'll see the main database editing window. To see the table, click the Tables icon at the left, select the table you created, then click on the dropdown list at the right and select Data. The data you entered will be displayed.

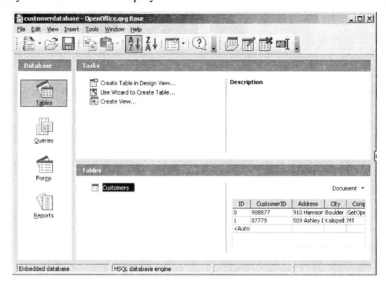

**7**    Important: The database and table still aren't saved. When you close the database editing window, watch for this window and be sure to click Save.

# Importing Content From Another Database or Spreadsheet

Typing content into a table from scratch might not be the most practical approach, if you've already got the data sitting there in a spreadsheet or other form. Fortunately, you can just copy and paste.

**1**    Create the database and the table that you want the data brought into. Be sure to set up fields, keys, and other items correctly for the existing data.

**2**    Get the data into a spreadsheet. If it's currently in another database, such as Access, then use that database's feature to export data. You should be able to find a feature like File > Export. Export it to a CSV or spreadsheet file, then open that file in an OpenOffice.org spreadsheet.

**3**    Open the spreadsheet containing the data and copy it, including the headings.

**4**    Open the database that you want the data brought into.

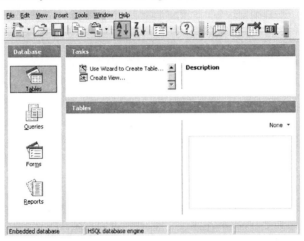

**5**    If you have already created a table that you'll be pasting the data into, double-click the table name and examine the field names, field definitions, and the primary key. The field names don't need to match but the field definitions—the type of data stored and the data length—must match the data you're going to bring in.

> Also, the data itself that you're bringing in must conform to the restrictions of the data. If the primary key for the table is the Customer ID, then every field you're bringing in must have a unique Customer ID and must not duplicate any ID already in the file. For this reason, it's usually most convenient to have an automatically incrementing primary key separate from the data. See step 9 on page 463.

**6**    Right-click in the table area and choose Paste.

**7** The Copy Table window appears. Type the table name you want, and leave Definition and Data selected. It is also usually a good idea to accept the option to create a primary key called ID; this can save you problems later. Click Next.

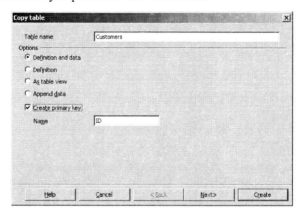

**Note** – If you're adding data to a table with data already in it, select the Append Data option.

**8** In the Insert Columns window, click the >> button to add all the fields to the table, or select each and click the > button to add selected fields. Click Next.

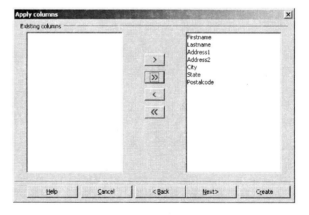

**Note** – If you're adding data to a table with data already in it, use the arrows to line up the fields you're bringing in with the fields that they correspond to. The names don't need to match but the field definitions do. For instance, if you're bringing in the field Address1, line it up with the existing field AddressLine1.

**9**   Check the field definitions in the Type Formatting window to be sure they're right.

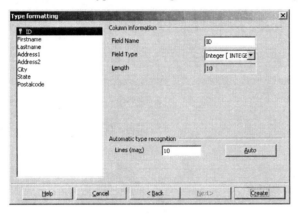

**10**   Click Create. You'll see the new table name in the tables area of the database window.

---

**Note –** To export data from a Base database table into a spreadsheet or text file, see http://openoffice.blogs.com and click the **Book Resources** link.

---

# Linking Two Tables With a Relation

Let's say that you have two tables, Customers and Invoices. You're going to use these tables together much of the time, since the Invoices table contains the invoices for your customers. The data goes together; it's just that you have applied standard database design and divided the data into two tables.

You can let the database know that these two tables are related with a relation.

**1**   Open the database file containing the tables.

**2**    Choose Tools > Relationships.

**3**    The database design window will appear.

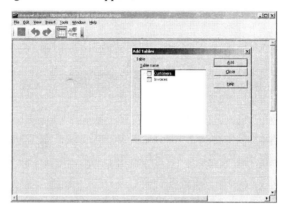

**4**    Click Add, then select the second table and click Add; both tables will appear.

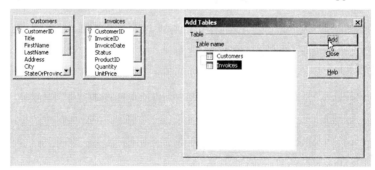

**5**    There must be at least one field that is the same in both tables. Click in field of the table at the
many end of the one-to-many relationship, in this case the Invoices table, and drag toward the
same field in the other table.

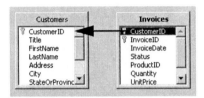

**6**    A line will appear showing that there's a relation.

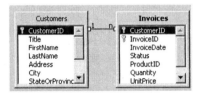

**7**    You can double-click the line to set options. Under Update Options, the default for both
columns is No Action. You might want to select the Update Cascade and Delete Cascade
options shown, so that when you delete a record in one table it's deleted in the other, and so on.
See the online help for more information about each option. Click OK.

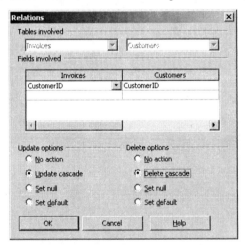

**8**    Click Save to save the relation.

**9**    Close the relation window, then close the database window and save again if prompted.

# Creating a Query

Let's say you've got an enormous database of 15,000 people who came to your last ice fishing convention. You'd like to invite the ones from Minnesota to attend your Minnesota Ice Fishing and Duck Blind Painting convention taking place in Duluth next month.

However, when you try to do a mail merge to create a personalized invitation for everyone you want to invite, all 15,000 of the attendees will show up, not just the good folks from Minnesota. And you're not about to print 15,000 invitations and throw away most of them.

The solution, luckily, is simple. Create a query for your conference attendees database that limits the records to the people who put down Minnesota as their state of residence. Then when you create your mail merge, you select the Minnesota query, not the entire database.

**Conference Attendees**
*Database*

| |
|---|
| John Banko  Colorado |
| Emily Rand  Minnesota |
| Kathy Sierra  California |
| Bert Bates  Wisconsin |
| Arthur Kavanaugh  Minnesota |

What you have (but
15,000 total records)

**Conference Attendees**
from Minnesota *Query*

| |
|---|
| Emily Rand  Minnesota |
| Arthur Kavanaugh  Minnesota |

What you want (probably
about 300 records)

You can also use queries to just sort your data the way you want it. Let's say you're sending out "Thanks for coming" postcards to 15,000 people, but the cards need to be printed in zip code order for the post office. Just create a query that has everything in the database, but sorted by zip code.

## Creating Views

The instructions here can be used to create views, as well. Views are like queries, but are treated like tables by the database program. Just click the Tables icon at the far left instead of the Queries icon and click the Create View option.

## Creating a Basic Query Using the Wizard

Here's how to make a simple query.

**1** Open your database file, the .odb file you created. Choose File > Open and find the file; you'll see the main database editing window.

**2** In the database editing window, click on the Queries icon on the left side, and choose to use the Wizard to create a query. (You can use design view or SQL view as well, but this procedure uses the Wizard.).

**3** You'll see the first window, and the fields in the database.

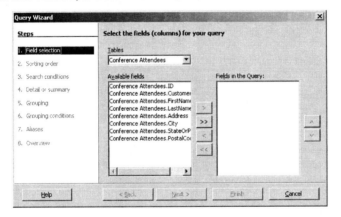

**4**    Use the >> and > arrows to add the fields that you want to the query. You might want all of them, or just a few. For this one, you don't really need the customer ID, so you could leave that one out.

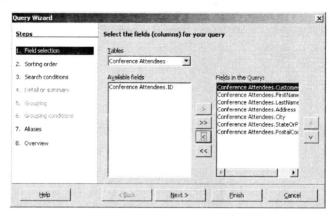

**5**    Click Next. You can sort the query any way you want. If you were doing zip code order, this is where you would choose to sort first by that field, in ascending order, then by anything you want, like last name.

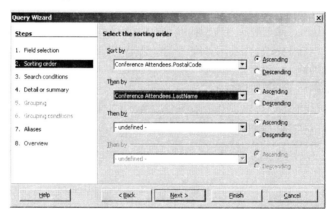

**6**    Click Next.

**7**    Here's where you restrict what information shows up in the query. To show only people from Minnesota, for instance, choose the State field, then the Equal To restriction, then just type the value MN. You also have options like Greater Than and Less Than.

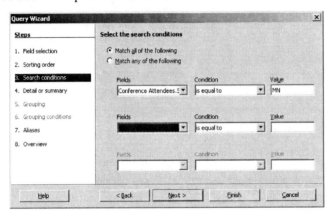

**8**    Click Next; you can ignore the next few windows. In the Alias window you might choose to use different names for the fields in this alias. Here's an example of what you might do. This is totally optional, however.

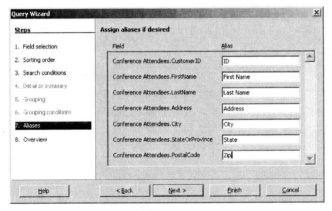

**9**    Click Next. Here's a review window. Name the query something clear that describes it.

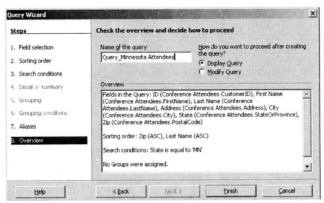

**10** Click Finish. You'll see the query, and only people from Minnesota are in it.

**11** Close the query. Select Queries on the left, select the query itself, and select Document. You'll see the query data on the right.

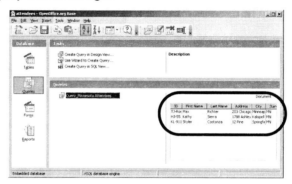

**12** Close the database, saving changes.

Now you'll see the query when you're creating mail merge documents, and you can base the documents on the query instead of the whole big database. The query will show up in different ways, so be prepared to dig just a bit.

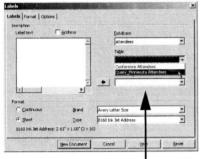

How you see the query when you create labels and envelopes; it shows up as another table.

How you see the query when you use the simple mail merge.

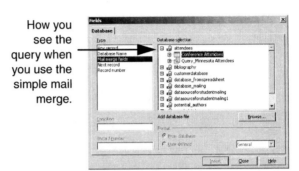

How you see the query when you choose View > Data Sources to "roll your own" mail merge document.

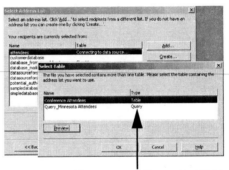

How you see the query when you use the advanced mail merge wizard; a window pops up and lets you select it.

## Creating a Query With Functions

The previous query showed you how to select specific data. However, what if you wanted to do more: for instance, calculate the average amount that each of your customers bought, or the number of purchases each of them had made? You can do this with functions.

Functions work only with the correct data. Your data needs to have one-to-many relationships. For instance, if you have a Customer table and an Invoices table, then for every record in the Customer table, there can be one ore more (many) records corresponding to that customer in the Invoices table. This is because every customer is allowed, and encouraged, to make multiple purchases.

The following illustration shows a simple example.

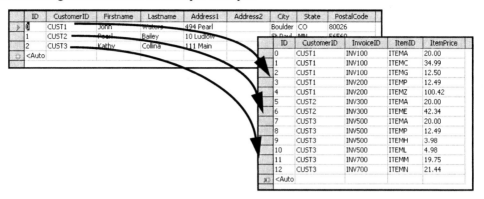

1    Open the database file containing your tables.

2    Click the Queries icon at the left and click Create Query in Design View.

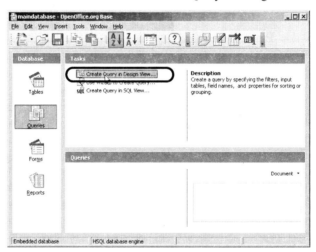

**3**    In the window that appears, click Add to add the table(s) you want to use. To use two or more tables, set up a relation; see *Linking Two Tables With a Relation* on page 468.

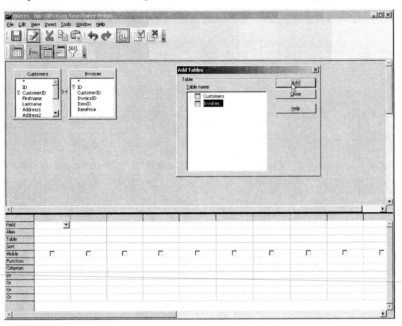

**4**    Double-click each field that you want to appear in the query, in the table it's in. It will appear in the design area.

**5**     In the Function row, for each of the fields select **Group**. However, for the field you actually want to perform the function on, select the function you want. If you want to find the average item price for each invoice, select **Average** as shown for the ItemPrice field.

| Field | CustomerID | Firstname | Lastname | InvoiceID | ItemPrice |
|---|---|---|---|---|---|
| Alias | | | | | |
| Table | Customers | Customers | Customers | Invoices | Invoices |
| Sort | | | | | |
| Visible | ☑ | ☑ | ☑ | ☑ | ☑ |
| Function | Group | Group | Group | Group | (no function) ▼ |
| Criterion | | | | | (no function) |
| Or | | | | | Average |
| Or | | | | | Count |
| Or | | | | | Maximum |
| Or | | | | | Minimum |

**6**     Click Run Query.

**7**     The query results will appear. Use any of the sort or filter icons, if necessary, to arrange or restrict the data further. See the online help for more information on those features.

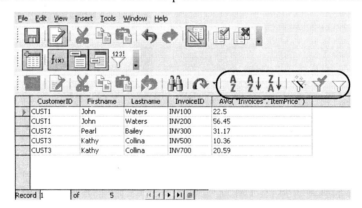

| CustomerID | Firstname | Lastname | InvoiceID | AVG("Invoices","ItemPrice") |
|---|---|---|---|---|
| CUST1 | John | Waters | INV100 | 22.5 |
| CUST1 | John | Waters | INV200 | 56.45 |
| CUST2 | Pearl | Bailey | INV300 | 31.17 |
| CUST3 | Kathy | Collina | INV500 | 10.36 |
| CUST3 | Kathy | Collina | INV700 | 20.59 |

Record |1    | of    5

**8**     Click Save.

**9**     Name the query and click OK.

| Save As | ✕ |
|---|---|
| Query name | Average Item Price |

OK     Cancel     Help

**10**  Close the query design window and the database window, saving changes if prompted.

The query will now show up in your data sources, when you choose View > Data Sources and when you do mail merges such as envelopes, labels, and when using the Mail Merge wizards.

To edit an existing query, right-click the query name and choose Edit.

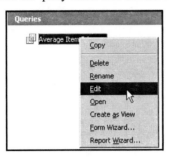

# Writing a Query Using SQL

Teaching SQL is beyond the scope of this book. However, to get into SQL view, click the Queries icon in the main database window and click the SQL item.

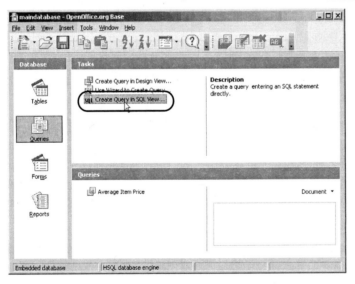

Type your query in the window that appears.

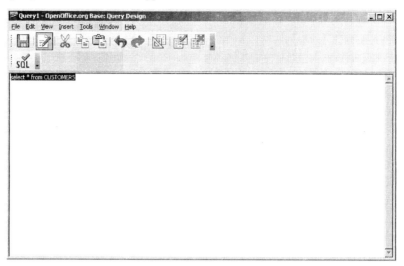

If you want to edit an existing query in SQL, right-click the query name in the main query area and choose Edit.

In the query design window, choose View > Switch Design View Off. The SQL for the query will appear.

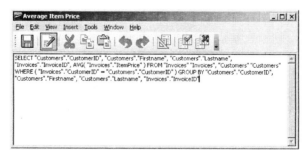

If you're having trouble seeing the SQL view, choose View > Switch Design View Off.

# Forms and Reports

Forms and reports are beyond the scope of this book. For an overview, see *Forms and Reports* on page 512 and the **Book Resources** link of the **openoffice.blogs.com blog**.

# Creating and Printing Mail Merge Documents

# Making Mail Merge Documents

**Note** – Be sure you've read or understand the content in *Creating Databases and Queries* on page 455 and *Introduction to Databases and Mail Merges* on page 613.

Now that you've got data and databases, it's time to create a document to put the information in. You can create envelopes, mail merges, and regular documents.

## Creating Mail Merge Envelopes and Labels

This works like *Simple Envelopes and Labels* on page 231. Instead of typing the information in the main content area, however, you select the database, the table, and the fields.

**1**  Select each field one by one, then use the arrow to insert the fields.

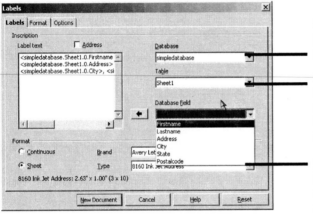

Select the name here that you specified when you saved the database.

Select the table here. This is the name of the sheet for spreadsheets, the text file for text files, or just the table for other database types.

Select the first field you want in the Databases Field list, and click the arrow. Add all other fields you want. Type any spaces, carriage returns, or other items you want.

**2**  Click the Options tab and pick the printer to print to.

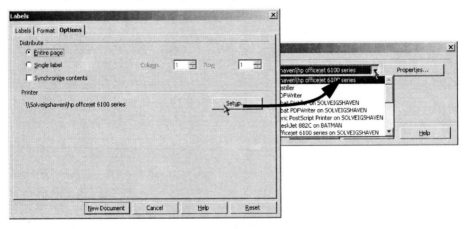

**3**    Then click New Document and you'll see the mail merge document. You can cut and paste, format, and rearrange the fields in the document if it doesn't look like what you want.

**4**    Print the envelopes or labels, and when you're asked to print a form letter, choose Yes. Printing is covered in *Printing Mail Merge Documents* on page 492.

If you have more records in your database than can fit onto one label sheet, don't worry—all the records will print. The label document you create is just kind of a template for the program. You'll get all the labels that are in your database.

# Using the Simple Mail Merge

There's a nice, simple little mail merge process that's the best approach if you don't need a lot of features. The only catch of course, is that it's not actually on any of the menus. However, it's pretty easy to add.

## Adding the Simple Mail Merge Wizard to the Tools Menu

**Note** – Add the wizard to any menu or toolbar; these steps use the Tools menu.

**1**    Choose Tools > Customize.

**2**    Click the Menu tab.

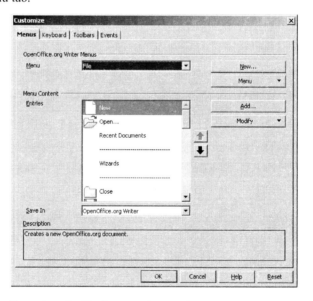

**3**    From the Menu list, select the Tools menu (or another menu you want to add the Mail Merge icon to).

**4**    Click the Add button.

**5**    In the Customize window, select Document in the left category and Mail Merge in the right category.

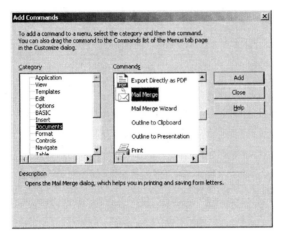

**6**    Click Add.

**7**    Click Close.

**8**    Use the arrows to move the icon to where you want it on the menu or toolbar.

**9**    Click OK.

**10**    The icon will show up on the Tools menu.

---

**Note – It's the Mail Merge option. The Mail Merge Wizard option is different, and is far more complex and unnecessary for any except the most advanced mail merges. For information on the Mail Merge Wizard, go to http://openoffice.blogs.com and click the Book Resources link.**

---

## Using the Simple Mail Merge Wizard

Now that you've added the wizard, here's how to use it.

**1**  Open the document where you want the mail merge fields to be in.

**2**  Choose Tools > Mail Merge, or whatever navigation you set up in the previous section to get to the mail merge.

**3**  You'll see this window; select Current Document and click OK.

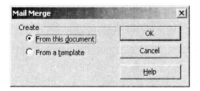

**4**  In the next window, choose to use an existing connection and click OK.

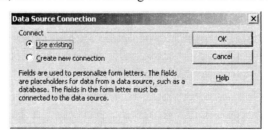

**5**   Here's the power window. Select the data source you want to use, expand it and select the correct table.

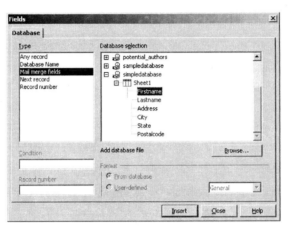

**6**   Click in the document where you want the first field to appear; you can keep the window open and click in the document at the same time. Select the field you want, and click Insert. The field will appear in your document.

**7**   Keep inserting until you have all the fields you want, where you want them. Space them and format them as you need them. When you're done, the document should look something like this.

**8**   Close the window.

**9**  You'll see this window, which is the window you need in order to print.

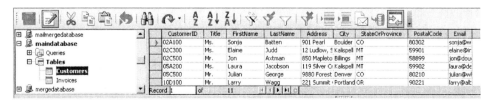

- If you're not ready to print, just click Cancel. You can format and cut and paste fields in your mail merge document as you want. Later when you want to print, just be sure the document is set up to print to the correct printer, then choose File > Print and click Yes to print a form letter.

- If you are ready to print, specify the range of records and where you want to print, and click OK. The documents will be printed to your default printer.

  You can learn more about printing in *Printing Mail Merge Documents* on page 492.

**Note –** There is a far more complex, though more powerful, mail merge wizard under the Tools menu. One additional feature that wizard has is the ability to automatically skip blank lines in addresses. For more information, see **htttp://openoffice.blogs.com** and click the link for **Book Resources**.

## Creating a Mail Merge Document From Scratch

This is useful in many situations: if you're sending a letter to multiple customers, friends, or need to create a document with information about every item in your Items database. If you don't need any of the power features in the mail merge wizard, creating a template from scratch works just fine.

**1**  Create a new Writer document, or open the document or template that you want to use as a mail merge document. Add any content you want to add prior to adding fields.

**2**  Choose View > Data Sources.

**3**  Select the database to use and expand to see the table.

**4**    Click on the column name for the first field you want to use.

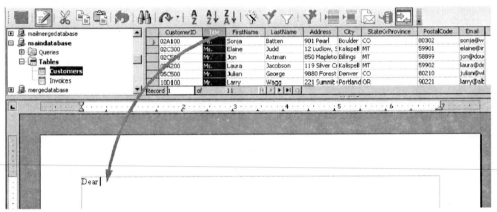

**5**    Drag the field you want to use into the document.

**6**    The field will appear, showing the name.

**7**    Continue to insert other fields, and add any other content, formatting, graphics, etc.

**8**    Save the document. To print, see *Printing Mail Merge Documents* on page 492.

# Previewing Data in a Mail Merge

When you create a mail merge document, regardless of the type, you'll see something like this.

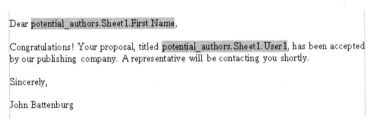

If you want to see the data, like the name **Bob**, rather than the names of the fields, here's what to do. Note that with letters, only the name of the first record will be displayed, and only the first page of labels will be displayed. Also note that you can't switch back after doing this.

With the mail merge document open, choose View > Data Sources.

**9**  In the area at the left, scroll to the data source you're using; it might be highlighted in bold. Select the database.

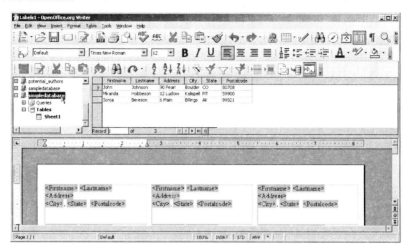

**10**  Click the blank gray square indicated in the data area of the preview window.

**11**  Click the Fields to Data icon.

**12**  The window will show data instead of field names.

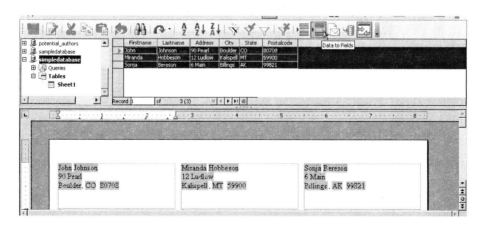

# Printing Mail Merge Documents

Printing isn't too complicated; you just have a few extra options that you don't have with regular printing.

## Printing a Mail Merge Document

**1**   Open any of the mail merge envelopes, labels, or letters you've created previously.

**2**   You can choose File > Printer Settings now to set the options, or later. Be sure that the printer you want is selected. Click OK.

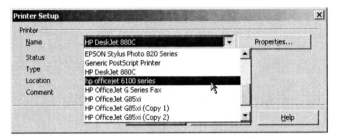

**3**   Choose File > Print.

**4**   You'll be asked whether you want to print a form letter. Click Yes. **Leave the checkbox unmarked.**

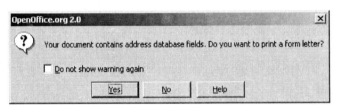

**5**   Select a range of records, or the entire range. You'll print all the letters to all recipients later when you're sure the letter looks the way you want.

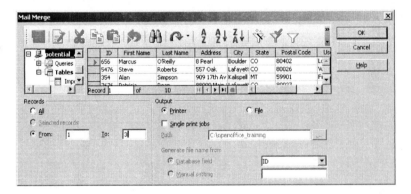

**6**    Be sure that the printing destination is correct. If you don't want to print to the printer and
you want to create OpenOffice.org Writer files instead, choose how you want to name the
files.

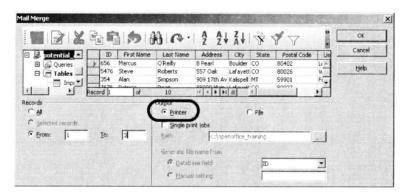

**7**    Click Print. You'll see the standard print window; select the printer you want. The
documents will be printed to the printer you chose earlier.

# Part VII: Appendix

# Installing OpenOffice.org

# Getting the Software

If you don't have the software, here's how to get it.

## Download the Software

1   Go to www.openoffice.org.

2   Click Download.

3   Choose the version for your operating system: Linux, Windows, Mac, Solaris, etc.

4   Download the file.

5   Double-click the downloaded file.

## Or Buy the Software

Go to one of the sites listed at http://support.openoffice.org. One of the vendors listed there is my site, http://www.cafepress.com/getopenoffice. Most CDs are in the range of free to $10.

# Installation

1   Double-clicked the file you downloaded, or follow the instructions on your CD. You'll see this window.

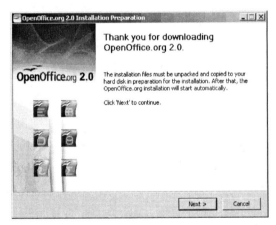

2   Click Next and follow the instruction onscreen in the installation wizard.

# Starting and Registering OpenOffice.org

When you start the program for the first time, you get a few different choices. Here's a walkthrough of how to start OpenOffice.org and register.

**1**   How you start OpenOffice.org depends on your operating system. Choose the type of document you want to create: Writer, Calc, etc. Here's what it looks like when you start it in Windows and in Linux.

Starting OpenOffice.org on Windows

Starting OpenOffice.org on Ubuntu Linux

**2**   The following window will appear. Click Next.

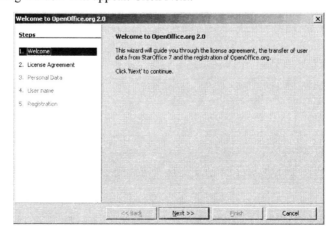

**3**   Follow the instructions in the registration wizard. When prompted, I recommend that you transfer over your settings from the previous version.

# Updating Documents

To update your old files from version 1.x to 2.0, or from Microsoft Office to OpenOffice.org format, use the converter wizard. See *Converting Documents to OpenOffice.org Using the Conversion Wizard* on page 31.

# Templates

There are templates all over the world to use with OpenOffice.org. Any templates you have, or that you can find online for free use, can be used. Here are some tips.

## Finding Templates

Your Word, Excel, and Powerpoint templates all work with OpenOffice.org. Use them if your license for Microsoft allows you to. You can just open them, or convert them and put them in a place where OpenOffice.org can find them. See *Converting Documents to OpenOffice.org Using the Conversion Wizard* on page 31, and *Preparing and Organizing Your Templates* on page 39.

You can also just google for other Microsoft templates; they're all over the place. WorldLabel has many templates for OpenOffice.org. I've also added links for finding book resources at **http:// openoffice.blogs.com**.

## Installing Templates

See *Saving Time With Templates and More* on page 37.

# Where to Find Other Resources

Google, of course, is a great place to start. Here are my recommendations, which is by no means to say I don't recommend anything else.

- I blog on using OpenOffice.org at **http://openoffice.blogs.com**
- There's a wealth of Calc knowledge at **www.openofficetips.com**
- Send an email to the **users@openoffice.org** mailing list. Check the archives first to see if your question has already been answered. Subscribe at **www.openoffice.org**; look for the Support tab.
- Go to **www.oooforums.org**, especially for more technical questions.
- For questions on master documents and other advanced techwriter topics, check the Writer category on my blog, **http://openoffice.blogs.com**. You should also go to the web site **www.taming-openoffice-org.com**.

# Learning More About Advanced Topics

# Everything Didn't Make It Into the Book

I decided that this 2.0 book would not weigh as much as some newborn children, so I focused on a practical and useful approach, writing a book that I thought would be most useful to most people, with the features that are:

◆   Most commonly used

◆   Most important or useful

◆   Most difficult to learn on your own

◆   Easy to explain quickly in not much space

That leaves us with less coverage of a few topics. I'm not going to cover those topics, but I'm going to let you know they're there so you can play with them or research them more on your own, if you like.

To learn more about any particular topic, go to my blog at http://openoffice.blogs.com and click the **Book Resources** link. You can also go to the search field for any blog entry, type in a keyword like gallery or master documents, and find my blog entries on the subject.

# The Gallery

The gallery is a place for storing frequently used graphics. Instead of navigating to Insert > Picture > From File and specifying where the file is stored, you can add graphics to the gallery and simply drag them into your file.

To see the gallery, click the Gallery icon on the toolbar. It's usually at the far right in the Standard toolbar at the top of the work area, except for in Draw and Impress where it's in the Drawing toolbar, below the work area.

There are existing graphics, and you can add your own themes (categories) and graphics.

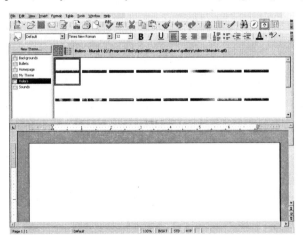

# Indexing

A lot of people add tables of contents to their documents, but fewer index. Here's how to get started. If you'd like to index the document, select the term to index in your document. Choose Index > Indexes and Tables > Entry to add entries. You'll see a window like this. Type the entry, then click Insert.

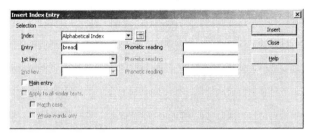

Do just a few entries, then generate the index to be sure the entries are working the way you expect. To generate an index, choose Index > Indexes and Tables > Indexes and Tables. Select Alphabetical Index, and set the other options you want. Many of the formatting options in *Tables of Contents* on page 241 apply to indexes, as well.

# Advanced Publishing Features

These are four powerful tools for techwriters and others who do heavy-duty publishing. They all have to do with the structure of the document.

## Master Documents

A master document is like a master file in Word or a book file in Framemaker. To create one, just choose File > New > Master Document. Insert the files you want in your book. You also need to insert a Text Item between the files.

# The Navigator

The window that pops up to show you what's in the master document is actually the Navigator. You can bring it up for master files and regular files by pressing F5.

Click the Toggle icon to switch between the expanded view here and the restricted view shown earlier with master documents.

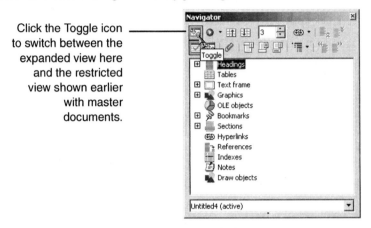

It lets you navigate among the headings, objects, tables, and other elements. The Navigator is very useful with large documents.

# Outline Numbering

Outline numbering is the backbone of your document structure. Tables of contents can be, and cross-references and running headers are, based on outline numbering. Outline numbering sounds like it's lists, but it has *nothing* to do with lists. Outline numbering is just specifying what styles define the structure of your document. If you use ChapterTitle as the top level of your book, for instance, and then Heading1, Heading2, and Heading3, that's what you specify in outline numbering.

Choose Tools > Outline Numbering to set it up and just select the style from the dropdown list, for each level. Ignore numbering unless you need numbered headings.

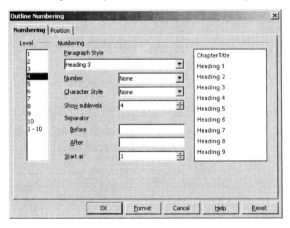

# Cross References (and Running Headers and Footers)

Once you've set up outline numbering, you can do cross-references. For instance, if you're writing about Southeast Colorado and you want to talk about how to get there, you might say "See *Transportation* on page 53," referring to the information you've already written about transportation. You don't want to just type that title and page number literally since the page and title might change, so you use a cross-reference so the title and page will automatically update.

First, create the reference. Select a title you need to refer to and copy it. Choose Insert > Cross Reference. Select Set Reference, then paste the name of the title. Click Insert.

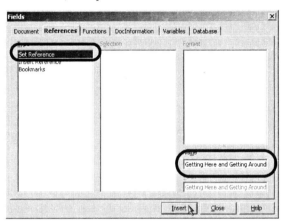

Later when you want to refer to that section, somewhere else in the document, choose Insert > Cross Reference. Choose Insert Reference and select the title you want in the selection list. For the format, choose Reference for the title and Page for the page number.

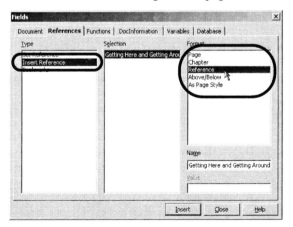

You use a similar function for running headers and footers. This will automatically show the name of the most recent heading used in the document. Click in the header or footer and choose Insert > Fields > Other. Click the Document tab and select Chapter. Select Chapter Name and then the level you want to refer to.

If you want to refer to a heading for which you use the ChapterTitle paragraph style, for instance, and that's at Level 1 in the outline numbering you set up, you'd specify level 1.

If you wanted to refer to a heading at a different level in the outline numbering, specify that level instead.

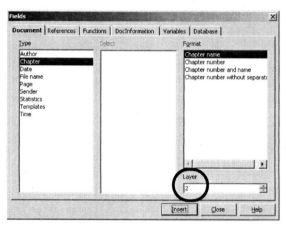

# Advanced Pagination

I want to make sure you know about two very handy pagination techniques. One lets you automatically switch from one page style to another, so that each page style is applied on one page, followed by the next. The other lets you automatically start a new page style, and a new page, every time a certain *paragraph style* is used.

## Automatically Switching Page Styles

This is a modification for page styles. Choose Format > Styles and Formatting, and choose to edit the first page style in the document, like CoverPage. In the first tab, select the next page style you want to use, such as Copyright, as the Next Style.

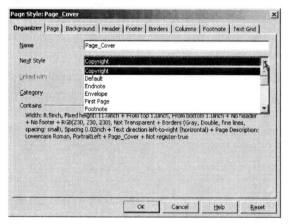

Keep repeating this. Modify the Copyright page style and set its next page style as the next one you want to use. Each page style will be used on one page, then the next page style will be applied.

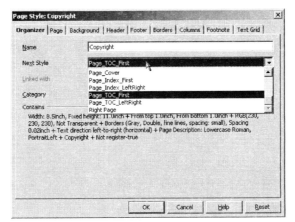

## Automatic Page Break With Page Style and Optional Page Number Restart

This is a modification to paragraph styles that can switch you from one page style to another. Let's say that you start each new main section at the top of a page with a title using the Heading1 paragraph style. And for every new main section you have a page style that has a centered bottom footer, but all your other pages are normal left-right with the page number in the header. That means that every time you use the Heading1 style, you want to have a page break and use the page style SectionFirstPage.

Modify the Heading1 paragraph style, and go to the Text Flow tab. Choose to make a page break before the content and switch to page style SectionFirstPage. You could also choose to restart the numbering at 1 (or -4, or 92) each time, but that wouldn't make sense in this example.

# Version Control and Change Tracking

You can save multiple versions of a document. You can also send out a document for edits and accept or reject each person's changes.

# Versions

Choose File > Versions. Save a version of the document, or revert to a previous version. Add notes if you want.

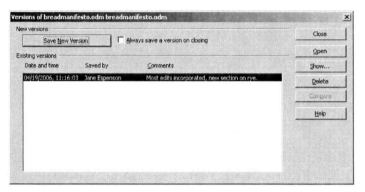

# Tracking Changes

Choose Edit > Changes. Make sure that your edits are showing and turned on.

Type your changes.

**Bump & Grind**

For the funky, arty, and open-minded type, try Bump &and Grind. Bright colors, quirky collectibles and local art adorn this Uptown joint and make it the hottest coffee spot in town. Vegetarians will be happy with lots of choices, and those with big appetites will love the homemade, super-sized scones and muffins. Lunch is also available, along with lots of coffee concoctions. Don't miss weekend brunch served by hilarious drag queens. 439 E. 17th Ave., 303-861-4841.

If you're the one receiving an edited document, choose Edit > Changes > Accept or Reject. Select each and accept or reject it, or accept or reject all.

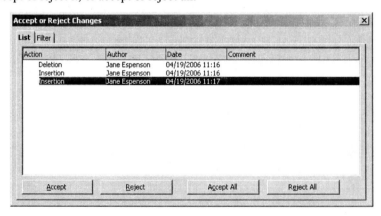

# Scenarios and Goal Seek

Scenarios and Goal Seek are two Calc features under the **Tools** menu that let you figure out what would happen with different variables. For instance, what would your net income be like with different values for rent, utilities, and 401(k) contribution? You could also see the results of your book deal for different royalty percentages.

## Scenarios

Here's when you might use scenarios. The lease agreement has fallen through for the bookstore so all the variables are up for grabs. You also have the opportunity to get a bunch of free labor from the local Children R R Future organization if you donate some money to their fund. However, to get that deal you need to lease their building for your bookstore. It's very complicated. So you need to figure out what kind of profit the Children's Palace is going to be turning based on all those variables, and make the right choice.

The following illustration shows an example scenario. See my blog for more details.

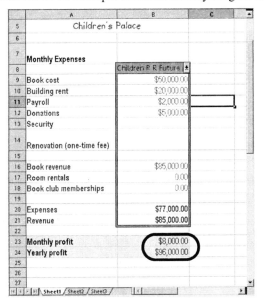

## Goal Seek

Here's an example of when you'd use Goal Seek. You've been told that the board would really a $50,000 profit in the first year their Children's Palace bookstore is in business. You know that various factors contribute to that—expenses, payroll, etc.

But the thing you can control the most is the book markup. Here's an example.

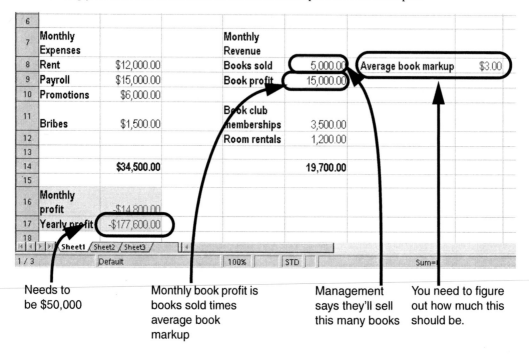

| Needs to be $50,000 | Monthly book profit is books sold times average book markup | Management says they'll sell this many books | You need to figure out how much this should be. |

# The Data Pilot

The Data Pilot is similar to Excel pivot tables. In the spreadsheet with data you want to play with, choose Data > Pilot > Start.

| | A | B | C | D | E |
|---|---|---|---|---|---|
| 1 | Date | Store | Book | Daily Sales | Units Sold |
| 2 | 09/15/2006 | Boulder | Open Source Case Studies | $6,576.00 | 219 |
| 3 | 09/15/2006 | Boulder | Living in Linux | $7,465.00 | 373 |
| 4 | 09/15/2006 | Boulder | Crossing the Digital Divide | $1,978.00 | 66 |
| 5 | 09/15/2006 | Boulder | Wide Open Source | $1,818.00 | 91 |
| 6 | 09/15/2006 | Denver | Open Source Case Studies | $2,722.00 | 91 |
| 7 | 09/15/2006 | Denver | Living in Linux | $1,767.00 | 88 |
| 8 | 09/15/2006 | Denver | Crossing the Digital Divide | $3,422.00 | 114 |
| 9 | 09/15/2006 | Denver | Wide Open Source | $1,711.00 | 86 |
| 10 | 09/15/2006 | Fort Collins | Open Source Case Studies | $1,499.00 | 50 |
| 11 | 09/15/2006 | Fort Collins | Living in Linux | $1,200.00 | 60 |
| 12 | 09/15/2006 | Fort Collins | Crossing the Digital Divide | $2,022.00 | 67 |
| 13 | 09/15/2006 | Fort Collins | Wide Open Source | $2,767.00 | 138 |
| 14 | 09/16/2006 | Boulder | Open Source Case Studies | $3,887.00 | 130 |
| 15 | 09/16/2006 | Boulder | Living in Linux | $1,899.00 | 95 |
| 16 | 09/16/2006 | Boulder | Crossing the Digital Divide | $6,576.00 | 219 |
| 17 | 09/16/2006 | Boulder | Wide Open Source | $2,476.00 | 124 |
| 18 | 09/16/2006 | Denver | Open Source Case Studies | $1,767.00 | 59 |
| 19 | 09/16/2006 | Denver | Living in Linux | $1,566.00 | 78 |
| 20 | 09/16/2006 | Denver | Crossing the Digital Divide | $1,480.00 | 49 |
| 21 | 09/16/2006 | Denver | Wide Open Source | $4,324.00 | 216 |
| 22 | 09/16/2006 | Fort Collins | Open Source Case Studies | $7,545.00 | 252 |
| 23 | 09/16/2006 | Fort Collins | Living in Linux | $5,454.00 | 273 |
| 24 | 09/16/2006 | Fort Collins | Crossing the Digital Divide | $7,465.00 | 249 |
| 25 | 09/16/2006 | Fort Collins | Wide Open Source | $2,978.00 | 149 |
| 26 | 09/17/2006 | Boulder | Open Source Case Studies | $4,343.00 | 145 |
| 27 | 09/17/2006 | Boulder | Living in Linux | $2,343.00 | 117 |
| 28 | 09/17/2006 | Boulder | Crossing the Digital Divide | $1,988.00 | 66 |

Sheet1 / Sheet2 / Sheet3

Choose the current document or another data source, then specify which fields you want to display, what type of functions to apply to the fields in the Data Fields area, and any options such as whether to total the rows and columns.

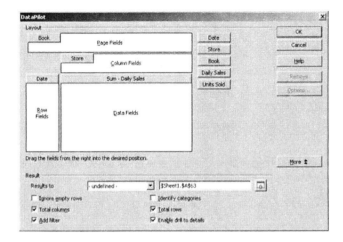

Click OK; the results will be displayed.

# Equations

Equations let you type complex equations. For instance, this equation looks like this typed in the equation editor box:

```
(%pi / rho) over 4.5
```

That equation shows up like this in your document, in a frame.

Choose Insert > Object > Formula. Type the formula in the box; it will show up in your document. When you're done, just click in the document. If you need symbols, click the equations icon on the toolbar.

For more information, use the excellent online help reference to the syntax.

# Macros

You can record or write macros by choosing Tools > Macros and the appropriate option. To record a macro, just choose Tools > Macros > Record. You'll see the Stop Recording button, so just click that when you're done.

To write a macro, choose Tools > Macros > Organize Macros > OpenOffice.org Basic. Then click New.

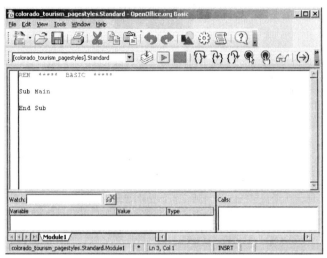

For more information, see *OpenOffice.org Macros Explained* by Andrew Pitonyak and the many other resources on the web, including http://api.openoffice.org.

# Forms and Reports

This is an enormous topic, and one that can be very useful. There are several articles on my blog about these tools, so check under **Book Resources** for more information.

When you open the .odb file for a database, there are several icons on the left side. Two are Forms and Reports. Click the one you're interested in. You'll then have two choices for how to create the form or report. The wizard is easiest to start with.

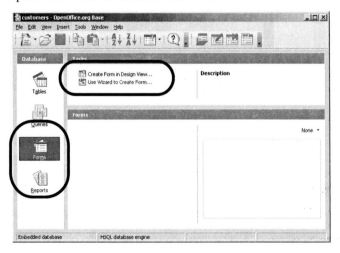

## Forms

When you choose to create a form in the wizard, you get a series of windows like these. Select
fields and make other choices when prompted.

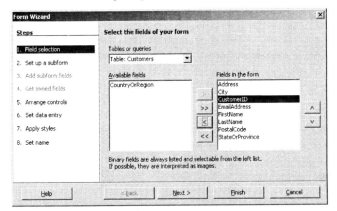

A finished form looks something like this.

## Reports

When you choose to create a report in the wizard, you get a series of windows like these.
Select fields and make other choices when prompted.

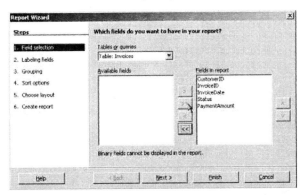

A finished report looks something like this.

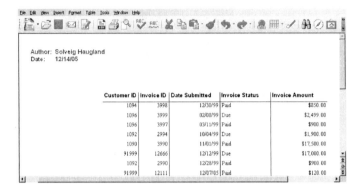

# Image Maps

If you're creating a web site, the easiest way to make a link is to type some text and hyperlink it. However, what if you want graphics for the links on the navigation bar? You could create 10 or 20 different graphics for each item. Or you could make one graphic and specify the location on each graphic that links to each different page. This is an image map.

An example of an image map is shown at right. This is just one .gif file, with different rectangles defined so that **Training** links to a different page than **Workbooks**, and so on.

To make an image map, create your HTML page and insert the graphic. Then click on the graphic and choose Edit > Image Map.

In the window that appears, use the drawing tools to specify the areas where people will click, and the URLs where the links should take them.

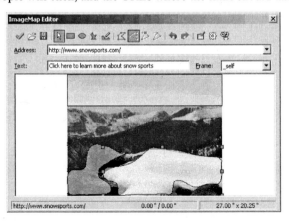

# OpenOffice.org Guidebook Online Supplements

To find out more about any topic, please visit my blog at **http://openoffice.blogs.com** and click the link for **Book Resources**. At that location you'll find the key topics left out of this book, blogs and articles where you can learn more, and PDFs that supplement this book.

You'll also find additional templates, comments from readers, and other book-related content.

# Index